Pleasure, preference and value

Pleasure, preference and value

Studies in philosophical aesthetics

EDITED BY EVA SCHAPER

Professor in Logic
University of Glasgow

CAMBRIDGE UNIVERSITY PRESS

Cambridge
London   New York   New Rochelle
Melbourne   Sydney

Published by the Press Syndicate of the University of Cambridge
The Pitt Building, Trumpington Street, Cambridge CB2 1RP
32 East 57th Street, New York, NY 10022, USA
296 Beaconsfield Parade, Middle Park, Melbourne 3206, Australia

First published 1983

Printed in Great Britain by
Redwood Burn Limited
Trowbridge, Wiltshire

Library of Congress catalogue card number:
82–14775

British Library Cataloguing in Publication Data

Pleasure, preference and value.
1. Aesthetics
I. Schaper, Eva
111'.85   BJ46

ISBN 0 521 25101 X

Contents

Contributors

John McDowell is Fellow of University College, Oxford.

Philip Pettit is Professor of Philosophy, School of Interdisciplinary Human Studies, at the University of Bradford.

Eva Schaper is Professor in Logic at the University of Glasgow.

Barrie Falk is Lecturer in Philosophy at the University of Birmingham.

R. A. Sharpe is Senior Lecturer in Philosophy at Saint David's University College, University of Wales.

Anthony Savile is Lecturer in Philosophy at Bedford College, London.

Ted Cohen is Professor of Philosophy at the University of Chicago.

Malcolm Budd is Lecturer in Philosophy at University College London.

J. M. Cameron is Emeritus Professor, St Michael's College, University of Toronto.

Introduction

In the last three decades, philosophical aesthetics has undergone something of a transformation. Back in 1954 William Elton, the editor of a collection of essays entitled *Aesthetics and Language*, openly admitted to the scarcity of good work applying philosophical expertise in an area as yet hardly disturbed by the techniques of linguistic analysis. The talk was of the 'present stone age of aesthetics', of barrenness, dullness, dreariness, pretentiousness and vacuity, and contributors to that volume seemed more than a little apologetic about turning their hands to the subject at all. Thanks to their labours, and the labours of others in the field over the next two decades, aesthetics, one dare hope, has once more achieved respectability as an object of philosophical study, and with the new vitality has come a more just assessment of the much-maligned tradition. The contributors to the present volume may not agree with the recent somewhat exaggerated claim of Joseph Margolis that 'aesthetics is the most strategically placed philosophical discipline of our time' (*Art and Philosophy*, 1980), but they clearly find the subject rewarding and anything but dreary or dull.

Our three-word title is indicative not so much of a philosophical remit for the meetings from which the papers emerged, as of what, in the event, turned out to be persistent themes variously taken up and developed by the participants. The concept of pleasure, of course, has always and rightly been regarded as a crucial one in aesthetics. Bob Sharpe's paper and that of Eva Schaper concentrate on the role of pleasure in aesthetic judgement; Ted Cohen, exploiting a parallel between the enjoyment of jokes and the enjoyment of art, throws light on the thrill of felt rightness; Barrie Falk, probing the communicability of feeling, takes pity as his example of an emotion felt, evoking the shade of Aristotle: can we really enjoy or take pleasure in the piteous, the sad, or the tragic as it is presented to us in art?

Preference and its grounds is another prominent theme. Appraisals of taste traditionally so-called, value judgements and art critical evaluations all have to produce their credentials in the reasons and the rightness or appropriateness of the reasons adduced for them. Anthony Savile's paper links this explicitly with loving attachment to beauty, Eva Schaper's with taste preferences, and Malcolm Budd's paper, concentrating on the case of poetry, raises the question whether we can aesthetically prefer works which embody beliefs perhaps even antithetical to our own.

Where value belongs in the scheme of things, including aesthetic value, is the subject matter of John McDowell's critique of a once prevalent dogma – the separation of fact and value. The subjective/objective distinction, time-honoured but deeply suspect when it canonizes a world-view dominated by science, forms part of this critique, and it also figures in James Cameron's inward/outward contrast and his lament over the epistemological solitary as reflected in autobiography owing much to the Cartesian heritage.

One spectre, I notice with pleasure, haunts these essays: Kant's. This is no accident in the case of Barrie Falk's paper and Eva Schaper's: the approach here is explicitly Kantian though not primarily exegetical. Bob Sharpe, Anthony Savile and Ted Cohen are more obliquely aware of the Kantian ghost.

I shall not attempt to summarize the individual contributions; instead, I shall indicate what are for me points of particular interest. John McDowell takes up the common belief that our aesthetic experience is at least in part an awareness of value which we encounter in the world as belonging to (in John Mackie's phrase) the 'fabric of the world'. Though not concerned explicitly to defend this belief, he clears the ground of some of the obstacles to doing so. He takes issue with Mackie's claim that the belief just mentioned is illusory, and that value is only how the real appears to us. This basic distinction between reality and mere appearance, where only that is real which counts as 'objective' in the sense of being independent of any sentient creature's experience of it, McDowell also detects in Bernard Williams's recent attempts to defend Descartes's 'project of pure inquiry'. Such a defence, if it could succeed, would go far towards dismissing value from the world as it really is; but McDowell's argument is that this world-view is basically incoherent anyway.

Philip Pettit takes aesthetic characterizations such as aesthetic descriptions of pictures to be reports of experience, and argues that they standardly come out as assertions 'in the strictest and most genuine sense of that term', i.e. as utterances which can be shown to be either true or false. This is tricky ground indeed, as Pettit concedes when he acknowledges the difficulty for his position created by the use of metaphor in aesthetic descriptions: metaphors are precisely not literal assertions. Pressing as he does a realist claim, he has to defuse the anti-realist objections. And that too is no easy task since Pettit accepts the premise from which the anti-realist argues, that is, the essentially perception-relative nature of aesthetic descriptions, and their perceptual elusiveness. This would suggest rather that aesthetic descriptions are non-assertoric, at least in the sense that they are not tied to beliefs but to responses in immediate experience. You have to 'see' that something is graceful or sad or charming, and no argument can show that it *is* so. Pettit, however, argues for an alternative account which would allow us to maintain aesthetic realism after introducing suitable constraints on 'rectified' aesthetic descriptions.

These same issues of realism and anti-realism are latent in Eva Schaper's paper, which stands in sharp contrast to Pettit's on the issue of truth conditions for judgements of taste or aesthetic appraisals. The account here is Kantian but it would be foolish to claim that it was Kant's. Precisely where Kant would stand on this now much debated contrast is matter for dark conjecture.

Barrie Falk takes up another strand of Kant's thought: the communicability of feeling. He introduces the features of resonance and salience to illuminate what it means to relate to a situation emotionally. This opens the way to an understanding of why art works engage us so deeply: the fleeting poignancy of emotional experiences can be captured and prolonged in clusters of thought. Art works do not just communicate feelings but through them we may find ourselves in possession of truths about what the world is like. The idea that through subjective involvement with works of art our knowledge may be enriched in a way which only the experience of art can provide echoes those aspects of Kantian doctrine which most closely approach Aristotle's insights into the centrality of the notion of the plausible in fiction.

Bob Sharpe's contrast between 'solid joys' and 'fading pleasures' is not, as the title might suggest, critical of the relation between aesthetic experience and pleasure maintained in preceding papers. Rather, his is a study of the many ways in which pleasure for the wrong reasons can mislead and confuse the critic and the performer of art works. Sharpe speaks of providing a pathology of our reactions to art from the merely sentimental to what he calls 'false pleasures'. Indeed, his essay broadens out into a discussion of whether pleasure is properly to be regarded as an emotion at all, and here he engages in lively controversy with Bernard Williams and Terence Penelhum on causal and reason-giving accounts of pleasure. Sharpe seems to think that only a causal account could satisfactorily deal with those cases in which we misidentify our pleasures and those in which we misjudge the role of pleasure in our critical response to art.

Anthony Savile too is concerned with the link between experienced response to beauty – the aesthetic response – and the objectivity of values so discerned. What particularly engages his attention is the endurance of beauty in art over time, in spite of changes in habits of thought, sensibility and aspiration. It is not Kant here, but Kant's pupil Schiller, who helps Savile to make his point that the permanence or evanescence of critical assessments are a direct function of recognition, or the lack of it, of what he calls the benignity of beauty. Schiller's conception of beauty, he maintains, is capable of explaining that overworked platitude: a thing of beauty *remains* a joy for ever. Even when the benign possibilities displayed in works of the past are no longer open to us, we can love them still because we have the capacity for sympathetic understanding of those for whom they were once real. This also throws light, he suggests, on the poignancy that frequently colours our experience of past achievements in art.

The joke in Ted Cohen's hands proves fruitful material in unexpected ways. Cohen does not say that jokes are works of art, though he thinks some might be, and certainly he is convinced that metaphors may be quintessentially works of art. He does find that jokes are 'curiously like' works of art. Thinking about jokes in the way we might think about art, we may receive genuine illumination on some otherwise baffling features of both. Here considerations broader than those usually thought of as belonging to aesthetics emerge. Thus, a comparison between assenting to the conclusion of a sound argument and laughter at a joke's punchline proves not to be a digression, and the linking of intimacy with the community achieved in successful joke telling suggests, surprisingly, a contact of ideas between being moved to laughter and being moved by beauty. The community of personhood which Kant saw as ultimately the fundamental ground of the universal claims of aesthetic judgements, in spite of their irreducibly subjective nature, finds unexpected if still tentative support here.

Malcolm Budd's problems are those of the acceptability or unacceptability of beliefs that may be expressed in poetry. He carefully disambiguates the references to beliefs expressed in poems by distinguishing a poem's persona from its author – either or both being capable of 'speaking' in a poem, with their beliefs coinciding, varying, or even clashing. In the light of these distinctions, he clarifies the notions of sincerity and of insincerity of beliefs. The fictional status of poems, though relevant to these considerations, turns out not to afford *carte blanche* to the sins of poet and reader alike, sins of sentimentality, hypocrisy, wilful deception and self-deception. Imaginative integrity is equally difficult for poet, poem and reader, but once achieved, it affords a compelling reason for the reader's assent not being withheld – at least not the assent of the reader whose sensibility is a match for his intellectual powers of discrimination.

James Cameron claims that modern autobiography, that is, autobiography since Rousseau, is 'autopsychology' and not just a history of a life told in the first person singular. He sees a connection between the inward-looking accounts of the self displayed in modern autobiography and the dominant philosophy of the last few centuries with its egocentric orientation. The self as a distinct and idiosyncratic centre of consciousness, in search of itself as much as of 'its' world, is a product of a conscious or unconscious world-view with its peculiar perplexities, the most alluring as well as the most frightening being 'epistemological solitude' which feeds on as well as reinforces scepticism. This conception of the self and its self-made world lives on as a compelling picture long after the doctrinal basis has been questioned or undermined, and the lure of it is vividly memorialized not only in autobiography but also in some of the great fictional creations of searching selves.

All papers in this collection are here published for the first time. Draft versions of them were presented at a number of meetings of members of the Thyssen Philosophy Group and their guests. On behalf of the Group I express our thanks to the Fritz Thyssen Stiftung and its director Professor Dr Rudolf Kerscher. It was their generous financial support and constant encouragement that made these stimulating meetings possible.

Glasgow   EVA SCHAPER
May 1982

Aesthetic value, objectivity, and the fabric of the world

JOHN MCDOWELL

I

Aesthetic experience typically presents itself, at least in part, as a confrontation with value: an awareness of value as something residing in an object and available to be encountered. It thus invites the thought that value is, as J. L. Mackie puts it in his *Ethics: Inventing Right and Wrong*,[1] 'part of the fabric of the world' (p. 15). Mackie does not dispute, but indeed insists on, this phenomenological claim. But he contends that the appearance is illusory: value is not found in the world, but projected into it, a mere reflection of subjective responses.

Mackie's concern is primarily with ethical value, but he claims that 'clearly much the same considerations apply to aesthetic and to moral values' (p. 15). In this paper I want to consider the plausibility of Mackie's thesis for the case of aesthetic value in particular.

The issue I mean to raise is not one about the significance of some putative range of peculiarly aesthetic, or perhaps more generally evaluative, vocabulary. It may well be true that a helpful critic rarely, if ever, makes an outright attempt to characterize the value which, in experiencing the works he discusses as they should be experienced, one should find in them (as the phenomenology of the experience tempts us to say). In that case explicitly evaluative terms are less than centrally important in the vocabulary of criticism. But this need not suggest that Mackie's thesis is not fundamental to aesthetics; for it remains plausible that the point of the critic's activity is to help his audience towards a proper experience of any work he discusses (an experience whose content he need not try to formulate explicitly), and thus that the critic's aim is, by a careful directing or focusing of the audience's attention to the work, to enable the audience to find for himself the value there is in it (still speaking as the phenomenology invites). The question Mackie raises – whether this is genuinely a matter of *finding* – has an interest for philosophical aesthetics that is quite independent of the mildly comical idea that the subject-matter

[1] Harmondsworth, 1977.

of aesthetics is a set of judgements in which objects are explicitly appraised, ranked, or evaluated.

II

How should we interpret what our aesthetic experience purports, as it were, to tell us, when it represents value as part of the fabric of the world? What is the content of the appearance?

Mackie treats the thesis that value is in the world as interchangeable with the thesis that value is *objective* (see, e.g., p. 15). I believe this is not an innocuous variation of terminology; I think it insinuates, into Mackie's account of the content of value experience, a specific and disputable philosophical conception of the world (or the real, or the factual). This opens the possibility that when Mackie argues that the phenomenology of value experience embodies an error, his arguments involve a misconstrual of what the appearances invite us to believe.

The notion of objectivity that I think Mackie has in mind is one that would be explained by contrast with a suitable notion of subjectivity. A subjective property, in the relevant sense, is one such that no adequate conception of what it is for a thing to possess it is available except in terms of how the thing would, in suitable circumstances, affect a subject – a sentient being.[2] (Think of affective properties like amusingness, or sensory secondary qualities like colours, according to a familiar conception in which what it is to *be*, say, red is not adequately conceived independently of the idea of *looking* red; this would preclude identifying the property of being red with a categorical ground for something's disposition to look red in suitable circumstances.) What is objective, in the relevant sense, is what is not subjective. Thus Mackie's implied doctrine that whatever is part of the fabric of the world is objective, if it is interpreted in this way, amounts to the doctrine that the world is fully describable in terms of properties that can be understood without essential reference to their effects on sentient beings. (Categorical grounds for affective or secondary properties can be part of the fabric of the world, on this view, even though the subjective properties they sustain cannot.)

Mackie cites two traditional reasons for holding that value is not in the world, the argument from relativity and the argument from queerness. (He supplements them with the claim that the illusion which he takes them to reveal, embedded in the phenomenology of value experience, can be explained in terms of 'patterns of objectification' (pp. 42–6).) Both

---

[2] I do not say that a subjective property is one which must be analysed in terms of its effects on subjects, because of the difficulty of seeing how it can be an *analysis* of, say, greenness to characterize it as a disposition to look *green* under suitable circumstances (and how else is the relevant effect to be described?). See section IV below.

arguments seem to owe their apparent cogency to the prior assumption that the world is objective in something like the sense I have just sketched.

Mackie's presentation of the argument from relativity (pp. 36–8) is partly spoiled by a tendency to slide between variation in valuings from one community to another, or within communities, and disagreement in valuings, as if those were the same thing. A shallow subjectivism might start from the thought that striking differences between, say, the artefacts of different cultures must result from a *disagreement* in valuings. This would yield an argument against any serious use, in this connection, of the notion of truth or the notion of the world: at most one of a pair of incompatible sets of valuings could match the world, and, since there is no unprejudiced way of telling which, we had better conclude that neither does. But this line of thought would be very crude. Our appreciating what we do need not preclude our supposing that there are different values, to which we are perhaps insensitive, in the artefacts of remote cultures – as if, when we take the value we find in the objects we appreciate to be really there in them, we use up all the room the world might afford for aesthetic merit to occupy. In fact it is remarkable, and heartening, to what extent, without losing hold of the sensitivities from which we begin, we can learn to find worth in what seems at first too alien to appreciate.

I think the argument Mackie intends is not this crude argument, but one that starts from the fact of *variation* in valuings (not necessarily amounting to disagreement), and turns on the claim that such variation is 'more readily explained by the hypothesis that [the valuings] reflect ways of life than by the hypothesis that they reflect perceptions . . . of objective values' (p. 37).[3] Now the role of a way of life, in a plausible story about what presents itself as a sensitivity to the value in a particular range of aesthetic objects, is no doubt sufficiently analogous to the role of a specific sensory apparatus, in a plausible story about what presents itself as a sensitivity to (for instance) colours, to warrant the thought that the values are subjective in something like the sense suggested above.[4] But this rules out supposing that the sensitivity is just that – a capacity to detect and respond to something that is part of the fabric of the world – only if we make the prior assumption that nothing subjective, in that sense, is found in the world. The word 'objective' is essential to Mackie's formulation of the hypothesis he wants us to reject; if 'objective' were deleted, it would no longer seem so

---

[3] I have omitted some words which suggest, again, the idea that the divergent perceptions would have to be in competition. Certainly any sensible cognitivism must make room for the thought that many of the experiences which purport to be perceptions of value are, as Mackie says, 'seriously inadequate and badly distorted'. But sheer variation does not itself justify that thought.

[4] Membership of a community, or sympathetic understanding of its way of life, would constitute a point of view, in the extended sense to be introduced in section III below.

clear that we have to choose.[5]

As for the argument from queerness (pp. 38–42): there would indeed be something weird (to put it mildly) about the idea of a property which, while retaining the 'phenomenal' character of experienced value, was conceived to be part of the world as objectively characterized. It would be as if we tried to construct a conception of amusingness which was fully intelligible otherwise than in terms of the characteristic human responses to what is amusing, but which nevertheless contrived somehow to retain the 'phenomenal' aspect of amusingness as we experience it in those responses.[6] But the phenomenology of value experience sets up this strain only if we insist on interpreting it in terms of a conception of the world as objective in the sense I have sketched.[7]

What emerges, then, is the prospect of a debate about whether it is compulsory to accept the equation of the world (what is real or factual) with what is objective in the relevant sense. If it is not compulsory, the phenomenology can be differently understood, so as to be, perhaps, immune to the traditional arguments. (And if there is no illusion to explain, Mackie's supplementation of the traditional arguments falls away as superfluous.)

When we consider aesthetic value in particular, there is a special advantage in shifting discussion away from Mackie's arguments to the question whether those arguments attack the right target. The issue is this: if we grant that we cannot construct a conception of aesthetic value that is

---

[5] What emerges here is the possibility that the explanation of the perceptions as reflecting ways of life might not amount to an explaining *away* of what the perceptions purport to discover in reality.

[6] I should sympathize with anyone who found this idea incoherent; whereas Mackie insists that his target is a thought which is coherent (though, of course, false). This might cast doubt on my interpretation of Mackie, were it not that this issue about coherence is duplicated in the case of Mackie's views about colour. Here he takes it to be coherent, although false, that there are colour properties which are not secondary but primary (that is, which characterize things independently of their effect on perceivers), but which 'resemble' colours as they figure in our experience (that is, which retain the 'phenomenal' aspect of our ordinary notion of colours). This thought is rejected on grounds of explanatory superfluity rather than queerness (though one might well suggest that an argument from queerness would be pretty effective in this case). See Mackie's *Problems from Locke* (Oxford, 1976), pp. 10–11, 18–19. I believe this idea of primary qualities which 'resemble' colours as we see them can seem coherent only in the context of a quite disputable view of how colours figure in our experience: one which is at variance, moreover, with Mackie's official account of that matter.

[7] I have ignored the epistemological component of Mackie's argument from queerness, in which he claims that if one holds that value is in the world, one must postulate a special faculty ('intuition') to be what detects it. If the aim is, as Mackie takes it to be, to insist on the existence of primary qualities that 'resemble' value properties as we experience them, it is hard to see how inventing a sense-like faculty would help. For surely values would seem to stand to any such faculty in the same sort of relation as that in which colours stand to the faculty of vision, thus remaining stubbornly non-primary.

detached from the idea of an experience of an object's seeming to have it, any more than we can construct a conception of amusingness that is detached from the idea of the responses that constitute finding something amusing, are we thereby debarred from supposing that we find aesthetic value (or amusingness) in the world? This is a general question about the status of properties that are not conceivable independently of sentient responses to them. Now the precise nature of the response in question can vary from case to case. And this means that we can let Mackie's harping on the queerness of, in particular, objective *prescriptivity* fade into the background; which is an improvement, since 'prescriptivity' suggests a specific response involving value's appeal to the *will*, and this is at best questionably appropriate for ethical value in general, and surely inappropriate for aesthetic value.

Mackie claims (p. 43) that the inclination to take value experience to be cognitive is less entrenched with aesthetic value than with moral value. This strikes me as exactly the reverse of the truth: and I think the reason is connected with the irrelevance, or near irrelevance, of the will to an account of aesthetic value. The phenomenology of value experience in general suggests a visual model for our dealings with value. In the moral case we are prone to be tempted away from that model by the distracting influence of the concept of choice or decision; whereas in the aesthetic case – so long as we are not corrupted by an easy philosophical assimilation – that temptation is not operative. (I think the temptation should be resisted in the moral case too, but that is another story.)

III

The conception of the world as objective, in something like the sense I have sketched, is given an explicit and highly illuminating discussion by Bernard Williams in *Descartes: The Project of Pure Enquiry*.[8] In this section I shall set out some salient features of Williams's discussion, with a view to raising the question whether the conception he describes can succeed in underwriting Mackie's metaphysically disparaging attitude to values.

The fundamental idea is the idea of the distinction between reality and appearance (see p. 241). The way the world really is must be distinguished from ways the world appears to be only because the recipient of the appearance occupies some local or parochial point of view.[9] An illustration of this distinction, with a literal application of the notion of a point of view, is afforded by the way we correct for the angle from which we are observing

[8] Harmondsworth, 1978: see especially pp. 241 ff.
[9] For the phrase 'point of view' see, e.g., p. 245. Williams also uses, apparently interchangeably with the notion of a point of view, the notion of a perspective (see, e.g., p. 243). Ted Cohen has persuaded me that this is a misuse of the notion of a perspective; but I think the attractiveness of the line of thought Williams sets out is not affected.

a plane surface when we form a judgement about its true shape.[10] But this use of the notion of a special point of view, as something requiring to be transcended if we are to achieve a conception of things as they are in themselves, lends itself naturally to metaphorical extension. Thus it is natural to think of possession of the special perceptual apparatus involved in colour vision as constituting a special point of view; and a generalization of this line of thought is what underlies the familiar philosophical thought that a description of the world as it really is would leave out the secondary qualities. Again, a description of something as amusing issues from a peculiarly human point of view, constituted, in this case, by certain 'human tastes and interests' (p. 243); and a similar line of thought suggests that amusingness cannot belong to a description of things as they are in themselves.

Williams does not explicitly discuss the case of value as such. Perhaps amusingness is already an example of an aesthetic value. In any case, the evident analogy between relativity to tastes and interests and relativity to sensory peculiarities suggests a ready extension to value of the line of thought that Williams spells out about secondary qualities.

It is natural to wonder whether the idea of transcending special points of view really makes sense. Surely any conception of reality we could achieve would still be *our* conception of reality, from a point of view we occupied; the idea of a view from nowhere is incoherent.[11] Williams notices this difficulty, and responds as follows (p. 244):

> ... there is no suggestion that we should try to describe a world without ourselves using any concepts, or without using concepts which we, human beings, can understand. The suggestion is that there are possible descriptions of the world using concepts which are not peculiarly ours, and not peculiarly relative to our experience. Such a description would be that which would be arrived at, as C. S. Peirce put it, if scientific enquiry continued long enough: it is the content of that 'final opinion' which Peirce believed that enquiry would inevitably converge upon, a 'final opinion ... independent not indeed of thought in general, but of all that is arbitrary and individual in thought'.[12]

It is worth making explicit the distinctive character of the view of scientific enquiry that Williams here embraces. Scientific enquiry must be conceived as defined by a determinate method – one capable of yielding its

---

[10] The illustration is not Williams's: he goes straight to the metaphorical use of the notion of a point of view.

[11] It is important to remember how far we are from a literal application of the notion of a point of view. The thought that there cannot be a view from nowhere is not the Berkeleyan thought that any conception of how things are must be a conception of how things would strike a possible perceiver.

[12] The quotation is from 'A Critical Review of Berkeley's Idealism', in Philip P. Wiener (ed.), *Charles S. Peirce: Selected Writings (Values in a World of Chance)* (New York, 1966), p. 82.

practitioners some sort of assurance that they are on a path which, if properly followed, would lead at the limit to the ideal convergence that Peirce envisaged. And scientific enquiry, so conceived, is taken to be a pure mode of investigation of the world, uncontaminated in itself by relativity to anything local or parochial. When a candidate mode of investigation of reality is such that its upshot is vulnerable to the line of thought exemplified in the discussion of secondary qualities, someone can always complain, about the view of reality which that candidate yields, 'That is merely how things strike *us*, constituted as we are.' Facts about ourselves, additional to anything required of an investigator as such, prevent our achieving, in that way, an undistorted view of the world as it really is. But it is not so with scientific enquiry on the Peircean view which Williams endorses. Not that we cannot be engaged in scientific enquiry and still get reality wrong. But that will be because of our own fallibility; or perhaps because of our distance from the ideal end-point – perhaps there are some things we cannot get right until we are nearer getting everything right than we are. The method itself is conceived as intrinsically non-distorting; as a pure or transparent mode of access to reality.

So far we have been considering the conception of the world as it is in itself, that is, independently of the way it appears from this or that special point of view. What Williams calls 'the absolute conception of reality' is something arrived at by extending the conception of the world as it is in itself so as to encompass and be able to explain the various appearances (see p. 245; the extension will be considered further in section IV below). Now Williams's need for something to play the role he envisages for scientific enquiry emerges very clearly from a dilemma with which he confronts the absolute conception of reality in an important earlier passage (pp. 64–7). If, on the one hand, the absolute conception does not involve any determinate substance (any determinate conception of things as being one way rather than another), but is a matter of conceiving the world merely as whatever it is of which the various particular appearances are appearances, then it would be self-deceptive to suppose we have anything against which we could assess, and in terms of which we could explain, the various appearances; as Williams puts it (p. 65), 'the conception of an independent reality ... slips out of the picture, leaving us only with a variety of possible representations to measure against each other, with nothing to mediate between them'. If, on the other hand, we require the absolute conception to be a determinate conception of the way things are in themselves, then we are vulnerable to the worry that attaining such a conception is only attaining another particular point of view, so that all we have is a conception of how things appear from there – another appearance to add to the others, not something transcending appearance, in terms of

7

which all appearances could be explained.

It seems clear that this dilemma can fail to be fatal to the absolute conception only if we take ourselves to be equipped with a pure or transparent mode of access to reality as it is in itself, such as is constituted by scientific enquiry on Williams's Peircean conception. (It was not inevitable that this abstract requirement should seem to be met by science, as opposed to, for instance, divine revelation; but in our culture the casting of science in the necessary role is overwhelmingly natural.) The idea that we have a transparent mode of access to reality can permit us to occupy something like the second horn of the dilemma. It entitles us to claim to have, if not 'a determinate picture of what the world is like independent of any knowledge or representation in thought' (p. 65), at least a determinate picture of a determinate picture of what the world is like in itself,[13] and an assurance that at least the general shape of current science's (first-order) world-view is on the right lines. And the conception of science as transparent blunts the point of the second horn as Williams presents the dilemma. The determinacy in the scientific picture of the world does not carry with it any vulnerability to the accusation that that picture is only how things appear from another point of view (the scientific point of view); scientific enquiry is conceived as progressively revealing to us reality as it is in itself. So the idea of a transparent mode of access to the world disarms the dilemma. And it seems clear that nothing else would serve; if the absolute conception is not to be empty (the first horn), it requires the idea of a mode of investigation that gives us the world itself, as that against which all mere representations of it are to be measured.

Williams himself does not use the absolute conception of reality in order to recommend an anti-cognitivist position about the properties that would be excluded from the Peircean description of the world. Indeed, he is explicit to the contrary about the case of colour (see p. 254, n. 19): his claim is not that we can know only what figures in its own right in the absolute conception of things, but only that our knowledge must be 'comprehensibly related' to the absolute conception, and this allows, he says, the possibility of knowing that something is, say, green. But it would be unsurprising if this hospitality to an apparent cognitivism struck someone as a merely superficial terminological tolerance. (This would be particularly unsurprising in someone who was less cautious than Williams is committed to being about the precise manner in which the non-absolute parts of our knowledge – or, as such a person might prefer, 'knowledge' – are to be comprehensibly related to the absolute conception of reality. I

---

[13] For the retreat to the second-order, cf. Williams, p. 301: 'a view of the world (or at least the coherent conception of such a view) which contains a theory of error: which can explain the existence of rival views, and of itself'.

shall return to Williams's caution, about the case of colour in particular, in section IV below.) If the absolute conception is the frame within which all reflection on our cognitive dealings with the world must take place, then the contrast between reality and appearance is irresistibly brought into play – that is, after all, where we began – with secondary and affective qualities, and value, on the side of the appearances. Williams indeed speaks with apparent approval of 'the idea ... that the scientific picture presents the reality of which the secondary qualities, as perceived, are appearances' (p. 245). Perhaps it is only a matter of temperament whether one finds it natural at such a point, as Williams evidently does not, to say not just 'appearances' but 'mere appearances'. In understanding the inclination to add 'mere', we can understand how the thesis that all our knowledge must be comprehensibly related to the absolute conception might seem to leave no room for any substantive objection to Mackie's implied doctrine that what is *strictly* real, or part of the world, is objective. Perhaps this view might allow a more relaxed use of 'world' or 'reality' to pass muster on occasion, if explicitly recognized as non-strict. But the absolute conception cannot let such a relaxed use pass for all purposes, on pain of blurring the indispensable distinction between reality and appearance.

I conjecture, then, that what seems to justify Mackie's assumption that what is real, or part of the world, is objective – or perhaps what accounts for his not seeing that thesis as something for which a justification may be demanded – is something like the absolute conception of reality. But there is room for scepticism about the strength of any justification it can afford. I shall suggest two different grounds for scepticism in the two sections which follow.

IV

The absolute conception owes what credentials it has, as the frame for all reflection about our cognitive relations with the world, to its explanatory aspirations. The conception of the world as it is in itself is not supposed to be a mere highest common factor, 'the most that a set of very different observers could arrive at, like some cosmic United Nations resolution' (p. 244). Mere consensus could not by itself justify the claim to present the reality of which the non-agreed residues are appearances. The claim of the conception of the world as it is independently of observers (the objective conception of the world) to monopolize the 'reality' side of the distinction between reality and appearance depends on the possibility of extending it so as to become the absolute conception: that is, extending it so as to embrace and explain the particular points of view it transcends. (See especially pp. 245–6.)

But there is room for doubt about this extension. Can the expansion to embrace the various local points of view be undertaken in the objective spirit that would be required for its upshot to sustain the correlation between objectivity and reality? Or would it necessitate – surely defeating the project – a regression from the attempt to transcend particular points of view, in order to achieve an undistorted picture of reality as it is in itself, to an unregenerate occupation of the points of view that were to be transcended?

Take the case of colour. Williams considers an account of colour properties as dispositions to look red, green, etc., in certain circumstances; but he expresses scepticism about it, on the ground that 'it leaves us with the discouraging task of explaining "... looks green" in some way which does not presuppose any prior understanding of "... is green"' (p. 243). This pessimism seems well placed; and what it amounts to is the thought that the content of the appearances to be explained in this case – how it is that things appear from the point of view in question – is not so much as intelligible except on the basis of occupying the point of view. (Not that one has to suppose always that things are coloured the way they appear to be. But only someone who has, or at least might have, a use for '... is green' can understand what it is for something to look green.) Thus an explanation of the appearances in this case would have to address itself exclusively to occupants of the point of view in question, on pain of unintelligibility in its formulation of its explicandum. And how could such an explanation help show us how to transcend that point of view, let alone help convince us that transcending it is necessary if we are to achieve a correct conception of our relation to reality?

Williams writes of 'understanding ..., at a general and reflective level, why things *appear variously coloured* to various observers' (p. 242, my emphasis). Of course there is no disputing the possibility of such understanding, on the basis of information about the behaviour of light and the construction of visual equipment. But it seems to be an illusion to suppose that such understanding could still be forthcoming after we had definitively left behind a view of the world which represents colours as properties that things have (it would be a mere pleonasm to say 'really have'): in such a position, we would no longer understand what it was that we were supposed to be explaining. And it is mysterious how we are to be sustained in our resolve to abandon, or at least disparage, a point of view by a thought that is not thinkable anywhere else.

This is not a difficulty about the case of colours alone. Williams remarks that the problem about colours 'is part of a larger question, how the partial views and local experiences are themselves to be related to the world as conceived in independence of them' (p. 244). The general idea is that in an overarching objective account (the absolute conception of reality), the subjective properties (like colours) that figure in common-sense pictures of the world would be revealed as mere reflections of subjective responses to objective reality, 'projected on to the description of the world' (p. 245). To achieve the overarching objective account, one needs to transcend the point of view from which a given range of subjective concepts appears to be required in order to describe how things are, while nevertheless retaining as objectively factual the use of those concepts, or something close enough to them to serve as a basis for the supposed projection, in describing the content of the experiences characteristic of that point of view. This would work if the occurrence of the relevant predicates in describing the content of the experiences were intelligible independently of understanding their use to say how (as one takes it) things are.[14] But that is just what Williams is sceptical of in the case of colour predicates; and the point of the scepticism cannot be confined to the case of colour, but applies quite generally to the relation between the notions of *appearing* thus and so and *being* thus and so. There is a general difficulty about the idea that we can firmly detach subjective properties from objects in the world, eschewing all need for the idea of an object's really possessing such a property, while retaining the thought that such properties 'figure in our experience', so that we can regard them as projected on to the world from there.[15]

Williams returns later in the book to the question of what is involved in incorporating states of consciousness into an objective conception of the world. In a strikingly illuminating passage, he draws a connection between the difficulties in a certain familiar model of self-knowledge, on the one hand, and a misguided attempt to locate the *contents* of states of consciousness in the objective world, on the other (p. 295):

If I ... revert to the third-personal or objective point of view, and try to form a conception from there of just what is in the world when A is in pain, the temptation is to try to write into the world, in some hazy way, the appropriate content of A's experience – as we might naturally, but too easily, say: the pain. But in taking the content of A's experience, and putting it into the world as a thing we can conceive of as there, we are in effect trying to abstract from *how it is for A*, the *how it is* and leave

14 It is important that the predicates have to be *used* in describing the content of the experiences. There is no problem about the absolute conception's capacity to encompass, as a possible explicandum, someone's inclination to utter the word 'green' when confronted with something. But that is not the same as crediting it with a capacity to encompass the fact that something *looks green* to someone.
15 The idea may be encouraged by the perennial temptation to fall into a traditional sense-datum view of perception, which allows the thought that phenomenal redness, say, is a genuine property of *something* in the objective world, namely some sense-data. (I think Mackie's talk of 'resemblance' – see n. 6 above – really only makes sense in this sort of context, though it is not the theoretical framework in which Mackie claims to be operating.)

it as a fact on its own, which however has the mysterious property that it is available only to A, and can only be known directly to A, though it can be conceived of, guessed at, and so on by others. But there must be a misconception here. The *only* perspective on the contents of A's consciousness is the perspective of A's consciousness. When *it is so for A* (e.g. *it hurts for A*), the only way of one's conceiving the appropriate *it is so* at all is that of adopting ... A's point of view and putting oneself imaginatively in a state which one expresses (if it can be verbally expressed) by saying, as A, *it is so* (e.g. *it hurts*).

But one can fully concede how perceptive this is, while remaining sceptical about what Williams aims to protect by distinguishing it from the misconception he discusses here: remaining sceptical, that is, about the claim that an objective conception of the world can embrace the relevant states of consciousness themselves – facts of Williams's form *it is so for A*, where the appropriate *it is so* has an essentially phenomenal character. It ought not to be controversial that such facts can be grasped from a *third-personal* point of view. But it does not follow that they are *objectively* graspable in a sense that affords any comfort to the absolute conception of reality. It seems inescapable to suppose that facts of the form in question are intelligible (third-personally, by all means) only at, or from, a sentient standpoint whose phenomenological character is sufficiently similar to that of the facts to be understood.[16] This is a claim about the difficulty of finding room in objective reality, not for the abstracted *it is so*, but for the composite *it is so for A*. And in the light of this claim, Williams's easy equation of 'third-personal' with 'objective' (which has to mean 'independent of any special point of view') seems simply mistaken.

There is, then, a difficulty about the absolute conception's capacity to encompass the relevant subjective responses; and this raises a doubt about the absolute conception's capacity to justify the view that subjective properties reflect a projection of subjective responses on to the description of the world.[17]

---

[16] This has been argued by Thomas Nagel. See, for instance, his *Mortal Questions* (Cambridge, 1979), at p. 172: 'There is a sense in which phenomenological facts are perfectly objective: one person can know or say of another what the quality of the other's experience is. They are subjective, however, in the sense that even this objective ascription of experience is possible only for someone sufficiently similar to the object of ascription to be able to adopt his point of view – to understand the ascription in the first person as well as the third, so to speak.' Nagel's point is not at all met, as Williams seems to imply at pp. 296–7, by the thought that the totality of objectively graspable facts may *determine* the facts about consciousness. That thought – which is indeed highly plausible – is quite compatible with the falsity of any physicalism strong enough to rule out attributive dualism.

[17] I am not under the illusion that this section will have carried any conviction with anyone whose view of the mental is, in a broad sense, Cartesian. There is something to be said for including under this label the sort of physicalism that Williams envisages at p. 297. The

V

The second ground for doubt is over the idea of scientific enquiry as a transparent mode of access to reality itself. Without falling into scepticism about the general reliability of science, one may well suspect that there is an element of philosophers' fantasy in the thought that the idea of science can yield a conception of an 'Archimedean point' (Williams, p. 67), from which a comparison could be set up between particular representations of the world and the world itself.[18]

Surely whatever is substantive in any actual view of scientific method is itself part of a substantive view of what the world is like, which cannot escape being the product of a particular location in the history of science. One's beliefs about which sorts of transactions with the world yield knowledge of it are not prior to, but part of, one's beliefs about what the world is like; necessarily so, since the transactions themselves take place in the world. If a characterization of scientific method is to be general enough to be able to survive radical alterations in scientific theory, it needs to appeal to highly abstract notions like that of simplicity; and such notions acquire determinate content, and practical bite in the selection of one hypothesis as superior to others, only in the context of some specific beliefs. What looks simpler against one scientific background would look more complicated if the theory into which it is to be incorporated were different. This suggests a difficulty for the idea that scientific method can yield a conception of the Archimedean point. If we describe scientific method sufficiently abstractly not to seem vulnerable to accusations of historical parochialism (supposing we are worrying about Williams's dilemma at all), then the description will be insufficiently determinate to yield the idea of a standpoint from which to conceive the comparison between particular representations of the world and the world itself (the idea of a determinate conception of the world as it is in itself). We shall be impaled on something like the first horn of Williams's dilemma. If, on the other hand, we make our account of scientific method substantive enough for it to be plausible that it counts as a representation of a determinate representation of the world, then we shall be impaled (again, supposing that we have a worry that makes us inclined to think this way at all) on the second horn of Williams's dilemma: 'open to the reflection, once more, that that is only one particular representation of [the world], our own, and that we have no

common feature, which makes the label not inappropriate, is an inability to accept the point on which Nagel insists: namely that mental facts cannot be incorporated into a wholly objective conception of reality.

[18] The idea of such a comparison is of course characteristic of traditional correspondence theories of truth.

independent point of leverage for raising this into the absolute representation of reality' (p. 65).[19]

Williams seems to suppose that scepticism about the idea of the Archimedean point could issue only from a relativism whose ultimate tendency would be anti-scientific. A demand which the absolute conception is meant to satisfy is the demand 'that we should be able to overcome relativism in our view of reality' (p. 301). Again, part of the point of the absolute conception is that it 'would allow us, when we reflect on our representation of the world as being one among others, to go beyond merely assessing others, relativistically, from the standpoint of our own' (p. 211). It is hard to understand this except as suggesting that if we gave up the idea of the Archimedean point, we should leave ourselves uncomfortably vulnerable to some such thought as this: objectively speaking, there is nothing to choose between our own largely scientific view of the world and (say) some primarily animistic world-view which we might have presented to us, as a possible alternative, by anthropological investigation. (We should be unable to combat the animistic world-view except 'relativistically, from the standpoint of our own'.) But if this gave us any discomfort, it would depend on our incoherently combining conviction that the Archimedean point is unavailable with the thought that there ought still to be, so to speak, an 'Archimedean' meaning that we could confer on the words 'objectively speaking'.[20]

The right response to the claim that all our assessments of truth are made from the standpoint of a 'conceptual system' that is inescapably our own is not to despair of our grip on reality but to say, with Hilary Putnam, 'Well? We should use someone else's conceptual system?'[21] It is pointless to chafe at the fact that what we believe is what *we* believe. We can justify beliefs we hold about how things are (for instance, combat offered alternatives) only by appealing to what are in fact further beliefs we hold about how things are; but it would be a mistake to let this tend to undermine our confidence in the beliefs, or in their possession of a subject-matter largely independent of themselves – our confidence that we have reality more or less within our cognitive grasp. Occupation of the second horn of Williams's dilemma, unblunted by the idea of a somehow impersonal and ahistorical mode of access to reality, ought not to seem to

---

[19] Williams says, on p. 246, that the absolute conception 'is not something transcendental, but is an historical product of consciousness in the world'. But it seems that there must be something transcendental about the idea of the view from the Archimedean point. If that view is 'an historical product of consciousness in the world', then the thought of it does nothing to save us from the dilemma.

[20] For a parallel point, see pp. 41–2 of Williams's own *Morality: An Introduction to Ethics* (Harmondsworth, 1973, reissued Cambridge, 1976).

[21] *Meaning and the Moral Sciences* (London, 1978), p. 32.

threaten anything we should want to mean by Williams's thesis 'Knowledge is of what is there *anyway*' (p. 64).

This scepticism about the Archimedean point has no need to ally itself with the claim that the idea of convergent progress in science is a myth.[22] It is simply that convergence in science occupies a different position, in the right general picture of our relation to reality, from the one that Williams envisages. For Williams, the thesis that scientific enquiry converges on the truth plays a metaphysical role, in serving to introduce the idea of the Archimedean point. Once we have the idea of the Archimedean point, it is irresistible to suppose that all *genuine* truth about the world and our relation to it should be discernible from there. And since the Archimedean point has been introduced on the basis of the Peircean conception of scientific enquiry, we seem now to have been given a metaphysical foundation for the view that science constitutes the frame for all reflection on our relation to reality, and consequently a metaphysical justification for the projectivist rhetoric that seems forced on us if we try to say something suitable to such a frame about secondary qualities, affective qualities, and values. Without the Archimedean point, we can still usefully distinguish a scientifically objective component within a world-view we can concede to be inescapably ours (giving up the aspiration to render that component impersonal and ahistorical). There is nothing to stop us using whatever first steps towards Peircean convergence we think we can detect, in the history of science so far, as an internal check on the content of the objective component. This would be a scientific rather than metaphysical employment of the notion of scientific convergence. What we no longer have is a metaphysical reason to attribute to the objective component of our world-view the status of a framework within which any philosophical reflection on the remainder of our view of reality must take place.

In short: the idea of the Archimedean point, in its Peircean version, appears to constitute a metaphysical underpinning for the tendency of science to arrogate to itself final authority over the use of the notion of the world (which is a metaphysical notion, not *ex officio* a scientific one);

[22] Williams considers this as a source of opposition to the absolute conception: see p. 248.

without the idea of the Archimedean point, that tendency stands revealed as nothing but a familiar scientism – which we can recognize as such without that relativistic disrespect for science itself which Williams rightly deplores.

VI

Nothing I have said in this paper casts any doubt on the thesis that value is not objective in the sense I have attributed to Mackie. The point is, as I suggested earlier (section II), that if we can disconnect the notion of the world (or its fabric or furniture) from that notion of objectivity, then we make it possible to consider different interpretations of the claim that value is part of the world, a claim which the phenomenology of value experience has made attractive to philosophers and ordinary people. Of course this paper is at best a preliminary to that enquiry.[23]

It would be pointless to pretend that the correlation between reality and that notion of objectivity is the only obstacle to taking the phenomenology of value experience at face value. I have already mentioned the difficulties posed by the relation which the experience of moral value apparently bears to the will (section II above). A plausible connection between the experience of aesthetic value and the feeling of (in some sense) pleasure generates a problem about aesthetic value in particular, which might be summed up in this question: how can a mere *feeling* constitute an experience in which the world reveals itself to us? All I have done in this paper is to try to cast doubt on a line of thought which would prevent us from finding this question, and similar questions, so much as worth raising.

[23] In considering these different interpretations, we ought to contemplate the possibility of connecting the notion of the world with *different* notions of objectivity. One different notion of objectivity that might repay examination is one according to which an experience is of an objective reality if what the experience is an experience *of* is independent of the experience itself. This is something we might make out to be true of particular experiences of value, even if not of value experience in general; and we should ask ourselves whether something's being independent of each particular experience might not be enough to secure the truth in this case of the thesis that 'knowledge is of what is there anyway'. Again, we ought to consider David Wiggins's suggestion that convergence need not be Peircean; that a notion of objectivity suitably explained in terms of a different conception of convergence does not, after all, exclude from objective reality all features that are subjective in the sense with which this paper has been concerned. (See 'What Would be a Substantial Theory of Truth?', in Zak van Straaten (ed.), *Philosophical Subjects: Essays Presented to P. F. Strawson* (Oxford, 1980), especially at pp. 218–19.)

The possibility of aesthetic realism

PHILIP PETTIT

I

My concern in this essay is with aesthetic characterisations of works of art, in particular works of pictorial art. I want to raise the question of whether there is any general reason why such characterisations should not be taken in the realist's manner. My personal belief is that there is not and I should like to do something to bear this out: that is, to establish the possibility of aesthetic realism. What I shall do is to consider two objections that have been brought against the realistic view and to provide a sketch account of how the realist can hope to evade these.

What are aesthetic characterisations of works of art? In response I might simply say that they are characterisations with which the objections that we shall be considering engage; that would be to thrust the onus of definition on to my opponent. It would be unhelpful of me, however, to take such a short line and I propose to make three comments which may serve to focus the class of judgments that we shall be discussing.

The first comment is that aesthetic characterisations of pictures are distinct from pictorial ones. Pictorial characterisations are descriptions of the colours displayed by pictures. Nelson Goodman gives a convenient, though avowedly rough, account of them in the following passage.

An elementary pictorial characterisation states what colour a picture has at a given place on its face. Other pictorial characterisations in effect combine many elementary ones by conjunction, alternation, quantification, etc. Thus a pictorial characterisation may name colours at several places, or state that the colour at one place lies within a certain range, or state that the colours at two places are complementary, and so on. Briefly, a pictorial characterisation says more or less specifically what colours the picture has at what places.[1]

---

[1] *The Languages of Art*, Oxford University Press, 1969, p. 42. The account is rough; for example in ignoring the three-dimensional properties that a picture may have. Notice that if a painting changes shade of colour at some place it will alter in respect of the pictorial characterisations it sustains, though it may not invite a different colour name: this, because pictorial characterisations include comparisons with colour charts. The fact is important, since if pictorial characterisations were insensitive to such a change, they could not provide a base on which aesthetic characterisations supervene: see below.

My second comment on aesthetic characterisations is that they are ordinarily taken as relatively primitive reports of experience rather than as reports which have been rectified by background information. The distinction in question arises with pictorial characterisations as well as with aesthetic. Taken as primitive, 'It's red' is a report of how something looks here and now; taken as rectified, it is a report of how it would look to a normal eye under normal illumination. Aesthetic characterisations are taken as relatively primitive in so far as the only rectification that is thought to be relevant to them is that which is already assumed for pictorial reports.

In the last section of this essay we shall find ourselves forced to introduce a distinction between primitive – that is, relatively primitive – aesthetic characterisations – and characterisations that have been submitted to a distinctive process of rectification. Until then, however, we shall go along with the common assumption and treat them as primitive reports of experience. Their primitiveness comes to this: that if a characterisation applies to one work, then it applies to any which, subject to rectification for colours, is observationally indistinguishable from that work; there is no possibility of an unobservable difference affecting how the works are respectively characterised.[2]

My third comment spells out something implied in the first two. If aesthetic characterisations are non-pictorial, and if they apply to any two works which are indistinguishable in pictorial profile, then this is to say that they are supervenient on pictorial characterisations. The indiscernibility of any two works with respect to their pictorial characterisations entails their aesthetic indiscernibility; equivalently, there cannot be an aesthetic difference between two works unless there is also a pictorial one.[3] Such supervenience on the pictorial – henceforth, I shall use the term 'pictorial supervenience' – comes to what Nelson Goodman describes as constancy relative to pictorial properties. 'A property is thus constant only if, although it may or may not remain constant where pictorial properties vary, it never varies where the pictorial properties remain constant. In other words, if it occurs anywhere, it also occurs whenever the pictorial properties remain the same.'[4]

The three comments which I have offered are designed to focus the class

---

[2] My account of primitiveness draws on the account of observational predicates in Crispin Wright, 'Language-Mastery and The Sorites Paradox' in Gareth Evans and John McDowell (eds.), *Truth and Meaning*, Oxford University Press, 1976, pp. 223–47.
[3] For a useful account of supervenience see J. Kim, 'Supervenience and Nomological Incommensurables', *American Philosophical Quarterly* Vol. 15, 1978, 149–58. Like Kim, I leave open the question of whether the necessity involved in supervenience is logical necessity or some weaker variety.
[4] Goodman, p. 86.

of aesthetic characterisations. They culminate in this third remark, that it is at least a necessary condition for such characterisations that they supervene on their pictorial counterparts. In conclusion, I should like to point out that the usual examples given of aesthetic characterisations do seem to meet this condition. For a list of examples we may turn to Roger Scruton, a writer who sponsors the objections which we shall later be considering. He writes as follows about the predicates used in the aesthetic characterisation of art, pictorial and non-pictorial.

Among these predicates we find a great variety. For example, there are predicates whose primary use is in aesthetic judgment, predicates like 'beautiful', 'graceful', 'elegant' and 'ugly'. These terms occur primarily in judgment of aesthetic value. Then there are descriptions referring to the formal or technical accomplishment of a work of art: 'balanced', 'well-made', 'economical', 'rough', 'undisciplined', and so on. Many aesthetic descriptions employ predicates that are normally used to describe the mental and emotional life of human beings. We describe works of art as sad, joyful, melancholy, agitated, erotic, sincere, vulgar, intelligent and mature ... Aesthetic descriptions can also refer to the expressive features of works of art. Works of art are often said to express emotion, thought, attitude, character, in fact, anything that can be expressed at all ... Closely connected with expression terms are the terms known philosophically as 'affective': terms that seem to be used to express or project particular human responses which they also indicate by name – examples include 'moving', 'exciting', 'evocative', 'nauseous', 'tedious', 'enjoyable' and 'adorable'. We must also include among aesthetic descriptions several kinds of comparison. For example, I may describe a writer's style as bloated or masculine, a colour as warm or cold, a piece of music as architectural ... Finally there are various descriptions of a work of art in terms of what it represents, in terms of its truthfulness, or its overall character or genre (whether it is tragic, comic, ironical or what) which cannot easily be fitted into these classes, but which have an important role, despite this, in aesthetic judgment.[5]

Looking at the aesthetic characterisations of pictures towards which Scruton points, we must certainly judge the bulk of them to be pictorially supervenient. Three possible exceptions come to mind but none calls to be taken very seriously. The first is the characterisation of a work by reference to the motive of the artist, as sincere or whatever. Might not such a motive have differed while the work remained pictorially the same? In one sense it might, but not in the sense in which the characterisation which mentions it would really be of aesthetic interest. When we focus on such properties as the sincerity of a work of art we are interested usually in the sort of sincerity that shows through in the painting itself; thus were the work to differ in the sincerity it displays, it would also have to differ pictorially.

A second possible exception is the characterisation of a work by

---

[5] *Art and Imagination*, Methuen, London, 1974, pp. 30–1.

reference to that which it represents. Whether a picture represents this or that person, this or that scene, would seem to depend on factors other than its colour properties: in particular, it would seem to depend on the painter's intention. Thus any judgment of representational value must fail to be pictorially supervenient. Once again, however, it is not clear that such representational value is aesthetically interesting. What is of more direct aesthetic interest is the characterisation of a picture by reference to the sort of thing it represents: that is, as a child-picture, a landscape-picture, a Christ-picture, or whatever. Such a characterisation, unlike the judgment of particular representational value, must be expected to be pictorially supervenient.

The third possible exception to the pictorial supervenience thesis is the characterisation of a work of art as inventive or creative. Whether a picture has such a property would seem to depend as much on what other pictures are in existence as on the work itself; thus the characterisation of a picture by mention of it would not be pictorially supervenient. Here there is no accommodating response which I can immediately make but I hope to be able to describe one in section IV. In the meantime; it does not seem unreasonable to ask for charity towards the supervenience claim. That claim formulates a necessary condition on aesthetic characterisations and with respect to the utterances which it identifies, we now have to raise the realism versus non-realism issue.

II

What does it mean to regard aesthetic characterisations realistically? At a first level it means two things: that one believes that under their standard interpretation, under the interpretation which respects speakers' intentions, they come out as assertions; and further that one believes that the standard assertoric interpretation is unobjectionable. For the purposes at hand assertions may be taken as utterances which are capable of being true or false in a manner that distinguishes them from questions, commands and the like.[6] What exactly it is to be true or false is a question which we may for the moment ignore.

Under their standard interpretation, there is little doubt but that aesthetic characterisations generally come out as assertions. Under that

---

[6] Notice that not every characterisation must be said by the realist to be true or false; he may deny bivalence. See John McDowell, 'Truth Conditions, Bivalence, and Verificationism' in Evans and McDowell, pp. 42–66. Notice too that the following case is assumed not to arise: that of an utterance which is standardly taken as non-assertoric but which the realist wishes none the less to construe as an assertion. Notice finally that the reductivist who tries to fix the truth conditions of the assertions by reference to the truth conditions of certain other statements will be a non-realist only if he sees himself as combatting the standard interpretation of the original assertions.

interpretation they have the syntactical form of assertions and they have the distinctively assertoric mark of committing someone who utters them to a particular line of action, linguistic and non-linguistic: this, by contrast with non-assertoric utterances such as questions and commands.[7] There may be some utterances which would pass as aesthetic characterisations and which do not count as assertions, but it seems that they must be less than typical. The obvious examples of non-assertoric aesthetic remarks – 'Think of the painting as a coloured canvas', 'Imagine the line of the shoulder raised' – will not do because they are not examples of characterisations of pictures.

One putative class of non-assertoric aesthetic characterisations which may be mentioned for illustrative purposes is that of metaphorical descriptions of pictures as sad or gay, heavy or light, or whatever. On one theory of metaphor such utterances are not assertions under their standard interpretation, or at least not assertions in the appropriate way. Taken literally, they are assertions, but taken with their proper metaphorical import they are distinguished by the non-assertoric intention to affect the hearer's way of seeing things; the intention is non-assertoric because the effect sought is not to be achieved just through changing the hearer's beliefs.[8] It would take us too far afield to consider this theory here, but, even if it is correct, it does not undermine the claim that generally aesthetic characterisations come out as assertions under their standard interpretation. I do not myself accept the theory, but I cannot set about defending my view here.

But if the standard interpretation casts aesthetic characterisations as assertions, is that interpretation unobjectionable? There may be objections forthcoming in respect of certain sub-classes: for example, it may be said that even if metaphorical characterisations are standardly taken as assertoric in the normal way, the cost of so construing them is for some reason unacceptable.[9] We may overlook such specific objections, on the assumption that they will leave us with some aesthetic characterisations still to discuss. The question is whether there is any general reason why the standard interpretation of such characterisations might be thought to be objectionable.

What may certainly be said is that the consideration which often leads

[7] For a discussion of the latter point see Michael Dummett, *Frege: Philosophy of Language*, Duckworth, London, 1973, Chapter 10. An aspect of their having the syntactical form of assertions is that they pass the Geach test discussed by Dummett: the form of words in which an aesthetic characterisation is formulated can occur as the antecedent of a conditional. See Peter Geach, *Logic Matters*, Blackwell, Oxford, 1972, Chapter 8.

[8] Such a view might be drawn from Donald Davidson, 'What Metaphors Mean', *Critical Inquiry* Vol. 5, 1978, 31–47; reprinted in Mark Platts (ed.), *Reference, Truth and Reality*, Routledge and Kegan Paul, London, 1980, pp. 238–54.

[9] It is also possible to read Davidson's position in this manner.

anti-realists to seek out non-standard interpretations does not apply in the present case. The consideration is this: that with the body of apparent assertions under examination, the standard interpretation of them would wish us to ascribe truth-conditions to certain utterances when the relevant speakers have no way of telling whether or not the truth-conditions obtain. This consideration certainly applies to statements about other minds and about the distant past: with some such statements we shall have to admit that the relevant speakers have no evidence as to whether or not the truth-conditions realistically ascribed to the utterances actually obtain. With aesthetic characterisations, however, it seems to be irrelevant. Here there is no question of some of the utterances having to be regarded as verification-transcendent, if they are taken realistically; the characterisations are equally subject to the prospect of verification or equally resistant to it.[10]

Let us grant that, so far, the way seems to be open to us to regard at least some aesthetic characterisations realistically: that is, to believe that under their standard interpretation they come out as assertions, and to believe that that interpretation is unobjectionable. There is yet a second level, however, where it may be said that realism has also to establish certain claims. At this level, so it will be held, to regard aesthetic characterisations realistically again means two things: that one believes that under their standard interpretation they come out as assertions of a strict and genuine kind or, probably the same thought, have truth-value in the most substantial sense of that term; and further, that one believes that in this respect too the standard interpretation is unobjectionable.

It is possible to argue that it is unnecessary for the realist to enter debate at this second level. David Wiggins has urged that the notion of truth-value assumed in taking utterances as assertions is already as substantial as we should wish it to be.[11] In that case there is no useful distinction to be made between loose and strict assertions, between assertions which have truth-value in a merely formal sense and assertions which have it in a more substantial one. Although I am sympathetic, I do not propose to adopt Wiggins's strategy of argument. Rather I mean to be charitable to the opponent of aesthetic realism and to assume that he can reasonably hold at once that aesthetic characterisations are assertoric but not genuinely assertoric, capable of having truth-value but not capable of having it in the most substantial sense.[12]

---

[10] In this they are like the evaluations discussed in my paper 'Evaluative "Realism" and Interpretation' in Steven H. Holtzmann and Christopher M. Leich (eds.), *Wittgenstein: To Follow a Rule*, Routledge and Kegan Paul, London, 1980, pp. 211–45.

[11] 'What Would be a Substantial Theory of Truth?' in Zak van Straaten (ed.), *Philosophical Subjects: Essays Presented to P. F. Strawson*, Oxford University Press, 1980, pp. 189–221.

[12] In the paper mentioned in note 10 I do not consider the possibility of such a position with

Exercising such charity, I need to say that the realist holds at least some aesthetic characterisations not just to be assertions, but to be genuine assertions. And how may we define that class of utterances? Happily, we can help ourselves to a definition constructed in another context by Crispin Wright. According to this, genuine assertions are

statements communally associated with conditions of such a kind that one who is sincerely unwilling to assent to such a statement when, by ordinary criteria, those conditions obtain, can make himself intelligible to us only by betraying a misunderstanding or some sort of misapprehension, or by professing some sort of sceptical attitude.[13]

The idea is that with a genuine assertion appropriate evidence leaves no room for discretion: someone presented with the evidence can sincerely fail to assent only through a failure of understanding or apprehension, or because of adopting some form of philosophical scepticism. By contrast the non-genuine assertion – the quasi-assertion, in Michael Dummett's phrase[14] – is an utterance with all the marks of an assertion except that the conditions with which it is communally associated leave room for discretion as to whether one should assent or not.

The most plausible threat to aesthetic realism comes at this second level of debate and the opponent whom I envisage in this paper takes his stand there. He says that the standard, or at least the proper, interpretation of aesthetic characterisations casts them as quasi-assertions, as assertions which have truth-value only in a weak sense. What might that sense be said to be? This, perhaps: that we can, and probably must, render them in an interpretative language using the formula, for any asserted sentence S, 'S is true if and only if p', where 'p' is a declarative sentence. Our opponent will wish to deny that such interpretability makes S-like utterances assertions in the genuine sense, for he will say that it may yet be the case, both for S and for 'p', that the appropriate evidence leaves room for the speaker's sincerely failing to assent. What may be required to motivate assent, he will say, is not only a belief that the circumstances associated with the assertion are realised but also a certain logically independent psychological response: say, an act of will or a visitation of feeling.

A denial of aesthetic realism on the lines just sketched can be found in Roger Scruton's *Art and Imagination*. Scruton takes his starting point from the following view about aesthetic characterisations: 'To understand such an aesthetic description involves realising that one can assert it or assent to it sincerely only if one has had a certain "experience", just as one can

---

respect to evaluations.
[13] *Wittgenstein on the Foundations of Mathematics*, Duckworth, London, 1980, p. 463.
[14] See Dummett, Chapter 10. Wright's distinction is developed from Dummett's notion of the quasi-assertion, as he makes clear on p. 448.

assert or assent to a normal description only if one has the appropriate belief.'[15] On the basis of this he constructs an alternative to realism which he describes as an affective theory.

The affective theory of aesthetic description argues that the acceptance condition of an aesthetic description may not be a belief but may rather be some other mental state which more effectively explains the point of aesthetic description. To agree to an aesthetic description is to 'see its point', and this 'seeing the point' is to be elucidated in terms of some response or experience that has yet to be described. Hence aesthetic descriptions need not have truth conditions in the strong sense, and to justify them may be to justify an experience and not a belief.[16]

From what we have already seen it will be clear that there are two possible forms for an affective theory such as Scruton's. The theory may be that the standard interpretation depicts aesthetic characterisations as non-genuine assertions or, in a revisionary spirit, that although the standard interpretation depicts them realistically, aesthetic characterisations ought properly to be taken as non-genuine assertions. From our point of view, it does not really matter which version of the theory is ascribed to the opposition. We shall be looking at two objections to realism and hoping to find a means of rebutting them. The objections might be invoked to support either form of the affective theory and it is no concern of ours to determine which of these is the more plausible.

III

So much for the delimitation of aesthetic characterisations and the definition of what it is to regard them realistically. We come now to the two objections mentioned: the objections which put in doubt the possibility of aesthetic realism. The objections each point to a problematic feature of aesthetic characterisations: the one is that the characterisations are essentially perceptual, the other that they are perceptually elusive. They are not the only objections imaginable but, among serious contenders, they are the most distinctively aesthetic ones; the others tend to be recast versions of objections more commonly raised against realism about secondary qualities or realism about values. I assume in what follows that such other objections are not overwhelming. The issue is whether there is

---

[15] Scruton, p. 49.

[16] *Ibid.*, p. 55. For a denial of realism in respect of ethics which resembles the position characterised here for aesthetics see Simon Blackburn, 'Rule-Following and Moral Realism' in Holtzmann and Leich. Both Blackburn and Scruton indicate that they ascribe truth-value to the utterances which they discuss only in the weak sense that the utterances allow of interpretation by means of the formula described earlier. See Scruton, Chapter 5 for a lengthy discussion.

any distinctive reason why aesthetic characterisations should not be taken realistically.

We may assume, as a matter of definition, that aesthetic characterisations are all essentially perceptual. What this means is that the putatively cognitive state one is in when, perceiving a work of art, one sincerely assents to a given aesthetic characterisation, is not a state to which one can have non-perceptual access. What I seem to know when, having seen a painting, I describe it as graceful or awkward, tightly or loosely organised, dreamy or erotic, inviting or distancing, is not something which you can know, or at least not something which you can know in the same sense, just through relying on my testimony. It may be that common parlance would allow you to say: 'I know that the picture is graceful and inviting; I have expert and reliable testimony on the matter.' The fact remains however that, phenomenologically, we must distinguish between the type of cognitive state I enjoy – we may assume for the moment that the state is properly cognitive – and that to which you have access. The difference is like that between someone who hears a joke, finds it funny and says that it is amusing and someone who says that it is amusing on the ground of having been told as much.

Aesthetic characterisations are essentially perceptual in the sense that perception is the only title to the sort of knowledge which perception yields – let us say, to the full knowledge – of the truths which they express. In this feature they contrast with pictorial characterisations, and sensory reports in general. The cognitive state of someone who sees and reports that an object is red is a type of state accessible to a companion who sees the object and fails to discern its colour, provided that the second person has good reason to trust the report of the first. Here, by contrast with the aesthetic case, one would find the following sort of remark quite reasonable: 'I don't have to look more closely; I know from my friend's testimony that it is red.' The remark signals the fact that the cognitive state of sincerely assenting on the basis of perception to the sentence 'The object is red' is one to which testimony may also give one access. Both perception and testimony may count as titles to the full knowledge of the truth which that sentence expresses.

The essentially perceptual nature of aesthetic characterisations is surprising in view of the contrast it marks with pictorial characterisations: one would have expected the two sorts of judgments to allow of the same titles to knowledge. It constitutes a difficulty for aesthetic realism because it is unclear how the realist is to explain the phenomenon. The affective theorist, on the other hand, can make ready sense of it. He will say that one is fully entitled to assent to an aesthetic characterisation only where one has had a certain non-cognitive experience in response to the work and that this naturally leads us to deny that there can be a non-perceptual title to full 'knowledge' of what the characterisation expresses. Just as one must be amused before one is fully entitled to describe a joke as funny – the opponent of realism will naturally take amusement as non-cognitive – so it will be said that one must be moved in some non-cognitive fashion, one must enjoy some appropriate non-cognitive flush, before one has a full title to endorse an aesthetic characterisation.

Roger Scruton sketches the affective theorist's explanation in the following passage:

> If φ is a visual property, say, then it is not true that I *have* to see φ for myself in order to know that an object possesses it: there are circumstances where the opinion of others can give me a logically conclusive reason for saying that φ is there, as indeed a blind man can have knowledge of colours. In aesthetics you have to see for yourself precisely because what you have to 'see' is not a property: your knowledge that an aesthetic feature is 'in' the object is given by the *same* criteria that show that you 'see' it. To see the sadness in the music and to know that the music is sad are one and the same thing. To agree in the judgement that the music is sad is not to agree in a belief, but in something more like a response or an experience; in a mental state that is – unlike belief – logically tied to the immediate circumstances of its arousal.[17]

The second problematic feature of aesthetic characterisations, and we may also take it as definitional, is that they are perceptually elusive. What this means is that visual scrutiny of a picture, necessary though it may be for aesthetic knowledge, is not always sufficient to guarantee it. One may look and look at a painting and fail to come to a position where one can sincerely assent to the aesthetic characterisations which are true of it. One may look and look and not see its elegance or economy or sadness, for example. This perceptual elusiveness is different from the lack of thoroughness that may affect any form of perception: the lack which may explain why one did not notice the blob of yellow in the bottom left hand corner of the canvas. Assuming a normal eye and normal illumination, pointing is sufficient to put such an oversight right, but there is no exercise which is guaranteed to bring the perceptually elusive into view.

The perceptual elusiveness of aesthetic characterisations can be dramatically illustrated by reference to the ambiguous *Gestalt*. Take the much discussed duck-rabbit drawing. The description of this as a duck-representation is a putative aesthetic characterisation of the drawing. Someone who sees the drawing as a rabbit, however, may not be able, even

---

[17] *Ibid.*, p. 54. I am grateful to John McDowell for drawing my attention to what I describe as the essentially perceptual nature of aesthetic characterisations. I should mention that, unlike Scruton, I would like to leave open the question of whether a congenitally blind person can have a non-perceptual access to knowledge of colours. Some of the data relevant to the question are presented in the next section.

with herculean efforts at visual scrutiny, to come to a position where he can sincerely assert that it represents a duck. Although the characterisation is said to be determined by nothing more than what is seen, all that is seen is insufficient to produce recognition of its truth.

The perceptual elusiveness of aesthetic characterisations is surprising for the same reason as their essentially perceptual nature: it marks an unexpected contrast with pictorial characterisations. The phenomenon may be quoted as a difficulty for aesthetic realism because it is unclear how the realist can explain it. On the other hand, the affective theorist has an explanation ready to hand. He will say that assent to an aesthetic characterisation involves more than seeing that the picture has such and such a quality; it also involves having a certain sort of non-cognitive experience aroused by the picture. Saying this, he can explain the elusiveness in question by the fact that sometimes visual scrutiny of a work fails to arouse the appropriate experience, with the result that the person is not in a position in which he can sincerely assent to the characterisation.[18]

IV

The challenge for the aesthetic realist is clear. What has to be shown with aesthetic characterisations is that their being essentially perceptual and perceptually elusive can be explained consistently with a realistic construal: consistently with the view that they are genuine assertions and that the presentation of appropriate evidence leaves no distinctive room for the sincere reservation of assent. The problem, intuitively, is this. If aesthetic characterisations are held to direct us towards real properties of the works they characterise, how then do we account for the rather unusual nature of those properties? Short of making them out to be almost magical, how do we explain why the only general title to full knowledge of the properties is perception and why the most exact perception may yet fail to reveal their presence?

In order to see how such an explanation might go, let us consider the case with regular pictorial properties, i.e. properties of colour. The characterisation of something X as red is associated with an uncontentious, if analytically useless, conditional about how X looks to a normally equipped observer under normal conditions of illumination and the like. 'X is red', we can say, 'if and only if it is such that it looks red under standard presentation.' Granted the association with such a

---

[18] Roger Scruton makes this point, among others, *ibid.*, Chapter 3. He later exempts representational characterisations from the affective thesis which he argues. 'Although the important facts about both representation and expression must be stated in terms of our reactions to works of art, the logic of these two notions is (or, in the case of expression, can be) a logic of description' (p. 205). However, it seems from Chapter 3 that he will have to treat the duck-rabbit case in the manner suggested.

conditional, we can understand why the colour characterisation is neither essentially perceptual nor perceptually elusive. If the conditional tells us what it is for something to be red, then, given that the notion of standard presentation is appropriately determinate, we can see why the characterisation allows a testimonial title to knowledge and why it admits of ready perceptual adjudication.

Take first the issue of testimony. Given a sentence 'p', under what conditions might we want to endorse the following: person 1 knows that p but person 2, whom he informs of the fact, cannot be said to know in the same sense that p, even though person 2 has good reason to trust person 1? If person 1 has good evidence that p, so surely has person 2: he has good evidence of the good evidence which person 1 has. What then might make a difference? Presumably just this: that for some reason one can understand properly what is expressed by 'p' only if one has the non-testimonial relation to it enjoyed by person 1. In such a case, and it seems to be the only candidate, we might well wish to deny that person 2 knows that p, or at least that he knows that p in the same sense as person 1.

The claim can be borne out by illustration. Take the case where 'p' involves a demonstrative and where a non-testimonial relation to what 'p' describes is necessary for properly identifying the referent of the demonstrative. Suppose 'p' is 'He is fair-haired', that someone whom I trust asserts that sentence in my hearing, and that I am not in a position to see the person to whom he is referring. In such a case I could not be said to have access to the cognitive state enjoyed by my informant. I might be said to know that the assertion 'He is fair-haired', on the lips of my informant, expressed a truth, but knowledge that such an assertion is true may not involve knowledge of the truth expressed. I might be said to know that the person referred to is fair-haired, but knowledge of this kind, not involving a direct relationship with the person in question, is also less than my informant enjoys: it is knowledge de dicto, not de re.[19] Because testimony does not enable me fully to understand what is expressed by 'p', as this is asserted by my informant, so it does not give me a title to full knowledge of what is expressed by 'p'.

If the claim just presented is correct, then we can see why a colour characterisation, barring problems with demonstratives and the like, should allow a testimonial title to full knowledge. What is expressed by 'X is red' is given by the associated conditional and one can understand this properly even if one does not enjoy a non-testimonial relation to the fact reported. One knows what it is for something to look red, and one knows what standard presentation involves, even if one does not see the red object in question. Thus there is no reason why one should not be said to have

---

[19] See Tyler Burge, 'Belief de re' in Journal of Philosophy Vol. 74, 1977, 338–62.

knowledge that X is red, in the full and only sense of such knowledge, if one has been given testimony on the matter by someone whom one has good reason to trust.

It is less difficult to show why the colour characterisation should be, not only not essentially perceptual, but also not perceptually elusive. If what it is for something to be red is as the associated conditional says, then we must expect visual scrutiny to reveal the redness in every case. Only if standard presentation were a condition which was problematic in a certain manner could one have any other expectation. Were standard presentation a condition of which one could never be sure that it was fulfilled, for example, then we might reason that visual scrutiny would often fail to reveal the colour of the object scrutinised, even though all appears as normal. Granted that there are independent and relatively straightforward tests as to whether an object is standardly presented, there is no room for colour to be perceptually elusive. In any case where someone looks and fails to see, one must expect to be able to explain the failure by reference to independently checkable factors such as sensory impairment or an insufficiency of light.

Let us turn now from pictorial to aesthetic characterisations. Since these are also reports of experience, at least on a realistic construal, we must expect them to bear an association with parallel conditionals that say how the objects characterised look. Take 'X is sad' as an exemplar of aesthetic characterisations.[20] If we are realists we must expect such a characterisation to be linked with a condition which plays in relation to it the role which standard presentation plays in relation to 'X is red': we must look for a conditional of the form 'X is sad if and only if X is such that it looks sad under circumstance C'. Circumstance C, if it is to support realism, must ensure that not every work of art is sad and that any which is sad is not also at the same time, and in the same way, not sad: we shall return to this issue at the beginning of section v. It will include standard presentation and, in order to explain the difference between the pictorial and the aesthetic cases, some further condition. Thus we must look for a conditional of the form 'X is sad if and only if X is such that it looks sad under standard presentation and ——'. The question is, how should the blank clause be filled?

Our discussion of colour characterisations may be of some help to us in dealing with this problem. It suggests two constraints which any filler must meet, if it is to enable us to explain the fact that aesthetic

[20] In taking 'X is sad' as an exemplar of aesthetic characterisations, I assume that its metaphorical character does not make it significantly distinctive. Unlike 'X is sad' other aesthetic characterisations, such as 'X expresses sadness', do not allow of a transformation exactly parallel to 'X is such that it looks sad under a certain circumstance.' I also assume that this does not mean that 'X is sad' is significantly distinctive.

characterisations are essentially perceptual and perceptually elusive. If aesthetic characterisations are to be essentially perceptual, then the filler must describe a condition which can be fully understood only by someone who has a non-testimonial relation to the fact recorded in the characterisation: this, because we saw that the necessity of such a relation for understanding what is expressed by a proposition 'p' is the only likely explanation for why reliable testimony does not constitute a title for claiming full knowledge that p. If aesthetic characterisations are to be perceptually elusive on the other hand, then the filler must describe a condition which is appropriately problematic. The elusiveness could be explained if, for example, the condition were one of which one could never be sure that it had been brought about; in that case, one could explain someone's failure to see the fact recorded in a characterisation by the non-realisation, despite appearances, of the condition.

Where then do we turn for cues as to the nature of the required filler? One promising source is the ambiguous *Gestalt* such as the duck-rabbit, for here the condition that the filler describes must have a different value as the figure is differently seen. What is it that might be said to vary, in a manner consistent with realism, as the figure is seen now as a duck, now as a rabbit? With the particular duck-rabbit example it is not easy to say, but there is another ambiguous *Gestalt* with which an answer readily suggests itself. The figure in question is the central one of the five in this display:

$$12$$

$$A \quad 13 \quad C$$

$$14$$

As the figure at the centre of the display shifts from being seen as a letter to being seen as numeral, what varies is the reference class in the background. Positioned in the row class the figure is seen as a letter, positioned in the column class it is seen as a numeral.

In this example, whether one sees the figure as a letter or a numeral depends on one's disposition to identify A and C on the one hand, 12 and 14 on the other, as relevant contrasts. But these contrasts might not have been visually presented or even visualised in fancy. Generalising, then, we can say that if such a figure looks like the second letter of the alphabet, that is because one knows that the other letters supply the relevant contrasts. This knowledge gives one the appropriate reference class and against the background which that class supplies, the figure looks like the letter B.

The generalisation suggests that for any property which an object can display in perception, the object displays that property only in so far as it is positioned in an appropriate class: that is, only in so far as the perceiver knows what the relevant contrasts are. The pictorial property of redness will be displayed only in so far as the bearer is positioned by reference to the colour paradigms or, allowing for denseness, the colour spectrum. The aesthetic property of sadness will be displayed only in so far as the bearer is positioned by reference to certain parallel contrasts.

There is a crucial difference, however, between the redness and the sadness case. Because the pictorial positioning is by reference to something given once and for all, that positioning can be taken as a further aspect, over and beyond normal sight and normal illumination, of standard presentation. The aesthetic positioning, on the other hand, is by reference to something which may change from case to case. It requires only normal information and memory to position an object appropriately for colour; it requires imagination to position it so that it displays a property like sadness. Henceforth we shall ignore the positioning necessary for something like colour and reserve the term only for the case where imagination is required. Notice that imagination does not seem to be required for the case where a figure appears as a letter or a numeral: the class of letters or numerals by reference to which the figure is positioned is normalised in the same way as the class of colours.

The generalisation from our original example, combined with this observation about the aesthetic property of sadness, points us towards a general hypothesis of the kind that we require. According to the hypothesis, X is sad if and only if X is such that it looks sad under standard presentation and under suitable positioning. The positioning of the work is determined by the reference class against the background of which it is viewed. This class is assumed to be available only on the basis of imagination, not by the introduction of normalised examples.

Leaving aside the complications of raised or round surfaces, a picture can be seen as a mosaic of equal square modules, each module being of just less than perceptually distinguishable area. An elementary pictorial variation on a given picture is a variation in which just one such module differs in its pictorial properties. A compound pictorial variation, on the other hand, is a variation in which more than one module is different. Among the compound pictorial variations many, like elementary variations, will not differ discernibly from the original, but some certainly will: these latter we may refer to as the discernible variations on the picture. It will be clear that for any picture the discernible variations will include all the pictures that can be painted on the surface in question.

The hypothesis put forward is that every picture on which an aesthetic characterisation is fixed is seen against the background of a certain class of discernible variations: for simplicity, we may ignore the possibility that other sorts of items also play a background role. These variations are made into a reference class for the picture; they are used to determine what we have called its positioning. The reference class may be of any cardinality up to that of the total class of discernible variations. As the class changes in membership, the positioning changes, and as the positioning changes, the property in question may come into, or go out of, view.

Granted that a picture will have many aesthetic properties, our hypothesis means that it will be positioned at once in many different reference classes. Each of these classes can be seen as a dimension and the different dimensions may be taken to describe a space within which the object is seen when the appropriate properties are in view. The concept of a multi-dimensional aesthetic space offers a useful way of thinking about what happens when a picture assumes an overall aesthetic character for an observer. The picture is given coordinates, as it were, and fixed within an appropriate system of reference.

How plausible is the hypothesis which we have put forward? We cannot go into a full assessment of the pro's and con's here, but it may be useful to note one respect in which it is intuitively a very attractive idea. If we are offered a pictorial object and are asked whether it sustains some aesthetic characterisation, it is almost always in place to say that the answer depends on what the object is compared with. Compared with one set of figures, O may come out as a facial representation; compared with another, it may not. Compared with one range of alternatives, (0) may exemplify great regularity; compared with another, it may depict the breakdown of form. These remarks are platitudes and the attraction of our hypothesis is that it seems to do nothing more than generalise such points as they make.

Another way of bringing out the plausibility of the hypothesis is this. Given a set of mutually exclusive predicates F and G (or F, G and H: the number does not matter), it is notorious how often we agree on which member applies to any object, even an object not normally described by either term. We agree that Wednesday is fat and Tuesday thin, that science is hard and art soft, even that soup is pong and ice-cream ping. Such agreement is forthcoming, and the examples make this clear, only when it is obvious, for any object characterised, what objects are meant to contrast with it in resisting application of the term in question. Compared with Tuesday, Wednesday is fat; compared with art, science is hard; compared with ice-cream, soup is pong. What our hypothesis does is to extend the point to works of art, so far as those works lend themselves to characterisation by such sets of predicates as 'elegant–inelegant', 'economical–lavish', 'monumental–delicate', or whatever: the sets may or may not be normally used to describe pictures. The point is that pictures display themselves as suitable subjects for a given aesthetic characterisation, only so far as they are cast in appropriate contrast: that is, only so far as they are assigned to an appropriate reference class.

In connection with the plausibility of our hypothesis, what may also be mentioned is that it enables us to explain how a characterisation of a picture as inventive or creative can be cast as pictorially supervenient, and not as dependent on the other pictures in existence. We postponed the explanation from section I because we were not then in a position to describe it. The explanation is that the sort of creativity that is of aesthetic interest is the creativity which shows through in a picture when that picture is suitably positioned. Creativity is on a par with all of the other aesthetic properties: it is something which displays itself in perception, but only when the perceived object is situated within an appropriate reference class. (But see section V.)

Granted that our hypothesis is not implausible, the telling question is whether it would enable us to explain the two troublesome features of aesthetic characterisations. It offers us the following formula: 'X is sad if and only if X is such that it looks sad under standard presentation and under suitable positioning.' Does the condition described as suitable positioning meet the constraints formulated earlier? Is it fully understandable only from a non-testimonial point of view, so that the essentially perceptual feature of aesthetic characterisations is intelligible? Is it appropriately problematic, so that equally we can make sense of the fact that aesthetic characterisations are perceptually elusive?

To both questions, encouragingly, the answer must be 'yes'. Only someone looking at a picture and putting it imaginatively through various positionings can understand what that positioning is under which the picture looks sad. One fixes the positioning, one finds the appropriate reference class, only in so far as one succeeds in making the picture display the appearance of sadness. There is no access to the positioning parallel to the access which we have to standard presentation. Thus if I learn from a trustworthy and tested informant that the picture is sad, I may claim to know that the sentence 'The picture is sad' expresses a truth on his lips, but I still lack full knowledge of the truth expressed by the sentence. The reason is the same as in our earlier example with the demonstrative-involving report. What is expressed by the sentence is something which can be fully grasped only by someone who identifies the suitable positioning of the picture: that is, only by someone who has a non-testimonial relation to the fact in question.

As for our second question, it transpires that the condition described as suitable positioning is also appropriately problematic. There are tests for whether a picture is standardly presented, but not for whether it is suitably positioned. This means that we can never be sure, on grounds independent of what aesthetic characterisations are endorsed, whether or not a picture is suitably positioned for a given observer. Thus it is unsurprising that some observers will look and look at a picture and yet fail to come to a point where they can sincerely assent, on the basis of what they see, to an aesthetic characterisation which we find totally compelling.[21]

V

The preceding is a sketch-theory of aesthetic perception which indicates how a realist might respond to the two objections mentioned earlier. Rather than seek to elaborate the theory, I should like to try, in the remaining paragraphs, to buttress it against an obvious rejoinder. The opponent of aesthetic realism may argue that he can embrace our theory without embarrassment, and I must show why I think that he cannot.

We noted in the last section that the circumstance described as standard presentation plus suitable positioning, if it was to support realism, would have to ensure that not every work of art had an aesthetic property like sadness and that any which had did not, in the same way, have the property of not being sad. An opponent may now argue that this realistic constraint is not after all satisfied. He will say that for any work of art and for any aesthetic property there is likely to be a positioning, however bizarre, under which the work displays that property. Thus every work of art will have every aesthetic property and among the properties possessed by any work will be properties which are directly opposed to one another.

We may wish to cavil at the universality of our opponent's claims, but that would hardly be useful: even if the claims are only true of some works and some properties, they are still inimical to realism. They mean that we cannot generally take aesthetic characterisations as genuine assertions. The purveyor of troublesome characterisations may say that no characterisation rules out any other; in this case they cannot be regarded as assertions at all, not engaging with the notion of truth. Alternatively, and more plausibly, he may say that whether one defends one or another of a set of conflicting characterisations depends on how one positions the work. In this case they cannot be regarded realistically either, for someone appropriately placed may now be sincerely unwilling to assent to our aesthetic characterisation, even though he does not misunderstand, misapprehend, or maintain a philosophical scepticism. The factor which

---

[21] Notice that properties for which there is a normalised reference class will naturally fail to be essentially perceptual or perceptually elusive. This rules out colours as aesthetic properties and also properties such as that of being a certain letter or numeral. It may also be taken to rule out some apparently aesthetic qualities, such as that of being a landscape picture. One might argue that for such bland properties, there are often normalised reference classes.

will explain such unwillingness is his positioning the work under characterisation in some deviant way. Deviant positioning is not an expression of scepticism and neither is it a product of misapprehension or misunderstanding. So at least it will be said.

The objection raised shows that aesthetic realism must be abandoned, if the positioning of a picture is taken to be unconstrained: if there is assumed to be no right or wrong way of positioning it. As against the objection, I wish to urge that there are at least two different sorts of constraints that must be acknowledged in the positional determination of a picture, and that where these are unsatisfied the positioning is incorrect. The recognition of such constraints, as we shall see, means a serious revision in our conception of aesthetic characterisations.

The first sort of constraints on aesthetic positioning are what might be described as holistic ones. These are the constraints on how we position a picture for one kind of aesthetic property which arise from the fact that we have positioned it in such and such a way for another. The reference classes for different kinds of properties, the different dimensions of aesthetic space, interact. If a picture is so positioned that it presents itself as a representation of a woman, for example, that naturally affects how it may be positioned with a view to displaying economy or lavishness, dreaminess or matter-of-factness, sadness or gaiety. This interactive influence means that for a given kind of property certain reference classes will be inappropriate, certain positionings wrong. The positioning for any one kind is bound by the constraint that it allows such positionings for other kinds of property that the picture presents itself as a coherent unity. A given positioning will be illegitimate if it means that we cannot make unified sense of the picture as a whole: that is, if it gives rise to a certain incoherence, or if it allows us only to make sense of part of the picture.

Holistic constraints may not be taken very seriously on their own, since the standards of what is a perceptual or aesthetic unity have been dramatically altered in modern painting. Among the lessons of the twentieth-century tradition we might number this: that not only is the duck-rabbit a unity when it is seen as a duck or as a rabbit, it is also a unity, although a different non-representational unity, when seen as a duck-rabbit. In order to salvage the force of our holistic constraints, we need to see that they do not operate alone but rather in combination with another set, a set which we may characterise as humanistic ones.

Humanistic constraints spring from the requirement, not that we see a work of art as a unity, but that we see it as something which it is intelligible that a human being should have produced. When we offer a positional account of a work of art, we necessarily suppose that the painter was moved by certain desires, and certain beliefs about how he might fulfil those desires: even if we invoke unconscious intentions and the like on his part, we must offer an account of the more mundane states of mind in which these are carried. That being so, we are obliged in putting forward our construal not to commit ourselves to the ascription of beliefs or desires which are unintelligible or which it is unintelligible that the painter, granted his milieu, should have had or should have acted upon.[22]

Humanistic constraints can be disregarded only at the cost of ignoring the human origin of pictures, or at a cost of ignoring the humanity of those with whom pictures originate. I assume that such a price is not worth paying. Together with holistic constraints they will have effects such as that of proscribing the construal of Egyptian pictographs as early cubist paintings, or the construal of pictures in the international Gothic style as paintings designed to dismantle perspective. If they seem to spoil sport in so undermining the cult of play, this may only be because art is not taken as a serious matter.

It may be said that if holistic and humanistic constraints are generally respected in the positioning, and consequently the aesthetic characterisation, of pictures, that is only a matter of changeable convention. It is certainly a matter of convention, just as it is a matter of convention that certain constraints define what is meant by standard presentation in ascertaining the colour of things. But might the convention change? Not, I would say, without a barely imaginable transformation in what is meant by artistic production and aesthetic appreciation.

Under our current and traditional conception of these matters, the artist and his ideal audience share a common knowledge in virtue of which each can expect the other to see a distinctive significance in certain painterly choices. Against such a background the artist seeks, and knows that he will be taken to seek, a certain unified effect in every picture he makes: in a sense, he speaks to his audience. This conception would be quite undermined if the holistic and humanistic constraints on aesthetic positioning were put aside. If it does not matter that a positioning makes only partial sense, or makes a sense that the artist could not have consciously or unconsciously sought, then the work of art might as well have been the product of chance. It ceases to be a challenge to enter into a perception sponsored by the artist and degenerates into an occasion for the play of whim and fancy.

The recognition that there are constraints of positioning forces us to recast what we have said in preceding sections about aesthetic

---

[22] As has often been noticed, holistic and humanistic constraints operate generally in the assignment of intentional characterisations to actions. See, for example, Graham Macdonald and Philip Pettit, *Semantics and Social Science*, Routledge and Kegan Paul, London, 1981.

characterisations of works of art. The sort of characterisation we have discussed satisfies the following schema: 'X is φ if and only if it is such that it looks φ under standard presentation and under suitable positioning.' The introduction of constraints of positioning forces us to recognise that our real interest is in a sub-species of this kind, namely the sort of characterisation which meets this more specific schema: 'X is φ if and only if (1) it is such that it looks φ under standard presentation and under suitable positioning and (2) it is such that the positioning found suitable, assuming that there is one, is allowed by the appropriate constraints.' The difference between the two classes of judgment is that which we mentioned at the beginning of the paper: the one class is that of primitive aesthetic characterisations, the other that of aesthetic characterisations rectified by appropriate background information.

What appears in this section is that aesthetic realism can only be defended in the last resort for characterisations which are appropriately rectified. We may stave off the two objections considered by recourse to the idea of positioning, but that idea will underpin realism only if we introduce constraints and distinguish rectified from primitive characterisation. We should not be surprised at the result, for it parallels the case with characterisations of colour. The unrectified colour report would have to be taken as less than a genuine assertion, since something other than misapprehension, misunderstanding or scepticism would make intelligible a subject's sincere unwillingness to assent to an appropriate judgment: for example, his wearing coloured contact lenses, his having been in bright sun, his being blinded by an intruding light, or whatever. We can construe colour reports realistically only because they are taken as rectified by the reference to standard presentation; this reference means that factors such as those just mentioned are recast as obstacles to apprehension.

This paper began with the discussion of primitive aesthetic characterisations because aesthetic characterisations are normally assumed to be such. The starting-point is also philosophically justified since rectified aesthetic characterisations can be defined only by reference to primitive. It must be noted, however, that rectified characterisations differ significantly from their primitive counterparts. The main differences spring from the fact that the characterisations depend on background as well as visual information. Thus they are not pictorially supervenient, for example: our background information will prevent us from characterising in the same way as the original a pictorial replica produced by some chance mechanism.[23] Furthermore, the realistic construal of rectified characterisations may be undermined by a non-realism in respect of the utterances, related to other minds and perhaps the distant past, which constitute relevant background information. If we defend aesthetic realism, we must assume that realism is appropriate in those other areas as well.

The theory sketched in the last section shows how one may hope to escape Scruton's objections and espouse aesthetic realism. The amendment constituted by the restriction to rectified aesthetic characterisations keeps open that hope. There is room for the endorsement of the following sort of remarks. In the sense in which it is usually assumed that the colours of a picture are there to be perceived, there to be more or less exactly characterised in pictorial description, so the aesthetic properties are there to be detected and characterised.[24] An aesthetic description of a picture may well fail to capture all that is there to be seen by the informed eye, but what it captures when it is a faithful record is something which properly belongs to the painting and something which is in principle accessible to all. Aesthetic characterisations, or at least those to which no special disqualification attaches, are both standardly and properly taken as assertoric, and as assertoric in the strictest and most genuine sense of that term.[25]

I am grateful for the helpful criticism that I received when an ancestor of this paper was read to the Thyssen Group. I am also grateful for the critical remarks made by the audience when the paper was read to the Philosophy Society, Lancaster University. Finally I must record my debt, and my gratitude, for written comments received from Jeremy Butterfield, Graham Macdonald and Eva Schaper. Peter Lewis has drawn my attention to an excellent article which contains similar ideas: Mark Sagoff, 'Historical Authenticity', *Erkenntnis* Vol. 12, 1978, 83–93.

[23] It may be wondered whether there is room for a distinction between primitive and rectified aesthetic characterisation of such objects as natural scenes. I tend to think that there is. I assume that such characterisation presupposes positioning and I believe that one's general view of nature will supply constraints to distinguish reasonable positionings from wholly artificial ones. Artificial positionings encourage the quaint and the whimsical, reasonable positionings the genuinely revelatory.

[24] The usual assumption may of course be questioned. It is often argued, for example, that colour ascriptions are improperly, if standardly, taken as genuine assertions. See, for instance, Bruce Aune, *Knowledge, Mind and Nature*, Ridgeview Publishing Co., Reseda, California, 1967, Chapter 7.

[25] The clause about special disqualification is meant to cover such possibilities as that raised about metaphorical characterisations in section ii.

The pleasures of taste

EVA SCHAPER

That the notion of taste is central to aesthetics is a well-entrenched idea. Exactly how it is to be understood is less clear. Traditionally, theories of taste have concerned themselves with how – or even whether – personal preferences are related to aesthetic value judgements. Such theories, from the eighteenth century onwards, have become associated with the idea of the beautiful, in line with aesthetics coming to be regarded as the science of the beautiful – an idea, Wittgenstein reminds us, 'almost too ridiculous for words'.[1] It is worth remembering that he would say the same about the good and ethics. Aesthetics, then, has as much or as little to do with the beautiful as ethics has with the good. When traditional philosophers, prominently Kant, hold that taste judgements are about what is beautiful, we could say that they are about *aesthetic* preferences, and that it is the analysis of what qualifies as a genuinely aesthetic judgement that separates personal preferences of a purely idiosyncratic kind from those preferences to which reason-giving is relevant in an appropriate form. This form must exhibit the logical difference of aesthetic judgements from moral, epistemological, economic, social and generally pragmatic judgements and thus confirm or establish the autonomy of aesthetics. We shall not, however, understand what this autonomy amounts to, except through an exploration of issues in the philosophy of mind, epistemology, logic and much besides. To seal off the aesthetic tank hermetically from the wide waters of philosophy is a move that has often brought the very undertaking of aesthetics into disrepute. It is not, I believe, a move of which the great contributors to its growth and understanding have been guilty.

In traditional theories of taste, one of the dominant questions was whether taste judgements – or statements of aesthetic preference – were subjective or objective, and in what sense. In one guise or another, this is still a prominent theme, despite the greater logical sophistication with which the contrast is now treated. Traditionally, also, theories of taste have insisted on a close connection between aesthetic appreciation and the

[1] *Lectures and Conversations on Aesthetics, Psychology and Religious Belief*, ed. C. Barrett, 1966, p. 11.

feeling of pleasure. What this connection is supposed to be, and the role assigned to pleasure, varies between theories and marks them off from one another. Over-simplifications to the point of caricature sometimes arise from the non-fortuitous ambiguity of 'taste' as picking out both the phenomena in which we are here interested and the sensations of the palate. Yet even the crudest exploitation of an analogy here points to something which seems axiomatic to any theory of taste: that the central role played in it should be a subject's experience of something or other, and the consequent pleasure or lack of it. The important question, then, is one of showing how the feeling responses are related to the causes and reasons which might be adduced for judgements of taste or aesthetic preferences.

There are many kinds of remarks we make about someone's responses to objects of appreciation. We say of his judgements that they are stupid or intelligent, that they show sensitivity or lack in delicacy, that they are sincere or bogus, alert or sluggish, discriminating or obtuse, precise or muddy, refined or vulgar, perceptive or crude. And so on. When we say that a person has taste, we are not adding something along the same lines. Rather, we think that a person has taste when he makes appreciative remarks that are intelligent, interesting, show sensitivity and discrimination, are not banal, trivial or boringly obvious. But we think that he has taste only if we believe that what he says arises from his own experience and is not parrotted or feigned. It is, of course, not just a matter of what people *say*; that only affords on the whole the easiest access to another's taste. A person may surround himself, with evident enjoyment, with just such objects and manifest his preferences in just such ways as allow us to conclude that he is capable of judgements of a certain kind. To have taste, we tend to think, is to have an ability which could, but need not, be expressed in judgements of taste.[2]

Yet we also tend to think that there is something paradoxical in our normal understanding of taste. On the one hand we believe that taste is bound up with the immediacy of feeling and that taste judgements therefore cannot be derived from principles or canons. On the other hand we believe that taste can be cultivated and educated and that taste judgements are reasoned appraisals. This tension has been felt ever since the heyday of theories of taste in the eighteenth century.

John Gilbert Cooper is a representative of one view: 'A *good* taste is that

[2] It will be noticed that I am not distinguishing between good and bad taste; the reasons for this may become obvious later on. 'Good taste' can often be substituted when I speak of taste – as in 'man of taste'; but I do not thereby acknowledge the distinction. If the objection is that 'bad taste' is something to be reckoned with, the answer is: yes and no. Yes, if what is meant by 'bad taste' is 'tasteless' or 'having no taste'; no, if someone enjoys what *others* call 'bad' taste, but enjoys it for the right kind of reasons. In either case, the distinction falls away. It has a place in the history of fashions – and of opinions.

instantaneous glow of pleasure which thrills thro' our whole frame, and seizes upon the applause of the heart, before the intellectual power, reason, can descend from the throne of the mind to satisfy its approbation.'[3] More soberly expressed, to have taste is to feel pleasure in something for which reasons can at best be found afterwards. Voltaire similarly observed that taste, like the sensations of the palate, 'anticipates reflexion'.[4]

Edmund Burke, however, argues against any such idea that taste is a 'separate faculty of the mind, and distinct from the judgement and imagination; a species of insight by which we are struck naturally, and at first glance, without any previous reasoning with the excellencies, or the defects of a composition'. What impressed him, and what he thought was incompatible with anything like the Cooper–Voltaire position, was that the operative factor in question was the understanding 'and nothing else'. Early and precipitate responses may be changed, he thought, by deliberation, and 'the taste (whatever it is) is improved exactly as we improve our judgement, by extending knowledge, by a steady attention to our object, and by frequent exercise'.[5] A taste that can be educated cannot be instinctive: to have taste is more like having learned to read than it is like having a taste for curry.

The contrast here is arguably overdrawn. The Cooper–Voltaire view does not have to be taken as supporting that shadowy figure, the man of innate good taste – him we can safely leave alone in this context. Also, it need not be incompatible with the fact (if it is a fact) that taste is educable. For someone who holds that in the beginning is the response may also believe, and reasonably so, that how someone responds is influenced by experience, education and culture. And there is room for debate, even if we grant the priority of feeling over reflection, or, in Voltaire's words, that 'taste anticipates reflexion'. Debate could arise when subsequent probing for the reasons of the initial feeling found that whilst there were such reasons, they hardly justified the feeling. Just as it may be true that my reason for being in a rage is that my neighbour is playing the piano, yet I am not therefore justified in feeling rage, so, it must seem, feeling pleasure may be a fact, yet the reasons for feeling it may turn out not to justify it. But if feelings are sometimes not justified by our reasons for them, it does not follow that feelings never have justifying reasons. That, then, suggests that even on the Cooper–Voltaire view, the subsequent reflection on feelings is relevant to the status allotted to them: the deliverances of putative taste may have to be disregarded if feelings, including those of pleasure or

[3] *Letters Concerning Taste*, 1755, p. 3.
[4] *Essay on Taste*, in A. Gerard, *An Essay on Taste*, 1759, p. 213.
[5] *Philosophical Enquiry into the Origin of our Ideas of the Sublime and the Beautiful*, 1757; ed. J. T. Boulton, 1958, p. 126.

displeasure, can be discovered to have been inappropriate. For clearly it must be appropriate feelings only that fill the bill of 'seizing upon the applause of the heart'. So our first view in question slides towards having it both ways: in one sense *de gustibus non est*, and in another *de gustibus est disputandum*.

If, on these considerations, we favour Burke, matters are not obviously improved. 'Whenever the best taste differs from the worst, I am convinced that the understanding operates and nothing else.' Here the objection must be that whilst this commendably stresses the importance of understanding the reasons for taste judgements, it is always possible that the reasons which would justify a person's feeling pleasure might not be *his* reasons even though he acknowledges them: he may not *feel* pleasure, but understand the kind of things others say when they do. But whether a person has taste, or what his tastes are, cannot be divorced from considerations of his feelings, from what he takes pleasure or displeasure in. (This is the point where the issue of sincerity enters the theory of taste.) Any reasons given must justify *his* feelings and not what, perhaps, he *thinks* he ought to feel. Thus Burke must be wrong when he insists that in matters of taste it is the understanding that operates and *nothing else*.

Though we have softened the contrast between the two positions somewhat, a feeling of bafflement remains. The beginning of wisdom might be to try, following Kant, a differentiation of judgements of taste from other judgements whose logical behaviour is both similar to and distinct from them. Taste judgements can be seen as a species of a genus of which culinary and moral judgements, for example, are species also. The leading idea, then, is that we have to look at the reasons, if any, for preferences to find the distinguishing features of the aesthetic ones, since the objects of preference do not by themselves dictate the kind of preference involved. In speaking of aesthetic preferences, nothing as yet prompts us exclusively in the direction of art objects at all, since preferences here might equally well be based on moral or pragmatic (e.g. monetary) considerations.[6] And in general it would be as unhelpful to say that moral considerations are moral because of their objects being, say, human actions as to maintain that taste judgements are aesthetic because their objects are, say, works of art.

Roger Scruton's treatment of aesthetic preferences illustrates the typically Kantian approach.[7] He points out that aesthetic preferences share some of the characteristics of both culinary and moral preferences.

---

[6] There is no reason even to exclude from the range of art objects constructions, say, of an edible nature that could be consumed analogously to music for instant consumption in supermarkets, psychiatric wards, therapy groups, or some television and screen plays.

[7] 'Architectural Taste', in *British Journal of Aesthetics*, 15, 1975, 304.

Culinary preferences are never actually in logical conflict, and we do not feel obliged to defend them. Moral preferences can be inconsistent and in conflict with one another and are always supported by reasons – they can be refuted and may be abandoned. Aesthetic preferences, by contrast, whilst never strictly inconsistent with one another, are yet justifiable by appeal to reasons. The outline is familiar, but a few of the more difficult details are worth dwelling upon.

With respect to culinary preferences, that we are not obliged to defend them is because there are no reasons (as against causes) which could possibly support them. This is not to say, though, that we may not have to defend our choices in this area. I may not be called upon to defend a preference for cod's roe to caviar, but my choice of the roes as against caviar at a dinner where the proceeds go to relief of Cambodian refugees is another matter. Similarly, the drug addict may not be called upon to defend his preference of heroin to alcohol, but the reasons for choosing to drink rather than to inject can be argued and may well be plain to him: he may actually wish he preferred them in that order though he does not. If statements of preferences are in this area simply reports of what is more pleasurable to the speaker, then choices may well be defended by appealing to or overriding them. But the preferences themselves are not the sort of thing for which reasons can be adduced.

It is not entirely clear how this feature of culinary preferences is related to the other, the logical independence of one such statement of another, so that no two declarations of preference can ever be inconsistent. A first look is reassuring. If I had reasons for preferring A to B, and these were also reasons for preferring D to E, then there would be a kind of inconsistency in not doing so. But there are no reasons. However, this leaves me with a doubt about the transitivity of preferences. Would it simply be a psychological quirk, then, if someone preferred caviar to cod's roes, cod's roes to chicken livers, and chicken livers to caviar? I find it hard not to see an inconsistency here, though I must grant that the person in each case just expressed a liking of one as against the other. Further – and although the relation between belief and pleasure is far too vast an area for me to explore here – would it not be the case that where beliefs and likes or dislikes interact, we do on occasion have at least a foothold for the suspicion of inconsistency? An obvious example is provided by the man who is revolted in retrospect on being told what animal he has just eaten with keen enjoyment, believing it to be quite another. And where parity of belief is concerned, there does seem to be scope for charges of inconsistency of a kind, even in pleasures of the table.[8]

---

[8] I suppose this is the sort of problem of which Donald Davidson said that it led to his

I have spent more time on gustatory preferences than on moral ones because one feature of the former, the alleged logical independence of one such preference of another, is said to carry over into aesthetic preferences. And this seems to me more problematic than the similarity with moral preferences, namely that both are supportable by reasons. Let's see how far we have got.

(1) (Contrasted with culinary preferences but similar to moral ones): aesthetic preferences or taste judgements are not merely capricious or idiosyncratic, as reason-giving is a legitimate move in the game. And if reasons can be given, then the reasons adduced for pleasure taken in one object or situation may in principle at least set up constraints on the justifying reasons for pleasure in some other objects.

(2) (Contrasted with moral preferences but similar to culinary ones): it is nevertheless possible to maintain that the felt delight is primary and that there is no reason in logic why feelings should be either consistent or inconsistent with one another.[9] With Burke we thus want to acknowledge a commitment to the idea that aesthetic preferences are rational in a way that culinary ones are not. We have reasons for the former and thus a right to assert them. A preference for which no reason *could* be adduced – like preferring wine to cider – is not aesthetic. At the same time, however, there is the pull of the Cooper–Voltaire view: something just appeals to us, even in our aesthetic preferences, and initially no reason can be given – the feeling of pleasure is the basic datum. Only afterwards do we start looking for reasons. Yet, again with Burke, finding reasons may modify our responses; it alters what we see in the object, and that in turn affects what we feel towards it. This compromise pinpoints the twin desire to show taste judgements to be based on reasons and yet to preserve the basis of such judgements in the immediacy of feeling. No wonder the compromise is an

abandonment of a brief career as an experimental psychologist: 'I do not think we can clearly say what should convince us that a man at a given time (or without change of mind) preferred *a* to *b*, *b* to *c* and *c* to *a*', the reason being that 'we cannot make good sense of an attribution of preferences except against a background of coherent attitudes' ('Psychology as Philosophy', in *Philosophy of Psychology*, ed. S. C. Brown, 1974, pp. 49–50. Also 'Mental Events', in *Experience and Theory*, ed. L. Foster & J. W. Swanson, 1970, pp. 51ff, 96).

[9] Roger Scruton in the article already cited discusses this tension with an example from architecture (p. 304). He accepts something like (1) and (2), but is uneasy about how they fit together. On (2) there is no formal inconsistency in a man's saying that he (aesthetically) very much likes St Bride's and very much dislikes St Mary-le-Bow. But, granting the truth of (1), 'it would be most odd if a man really thought that there was nothing in the basis for his dislike of St Mary-le-Bow that would not equally provide him with a reason for disliking St Bride's'. If, for example, he regarded the Baroque steeple as an unhappy compromise, should he not dislike them both? The answer, it seems to me, is that he probably should – but that he can be inconsistent in his aesthetic preferences only relative to the reasons given for them, not in the feelings as such – whilst for culinary preferences no reasons are relevant and they *cannot* therefore be inconsistent in any sense.

uneasy one, as each apparently compelling insight can readily reclaim a life of its own.

Kant had a name for it – the 'antinomy of taste'. As such, it is no more than a label for the location of a problem area which he tried to clear up. Even if, in the end, Kant cannot be said to have succeeded fully, it is worth going with him beyond the point reached so far.

His approach is oblique, via the characteristic transcendental mode of arguing – which is, in the *Critique of Judgement*, even less clear than in the other two Critiques. And if we are puzzled already about the notion of taste, this might seem to reduce the significance of Kant's contribution. However, I believe it would be our loss to disregard it on that ground alone. The strategy, roughly, is this. He first presents what he calls 'expositions' of the concept of taste, that is, delineations of those features which can be discerned as belonging necessarily to it – or, at least, those features which Kant found central to it. Among them, importantly, are the following. Anyone who as a subject makes a pure judgement of taste – that is, a judgement of the form 'This is beautiful' – claims for it universal validity for every subject (§20). But such a subjectively necessary judgement has, as Kant puts it, 'its foundation in the object'. Whilst subjective, then, it is not idiosyncratic. Now, with these features alone, taste judgement requires a 'deduction', that is, a demonstration of how it is that judgements possessing these features may legitimately be made. The deduction is, of course, to be a transcendental one, and we need to remember in what circumstances such deductions are called for.

In the *Critique of Pure Reason* a deduction was required in order to explain how certain concepts, the categories, can apply *a priori* to objects of possible experience (B 117). In respect of cognitive judgements, this deduction would explain how, and justify that, certain *a priori* principles (such as the causal one) can be affirmed as holding good of nature and are presupposed in all our knowledge claims. A parallel with the status of the judgements of taste is then tenuously established: 'The obligation to furnish a Deduction, i.e. a guarantee of the legitimacy of judgements of a particular kind, only arises where the judgement lays claim to necessity', Kant says in the third *Critique* (§31:1–3). So all that is needed for taste judgements to require a deduction is that they imply claims including prominently those to necessity and universality. And so they do, according to the expositions of the concept. What must be shown, then, is the principle or principles we can appeal to in their justification. And such principles, if they exist, must be *a priori*.[10]

---

[10] The following should not need pointing out, but in view of a widespread misunderstanding, unfortunately it does. Kant, it is sometimes said, held that judgements of the form 'This is

That said, however, the parallel seems to break down in another direction. For the problem of the deduction of the *Critique of Pure Reason* was precisely that of showing the legitimacy of *objective* application of certain concepts – thus showing how *objective* cognitive judgements are possible. Coming to the legitimization of taste judgements, however, we have to deal with judgements that have among their necessary features that of *subjectivity*. That is to say, although the judgement of taste necessarily, according to Kant, lays claim to the agreement of others 'just as if it were objective' (§32:25), it is not in fact objective. There are no criteria for determining true or false judgements of taste – as there are in the case of empirical judgements. But if it is this combination of subjectivity with the necessity claim that characterizes taste judgements and that now needs a certificate of legitimacy, then, we might feel, so much the worse for Kant's argument. A question of justification certainly arises, but it surely does so in a very different way from that in which it intelligibly emerges in the *Critique of Pure Reason*.

There are, indeed, thorny problems here for the Kant interpreter into which I cannot go. But I think one can at least lessen resistance to Kant's enterprise in this way. We have seen Kant affirming that certain features of the judgements of taste are necessary features, in particular that they claim universal validity but are nevertheless subjective. They then need a deduction, something that would show our entitlement to make such judgements. But we may feel that the deduction is redundant as judgements with those features are impossible anyway. Against this Kant would say that what his argument would show, if it went through, would be precisely how, appearances to the contrary, there can be judgements having those features. A justification would show both intelligibility and legitimacy of the claims of taste. 'The solution of these logical peculiarities, which distinguish a judgement of taste from all cognitive judgements, will of itself suffice for a Deduction of this strange faculty . . .' (§31:12–14).

Intelligibility can be granted, I think, even without the full solution to these peculiarities. Let me put what seems to be the problem in a very simple way. Everybody would agree, I suppose, that to say something is beautiful because it comes up to standards for which one can give a specification in terms of a set of rules, is intuitively false. That is not to show that it *is* false, but merely to indicate where most people now would

---

beautiful' were *a priori* synthetic judgements. This, of course, would be sufficient to discredit his entire enterprise. But it confuses the status of particular taste judgements with the conditions of making such judgements. In this respect taste judgements are exactly parallel to particular empirical judgements: it is not they that are synthetic *a priori* but the principles yielded by the categories which they presuppose.

take their initial stand. It has not always been so, but even in the eighteenth century, accounts of taste judgements have rarely taken the form I am now simply rejecting. There are no rules straightforwardly applicable on the analogy either of rules of a game which determine what the correct moves in it are, or of standard exemplars (like the standard metre) which supply points of comparison, or of standards of behaviour or etiquette. Any of these analogies might profitably be suggested if our interest were in historical or sociological study of fashions in taste – a legitimate inquiry, no doubt, but not mine.

In the above cases, rules and standards are formulable in abstraction from the particular cases we measure against them. But even if we contrived to elicit from the practices of a group or a society something approximating to a standard in this sense, it would not be that standard which could legitimize any claim to objectivity in aesthetic judgements. Consensus, even if there were one, in these matters would not amount to a means of assessing the objective validity of individual judgements. It does not follow, however, that failing such standards the only alternative is to fall back on a simple subjectivism, considering taste judgements merely as statements of likes and dislikes about which dispute would be futile. We may not believe in rules of taste; but neither do we think that in matters of taste anything goes. There is a way to be found for speaking of errors and lapses of taste, and for the cultivation and education of taste.

Kant's way, as one would suspect by now, is not an easy one. He does speak of correct and erroneous judgements of taste (e.g. §8). This, however, must not be construed as his subscribing to standards or rules of taste. He has something quite different in mind, namely that a judgement to be one of taste at all must satisfy certain conditions. Accordingly, a judgement of taste is called 'correct' not when it conforms to rules of validity, but when it meets the conditions for being a taste judgement. Erroneous judgements of taste, then, are judgements erroneously thought to be taste judgements, the error or mistake lying in falsely believing that one sort of assertion has been advanced when in fact quite another sort has been made. So a judgement of taste, when 'correct', is so not because it can be shown to be either true or false, but because the conditions for making such a judgement have not, in Kant's words, been 'sinned against'. When the conditions are satisfied, it will precisely not be the case that a particular judgement can be justified by appealing to criteria of truth or falsity, correctness or incorrectness, or to standards in terms of which to assess objective validity. Kant speaks of such judgements as having 'subjective validity', but that has nothing to do with truth or correctness of a judgement as ordinarily understood.

47

This, I admit, cannot but strike one at first as an evasion of the problems of taste judgements altogether. Kant's use of 'correct' and 'erroneous' is not the customary one, according to which one would expect there to be a difference between not being a judgement of taste and being a wrong judgement of taste – roughly like the difference between an illegal and a bad move in chess. The latter is a parallel Kant would disallow – and one wants to protest. Surely, a further question of propriety must arise after one has granted that a judgement is appropriately a judgement of taste, a question, that is, about the grounds for *this* judgement being made rather than *that*? In granting that the judgement is one of taste at all, we have at best settled the question whether the grounds for the judgement are appropriate to the kind of judgement it is, but not whether they are appropriate to what we call the object of a specific judgement.

Kant's reply would be that the further question is not one that can be asked. In matters aesthetic, what *seems* right is right for the person making the judgement – if it is correctly made: it is subjectively valid. A question can indeed be asked, and presumably must be asked, about why a person finds, say, a certain object beautiful, for his reasons will be crucial to knowing whether he has made a taste judgement or not. The particular judgement, once we accept it as one of taste, does not allow of further questions such as 'Is it true or false?' For its being a taste judgement leaves things just there. But the subject nevertheless thinks that his response is appropriate, not merely idiosyncratic. Kant alleges that such a person would have the basis for an imputation of the consent to it from others – something which would be absent from a pronouncement on the agreeable.

If we take the Kantian line, the question 'By what right is consent presumed?' must be a theoretical question, concerning not the content of an individual taste judgement but the form, i.e. its being a taste judgement. There is, it is true, a Kantian answer to it which goes beyond a purely formal one (though it too is independent of the particular content of a taste judgement). It goes something like this. When we judge something, exercising taste, we endorse, it seems, a trust in our capacity for delight that is necessarily bound up with the conviction that the delight can be matched by others (even if it is not). That conviction has a foundation in our common humanity. It is not so much that the person making the judgement sets himself up as an adjudicator as that he recognizes a 'universal voice' in his own appraisal. I find this, whilst appealing, philosophically hard to justify. Whether or not the form of the judgement demands that we cannot but hope that our own sincere taste appraisals make a claim upon all, it is difficult to see why this hope should be satisfied by a common human nature. Anything as general as that seems too general to sustain it. I shall stay for the time being with the more manageable formal question and return to the universal voice briefly at the end.

How is it, then, that taste judgements claim a special kind of validity though there are no criteria by which the individual judgement could exhibit its objective validity and thus be binding on others? The formal turn here is again to the *kind* of judgement it is: the universality that characterizes all genuine taste claims is subjective only. So let us concentrate on the principal condition whose satisfaction is central to something's being a taste judgement. Indeed, it even demands the subjectivity of such judgements. It emerges when we reflect on just two ways in which a putative taste judgement could fail to be accepted as such.

First, there is the case of someone who adopts another's judgement because he, rightly or wrongly, believes that the other has good taste. He does so without feeling either pleasure or displeasure in what he says he appraises. This may show a certain amount of intelligent awareness of what is usually valued or appreciated; it may even help eventually towards authentic taste appraisals. But as such it is a prudential assessment, and what the person actually prefers is irrelevant to his pronouncements.[11]

Secondly, there is the case in which someone does respond directly with pleasure or displeasure to something and would yet, on reflection, withhold the title of a taste judgement because the pleasure or displeasure was or became known to be fully conditioned by circumstances only contingently related to the ostensible object of delight or disgust. (For instance, I respond directly and strongly to Wagner: a single phrase is usually enough to give me intense displeasure. I do not doubt my response; occasionally I may even regret it. But I know, if not perfectly, why I respond as I do, and this knowledge, which I shall not here reveal, speaks against my displeasure's being the basis for a judgement of taste.)

So taste judgements must, in the first place, be based on the individual response of the person making them, that is, on felt pleasure in, or repugnance to, something; and, secondly, this pleasure or displeasure must be felt for appropriate reasons or from appropriate causes. Together that gives us the criterion of disinterestedness. For an appraisal to be that of taste, it must proceed 'by means of a delight or aversion *apart from any interest*' (§5:14–15).[12]

The notion of disinterestedness is often misinterpreted. The most

[11] Martin Hollis pointed out to me: 'I'm told there are expert tea tasters who don't like tea. They are not expert *merely* in what other people fancy.'

[12] Let me say at once that I do not go along with Kant's next move which seems, if not a *non sequitur*, then at least unsupported at this stage in the argument: 'For where anyone is conscious that his delight in the object is with him independent of interest, it is inevitable that he should look on the object as one containing a ground of delight for all men' (§6:23–6). Even if this conclusion can be reached eventually, the universality claim can hardly be said to follow immediately from the fulfilment of the disinterestedness requirement.

damaging of the readings that get in the way of seeing the link with the claim to subjective validity misconstrues disinterested pleasure (or displeasure) as a special sort of emotion, qualitatively different from interested pleasure (or displeasure). And if the question of what makes a judgement aesthetic hinged on its being an attitude exhibiting this special characteristic, then the enterprise would be doomed to failure.[13] But in any case that isn't Kant's point. In his scheme disinterestedness functions as a criterion concerning the origin of pleasure or what pleasure (or displeasure) is consequent upon. The notion of interest is a technical one in Kant's philosophy. The notion of disinterest is equally technical. Thus 'interested' pleasure would be, for instance, pleasure which on reflection one knows to arise causally from the consumption of something sweet, gratifying a desire or an appetite and inducing pleasurable sensations; or, to take another example, pleasure which upon reflection turns out to follow upon the achievement of ends, like the pleasure that may well result from the satisfaction of moral and practical goals. So when we affirm the disinterestedness of our pleasures, we have found the 'why' of them to be independent of gratified or anticipated desire on the one hand, and of moral or prudential satisfaction on the other. Part of what it is for a person to have taste is to have, among other qualities, those of sincerity and discrimination in respect of his sensibility, and to be able to recognize his feelings for what they are in respect of their antecedents.

It would be quite wrong to think of Kant as advocating detachment, aloofness, and non-involvement of the person who judges aesthetically. And even more bizarre is the interpretation of disinterestedness as not being interested in the object of one's pleasure or displeasure. This is nothing less than the opposite of Kant's view: because causal determinations of sensations and conceptual goals are ruled out as they relate pleasure or displeasure only externally to its object, what we are left with is a totally object-centred judgement. It articulates the structure of the object as nothing other than an object of appreciation.

Kant appears to disallow that interest in the object could even follow upon and, as it were, be created by, a judgement of taste. This surely must be wrong, and it is in any case not required by the criterion of disinterestedness. The exercise of taste reverberates through life, and the

---

[13] Thus George Dickie, 'The Myth of the Aesthetic Attitude', in *American Philosophical Quarterly*, 2, 1964, 56–64, wins the argument easily over Jerome Stolnitz, *Aesthetics and the Philosophy of Art Criticism*, 1960, Part I. Dickie's case rests on being able to show that, *qua* perceptual act, 'disinterested' attention does not differ from 'attention'. Equally misguided is Stolnitz's defence of disinterestedness as that quality without which an attitude would not be aesthetic. See also George Dickie, *Art and the Aesthetic*, 1974, p. 127: 'Stolnitz and others claim that a critic's relationship to a work of art is *necessarily* different from that of others because he attends to it differently.'

moments of aesthetic appraisals do not disrupt but deepen it. Desiring to possess, protect, preserve and exhibit what we value as the preferred objects of taste are natural extensions of appreciation and in no way affect the status of our taste judgements as satisfying the criterion of disinterestedness. Perhaps the closest analogue to the regard for an object of aesthetic preference is that of the love in which one person can hold another: not self-regarding but not self-forgetting either in the absorption in the loved one. And as the value attached to the object of love is not additional to what is already contained in the act of loving, so the values we place on the objects of our taste do not go beyond or outside what is grasped in the act of appraising them. Nevertheless, the emotion of love permeates the entire life of the person who loves. And so it is also with the pleasures of taste.

It is instructive at this point to compare Kant's approach to the problems of taste with that of Hume.

Hume characteristically goes to the heart of the matter. On the one hand, he says, there is the following view:

All sentiment is right; because sentiment has a reference to nothing beyond itself, and it is always real, whenever a man is conscious of it. But all determinations of the understanding are not right; because they have reference to something beyond themselves, to wit, real matter of fact; and are not always conformable to that standard.

On the other hand,

It appears then that, amidst all the variety and caprice of taste, there are certain general principles of approbation and blame, whose influence a careful eye may trace in all operations of the mind. Some particular forms or qualities ... are calculated to please, and others displease.[14]

Assuming that – as Hume thinks – the latter is so, he would like to give the simplest possible solution to the problem of taste, namely that 'there are qualities in objects which are fitted by nature to produce these particular feelings' (of pleasure or displeasure). That solution would work if certain qualities of objects did invariably produce the appropriate sentiment; in that case the notion of right or wrong sentiment would fall away: it would simply be a question of investigating what qualities produced what sentiments. Hume is aware that this will not do, since it is, as a matter of fact, not the case that the effects of the qualities of objects on people is always the same. Rather than give up this approach altogether, however, he concludes that if certain qualities 'fail of their effect in any particular instance, it is from some apparent defect or imperfection' of the sensibility of the person who therefore errs in his judgement. So Hume is led to

[14] 'Of the Standard of Taste', *Essays, Moral, Political, and Literary*, vol. I, ed. T. H. Green & T. H. Grose, 1875, pp. 268, 271.

introduce what we might call defeasibility conditions (not putting too much weight on the term): a person will make a correct judgement of taste provided he is not lacking in delicacy of discrimination, or good sense, is without prejudice, and so on. But then the question inevitably arises: with what justification does Hume assert that the appraisal of persons who make judgements satisfying these conditions will converge or coincide? An uncharitable answer might be that he has persuaded himself *a priori* of the truth of the view I rejected earlier: that there is an objective standard of taste. His own answer is interesting. He raises what he calls the 'embarrassing' question: supposing there are men of delicate discrimination, good sense and unprejudiced views, how will we know them as distinct from pretenders? We cannot say they will be the men who come up with the right judgements, for we only know which *they* are, as measured by the judgements of such men. Hume wants to say that who they are is a question of fact. But if that is so, then Hume's own prejudice – and it does not seem to amount to much more than that – that there is a standard of taste is really an irrelevancy to his account of judgements of taste. It would at best have to be something that emerged, if at all, from the individual judgements of these critical paragons.

Two comments on Hume's approach here will bring us back to problems in hand. The first is as follows. Hume is led, because of his adherence to the idea of a standard of taste, to make the crucial question one about the conditions under which someone can be said to be making a *correct* judgement of taste. He then introduces the man of delicate sensibility, good sense and unprejudiced eye. On Kant's approach this is the wrong question to ask anyway. What is important, as he sees it, is to be able to say when a judgement *of taste* is being made. Here too it is relevant to specify what I have tentatively called defeasibility conditions – they are implied in Kant's criterial use of disinterestedness. But they will not be conditions for a judgement of taste's being correct. The merit of Kant's approach is that it leaves as an open question what many of us feel must in any case remain so: whether there is, or can be, a consensus in aesthetic judgements. That also, of course, makes Kant's task harder, as it renders it impossible for him to adopt a Humean-type solution.

The other comment concerns the relation of pleasure and delight to its object. Hume, it seems, does not always endorse the view that 'sentiment has a reference to nothing beyond itself'; sometimes his considered opinion is that altering one's perception of the object or one's belief about it is the means by which one alters one's response, the response being the touchstone of taste. This would, of course, go some way towards explaining how education of taste comes about. But the picture is still a causal one, and in that respect supports only an external relation between response and object. What alteration of perception beliefs bring about is, according to Hume, a clearer perception of those qualities in objects which are 'fitted by nature' to produce the right feelings. No advance has been made on the original impasse.

Kant is mostly silent on the precise relation between what he calls the 'estimate' of the object and the consequent feeling of pleasure or displeasure, but there is good ground for thinking that he too would subscribe to a generally causal account. But since it isn't because of the presence or absence of a causal story that I think Kant's approach more promising than Hume's, something more will have to be said on pleasure and displeasure in relation to their objects.

Consider first a criticism often levelled against traditional theories of taste (Hume's and Kant's included), namely that their use of 'pleasure' is far too undifferentiated to be of any use. What could be more different, it is said, than the pleasure of a hot bath and the pleasure of listening to a Haydn quartet, or the pleasure felt watching the sun rise and that had in the sexual act, or the pleasure experienced in satisfying one's hunger and that in seeing justice triumph or virtue made manifest? Exactly. But if the suggestion then is that there must be a qualitative differentiation of pleasures, even if at present our language of expressing the shades is deplorably poverty-stricken, trouble looms. Two *prima facie* ways of differentiating pleasures are these. One, to attend more closely to the subtle shades of felt pleasure, that is, to introspectively available differences, and thus to obtain a scale ranging from the pleasures of sense to those in which intellect also is prominently involved. Unfortunately for this suggestion, any attempt to articulate such a scale needs reference points which fix the qualitative differences in something other than the mere feel. So the suggestion easily collapses into the second one: to account for the qualitative differences of pleasures by particularizing each in terms of what occasions it, its object, and then either ending up with as many distinct pleasures as there are distinct objects or situations, or making it true by definition that as objects are classifiable into kinds, so are pleasures. Clearly, there is little to be said for either approach. If we take it – as I think we must – that whatever objects of pleasure are, they are intentional objects, we see how both views miss the point anyway. For the analysis of a particular act of enjoying something can be neither in terms of introspected data nor in terms of independently describable objects. And even to talk about the relation between pleasure and its objects already obscures the advance Kant had made on his predecessors: he speaks of the relation between the *estimate* of the form of an object and the consequent feeling. The estimate *is* the aesthetic experience, and the joy is that of finding something beautiful.

It must therefore be the *role* of pleasure in the experience of estimating something that makes some pleasures pleasures of taste. The *nature* of pleasure may well be opaque until the judgement supervenes.[15] On the nature of pleasure Kant has nothing informative to say; but he suggests strongly that considered *qua* feeling it yields nothing to distinguish one sort of pleasure from another.[16] To say what role pleasure or displeasure has is, however, the same as determining under what conditions an experience is an aesthetic one. The pleasures of taste then will necessarily be individuated by reference to the circumstances under which they arise. Taste pleasures are those that arise in experiences meeting the conditions of disinterestedness. It is not the quality of the pleasure or displeasure that is different from other pleasures, but how they function in the larger economy of our experiences. This, I believe, does more justice to our intuitions about how tenuous our grip on our emotions often is: they are not invariably and immediately transparent to us, and the pleasures of taste in particular need our clear-headed honesty about their origin and reasons.

We can thus resist the temptation to regard aesthetic experiences themselves as a species of pleasure. Kant certainly leaves no doubt that such experiences are not always pleasurable: displeasure must not be forgotten. Even without appealing to Kant we should probably want to say that whilst pleasure can often be had from aesthetic experiences, there is no necessary relation between such experiences and pleasure. But if the idea of aesthetic autonomy is to make sense, we cannot admit a merely contingent relation either, for that would make it possible to say that we pursued aesthetic experiences for the sake of something else, a separate effect, namely pleasure. If pleasures are, however, individuated by reference to the circumstances under which they arise, taste pleasures are those that arise in situations which meet the conditions of disinterestedness. Pleasures in this role are consequent, then, upon finding something beautiful. We do not call something beautiful because it gives us

---

[15] I owe this point to Paul Guyer who, in his excellent book, *Kant and the Claims of Taste*, 1979, p. 119, observes that Kant's theory of aesthetic response does indeed seem to be 'an outmoded form of sensationalism' incompatible with the idea that pleasures have an intrinsically intentional component. On the other hand, the great merit of Kant's way of isolating the feeling of pleasure and then differentiating pleasures by investigating what gives rise to them is that 'by treating pleasures very much alike, and thus as internally opaque with regard to their diverse causal histories or relations to their objects, Kant undermines the traditional view that the nature of our mental states must always be immediately transparent to us'. Guyer even speaks of Kant's 'discovery of the opacity of pleasure'.

[16] Kant says in the *First Introduction* (viii, *Anmerkung*) to the *Critique of Judgement*: 'Here is it easily seen that pleasure and displeasure, not being modes of cognition, cannot in themselves be explained at all and have to be felt rather than understood...'

pleasure: but when the pleasure is that of taste, it has been occasioned by an aesthetic appraisal.

Thus, even though we may have to concede that Kant tells a causal story about pleasure and what brings it about, this hardly affects the criterial story of how to affirm a given pleasure as one of taste. For differentiating pleasures according to how they arise makes it necessarily true that they arise in circumstances such as those that warrant the description of the experience as aesthetic, i.e. that meet the conditions of disinterestedness. So Kant can be said to have shown that the pleasures of taste are internally related to aesthetic experiences – which is different from saying that there is a necessary relation between aesthetic experiences and pleasure, and different too from saying that the relation is purely contingent.

In conclusion, I am prepared to say now that a Kantian account does not rule out what is called the educability of taste. On the contrary. An account in which pleasure as a feeling does not bear the mark of its origin qualitatively on its sleeve makes room for and even demands the cultivation of that alertness to the ever-present dangers of self-deception that is a mark of the mature person. It demands constant exercise and training in that area in which sensibility and reflection intermesh; it demands practice in articulating and structuring one's emotions so that eventually one may trust them more and more. Not, however, as absolute arbiters. There is always room for uncertainty, not about whether one feels pleasure or displeasure, but why. Yet individual taste judgements are not on that account corrigible. Here I remain firmly with Kant. What is corrigible is a person's attitude to his feelings. Questioning what he thought to be the reasons for them may on occasion lead him not to revise a particular judgement but to see that it wasn't a taste judgement. Educated taste, I suggest, must admit that one's most powerful feelings may not always be immediately transparent as to their causal histories or the relations to their objects. And 'errors' and 'lapses' of taste are really, then, shorthand for errors in assigning one's pleasures and displeasures to those of taste, and lapses in one's vigilance against self-deception.

This seems to me more adequate to the complexity and the importance of taste judgements than any position that either rests with the immediacy of pleasure beyond which we cannot ask any questions, or insists that if taste judgements are debatable then the intellect alone is in the lead. The Kantian view is not a compromise between Cooper–Voltaire and Burke; rather, it shows where both went wrong from initially plausible premises. My conclusion, anyway, is not that Kant had all the answers: only that his approach does not foreclose too many of them.

A last word now on the presumption of taste to lay claim in its judgements to the agreement of others, the subjective universality claim, to use Kant's language. I think I dimly see a connection, but it only warrants a much weaker claim. When I can honestly say that I have eliminated as far as I know both rashness and conceit from my reflection on those appraisals which I affirm as those of taste, I think I do have some ground for appeal to the agreement of others. The universality, however, is narrower than Kant's: I appeal, I think, to all persons of taste, to those who know its pleasures. That they form a community in which communication is possible if not always easy seems to me undeniable. That this community is a changing one seems equally undeniable. That it should grow rather than contract seems an imperative less categorical than the moral one but nevertheless compelling. Perhaps it is here that Kant's 'universal voice' has its place. Not everyone, as a matter of fact, cultivates his aesthetic potential – and not everyone is given a chance to do so. But everyone is capable of it. And everyone has a right to it. So the appeal implicit in the taste judgements which I can share with members of the privileged community of taste is not that others should agree to my particular appraisals but that everyone should come to see that such appraisals are possible. Not everyone will share my views; but everyone could share the pleasures of taste.

My thanks are due to Terry Greenwood who helped throughout; to members and guests of the Thyssen Philosophy Group and especially to Martin Hollis; to the following who read an earlier draft and have let me have their comments: Malcolm Budd, Barrie Falk, Mary Haight, Peter Jones, Peter Lamarque, Michael Menlowe, Betty Redfern, Flint Schier, Bob Sharpe. My apologies for not always having taken their advice.

The communicability of feeling

BARRIE FALK

I

(i)

A question which preoccupied Kant in the First Critique was how creatures like us – discrete sensory systems, located in space and time – can come to have empirical knowledge which transcends that location and which we can communicate to others. A thought which pervades the answer Kant proposes is that for a state to be communicable in this sense and for it to be an epistemic state are necessarily equivalent. The link is conceptualization. If you and I are visually confronted by a book then of course the visual processes occurring in each of us will be numerically distinct. But there is no reason to suppose that they will not differ qualitatively too. Different viewing positions and differences in visual acuity are only some of the things which will make this likely. It is only if each of us conceptualizes the sensory events occurring in him – only if, according to Kant's theory of concepts, each of us relates the sensory events in a rule-governed way to other possible sensory events – that there is a possibility of our sharing the experience of the book. For then, we shall have applied the same conceptual procedure to numerically and qualitatively distinct sensory events. (The applyings, of course, will remain numerically distinct. But that is all right: Kant does not require that communicability should be anything more than common practice.) And given the further plausible assumption that (empirical) concepts are socially acquired, it will follow that conceptualization is a necessary and sufficient condition of being able to communicate one's experiences to others – at least to those others whose conceptual training has been much like one's own.

The other side of the equivalence is less anodyne than this. Kant has complex arguments purporting to show that, unless we conceptualize the sensory events occurring within us, we will have no notion or knowledge of the self whose current state the sensory events are part of. And without knowledge of that bit of the world which is oneself, we will have no knowledge of the world outside us. Without conceptualization therefore, no communication would be possible; but without it, also, the latter argument claims, there would be nothing to communicate, for there would be nothing that was being believed or known.

I am not concerned to defend these arguments here. I mention them in order to show the background against which Kant claimed, in the Third Critique, that there are certain feelings which are communicable. His reasons for thinking that this is so are complex and unfamiliar. I shall say something about them here. In the next section, I shall deal with his account of how such feelings are possible.

That I feel a pain is a fact about me; a psychological fact, no doubt, but, for all that, an ordinary objective event in the world. As such, it is something I can have a representation of and communicate to you. Actually feeling the pain, however, is not something I can communicate; but then, no more is it a knowing that something is so. Actually feeling the pain, Kant wants to say, is subjective. Whatever cognitive processes might come to be directed onto this feeling – my own awareness that I, who was feeling fine a few minutes ago, am now in the state properly called 'pain', the knowledge which an observer might have of my state – feeling the pain is not itself a cognitive state. It is a state of consciousness, but it is not a representing of how things are. Most importantly, the subjective state of feeling the pain is not to be confused with the state of reflective awareness that I am currently in pain, even though, in reflective creatures such as ourselves, the one state may be invariably accompanied by the other.

So far, then, it will seem that what is a candidate for communicability in this area is knowledge of feelings, not the feelings themselves, as understood in the strict sense of being subjective. But now consider what Kant is particularly concerned with in the Third Critique, namely aesthetic feelings, finding things beautiful. Again, *that* I find a thing beautiful is a fact about me, something I can have a reflective representation of and communicate to you. Actually finding it beautiful, however – 'being moved' by it, 'feeling its beauty' – is not a representing of what is the case, any more than is feeling a pain. To find something beautiful, Kant constantly insists, is not something one can be argued into: it is to have a feeling; it is something that happens to one. But here the analogy with pain ends. For, he wants to say, although one feels a thing's beauty and doesn't, except subsequently and reflectively, know that one's state is that of finding it beautiful – although, that is to say, the feeling is subjective and thus not a cognition – the judgement which we use to express the experience – 'That is beautiful' – concerns the object and not a state of oneself. It is not, Kant says, a judgement about a psychological fact.

The point needs elaboration. Suppose we take the exclamations 'Ow!' or 'It hurts!' and, on the other hand, the statement 'I am in pain' as, respectively, expressions of, and a reflective report on, my pain. The analogues in the aesthetic case would be something like 'Oh!' or 'That's marvellous!' and, on the other hand, 'I am finding this beautiful.' The two reporting speech events are, I take it, analogous and present no obvious difficulties. The two expressive speech events, however, are not analogous. I will take it for granted here that a Wittgensteinian treatment of 'It hurts!' is the correct one. That is to say, I will assume that the utterance of 'It hurts!', in appropriate circumstances, is not the product of an introspective survey of my sensation and a recognition of it as of the hurting, as opposed to the itching or tickling, kind. I will presume, secondly (and I take this, too, to be part of the Wittgensteinian picture) that the utterance is appropriate only when it occurs in the context of an *experience* of a pain, and not the experience of an itch. The difference between a pain and an itch is accessible to me only as the difference between what makes me say 'It hurts!' and what makes me say 'It itches!'; but, insofar as I make these different remarks in situations that can be assessed as probably appropriate, it will be reasonable to suppose that I do discriminate the experiences. (This point is essential, of course, to ensure that we have some purchase on the notion of an experience of pain as something distinct from its verbal expression.) The third point to make is that when I do manifest a discrimination of my state by saying 'It hurts!', what has caused me to be in that state – a pin piercing my skin, an inflamed joint – is no part of what I have thus discriminated. The pain experience itself takes me only as far as the location of the disturbance and any knowledge I have of what is going on beyond that will have to be achieved in some other, no doubt perceptual, way.

Now in the aesthetic case, the first two points apply. My access to the experience I express by saying 'That's marvellous!' is confined to knowing of it that it's an experience I want to express in that way. And the utterance is known or believed to be appropriate only when it is known of me that I produce tokens of that utterance only in some well-ordered way – that I do not, for example, commonly accompany it with gestures of rejection. It is with respect to the third point that the difference between the pain case and the aesthetic case can be seen. For the state of which I manifest my discrimination in saying 'That's marvellous!' is not just a (psychological) state of myself, like the state of pain, which makes no reference to anything external to the state; it is, making the minimal addition that is necessary, a relational state, one of the terms of the relation being the object I am perceiving. The feeling I am expressing is one *within which* there is awareness of something external to myself.[1] It should be noted that Kant is making a stronger point than that which is offered by so-called intentional theories of the emotions. He is not just saying that, accompanying any feeling, there is some belief about the object: he is saying that, to understand what is going on in the aesthetic case, we need to make sense of the idea that that something is so can be *felt*.

(ii)

It is clear that if indeed there are feelings which incorporate awareness in this way, it will be reasonable to suppose they have something like the communicability, and the possibility of truth and error, appropriate to awareness. And it may be granted that we do talk of aesthetic feelings, unlike pains, as if they were representations of how things are. But it may also be that to talk of them in this way is mistaken; and the claim that it is not must be defended. I shall give here a brief account of the defence Kant offers. My main concern is only to introduce the strategy he thinks appropriate. In section II, I shall make moves which are related to, but different from, Kant's in an attempt to answer questions which, again, are related to but different from his. I am not therefore primarily concerned to assess the cogency of Kant's theory in detail, and there will be many unresolved obscurities in what I say.

One of Kant's most basic epistemological claims, we know, is that to perceive that something is the case – that such and such an object is a book – is to subsume materials of sense under concepts. To judge an object beautiful, however, is not to subsume it under concepts. When I am in the state of finding a thing beautiful, my mind is in a state of free play: I do not conceptualize the object, but am aware of it as suitable for conceptualization. To use one of his favourite examples: an English garden, exhibiting a controlled irregularity of design, is something one might find beautiful; for although, as one scrutinizes the garden, one will find no ordering concept in the design, one will nevertheless be aware that it is ordered. The result of observing an object of this sort is that one's awareness of one's powers of representation is 'quickened': one will feel (in a way to be described) the suitability of one's understanding for the world it finds itself in. If the garden were completely regular – arranged in simple square blocks, for example – then the immediacy of one's recognition of it as so designed would preclude one's being aware, as one came into contact with the object, of oneself as that which was able to recognize it. On the other hand, if the garden were too irregular, it would simply baffle the

---

[1] 'External' is not quite the word, since the object that serves as one of the terms of the relation could be something like a taste I am savouring. I shall continue to use the word. But it should be kept in mind that it is meant to cover cases of this sort.

understanding and be found, not beautiful, but inane.

Kant's thought, as I understand it, is this. It seems reasonable to suppose that the more unsurprised and unhesitating one's recognition of a thing as being of a certain sort, the more entrenched one's concept of that sort is likely to be and the more cursory the scrutiny that leads to the applying of the concept. So that, when a brief inspection of something has led me to see that it is square, and if I should then happen to notice further how the sides are parallel, the corners right angles and so on, this will merely strike me as how, of course, things have to be, since the object is square. But suppose, taking the case of Kant's garden, I unexpectedly come across a curve in the stream; or that a lake suddenly comes into view as I emerge from the wood. Nothing I have previously seen in the garden will have elicited from me a concept the application of which *demands* that the stream will take this course or that there should be a lake just there. Nonetheless, if it is a good garden, it will strike me as exactly right that things are thus disposed, given what I have previously seen. On occasions such as this, when my perception of something (the surprised coming upon the lake) and my sense that it so exactly fits what I have previously perceived are as phenomenologically distinct as this, I become acutely aware of two things. First, that there are two processes going on here: on the one hand, my sensory encounters with the world; on the other hand, my activity of imposing order on what I encounter. And, secondly, I become aware that the two processes – the operation, as Kant likes to say, of the Faculties of Imagination and Understanding – are in harmony, that the sensory material is amenable to my ordering activity. For precisely because the rightness I find in the position of the lake is not a matter of its being in accord with some rule that I am following, not a matter of its consonance with some unthought-about expectation, finding it right will not be merely an element that is submerged in the process of ascertaining that the world is thus and so. Rather, it will be something that causes in me an awareness of a quite general feature of my experience: namely that I seek to impose order on what I encounter and that I succeed in doing so.

Let me elaborate on this with a more complex example. Suppose I see a flower and casually recognize what sort it is. It's reasonable to suppose, I take it, that this recognizing takes the form of some part of what I initially see arousing in me a set of concepts, each of which determines a direction of further scrutiny – to the petals, the leaf-structure and so on – and a set of expectations about what that scrutiny ought to reveal. As soon as enough that is distinctive of one of these (as one might say) covering concepts is established, I will take the flower to be of that sort. Typically, I will not then bother to look for its further distinctive features. But if I do happen to notice them, they will serve, not as further confirmation of my belief that the flower is of that sort – for I'm already sure of that; but as an example of the way in which the world is itself well ordered – the flower is of a certain sort and I now notice that it has the further characteristics proper to that sort. (It was this that I had in mind when I said that finding things right can be submerged in the process of ascertaining what is the case.) But now suppose that I notice something odd about the flower, and that further scrutiny reveals it to be of an unfamiliar kind. Consulting my books later, I identify the flower and read of other distinctive features. When I see it again, I will examine the flower closely and find that it has all the distinctive features I have read about. Such an experience provides a familiar kind of pleasure, which is to be explained, I believe, in this way. Although my recently acquired information has given me something like a covering concept, some knowledge of what to look for (and to this extent it is unlike the lake example), the thought of what has to be looked for does not occur to me in that impersonal or automatic way which having an entrenched concept provides. I must still, in this case, explicitly recall what to look for; and the result of this is that, although what I am doing can be described as discovering what sort of flower is there, a palpable part of the experience is the awareness of myself as that which knows what sort of flower is there. I am aware of having a sequence of thoughts or expectations about what should be so; and of the flower, in turn, meeting them. There is a reciprocity between what thoughts I have and what is there; and, on occasions, it can be this reciprocity, this suitability of my understanding for the world it has to deal with, which I become aware of, rather than merely of what is there.

We are not to suppose, of course, so far as Kant is concerned, that in the case of some ordinarily recognized object, the perceived rightness of its parts will have any source other than one's own imposition of order; or that the two processes of sensing and understanding are any less in harmony here. It is just that these facts are hidden from us in these cases: first, by the ease with which the ordering concept is evoked; and secondly, by the fact that when I perceive the world to be thus and so, concerns about how the pursuit of my current tasks might have to be modified quickly supervene.

Now, this awareness of the suitability of the understanding for the world it has to cope with cannot, Kant insists, be an intellectual awareness, something I have a representation of. I can have that of course: the knowledge that an object is having this effect on me is what I express when I *report* the fact that I am seeing something beautiful, or when I report, as a general fact about myself, that I find things beautiful. But the awareness of the object which I have when my awareness is of my understanding being in harmony with those sensory events which constitute my contact with it is not, itself, a representation of the fact that the object is having such an effect. That, recall, would be to conceptualize the events that are occurring; whereas, here, the faculty of conceptualizing is held in suspense – it is, so to speak, pointed at the object, but does not actually engage with it. My state, therefore, is analogous not to that state which is to be described as my knowing that I'm in pain, but to that subjective state which is feeling the pain. The crucial difference is that whereas the feeling in the pain case is a single *quale*, without internal structure, here the feeling is of myself as relating in a certain way to the world. It is, Kant believes,[2] a product of the confusion between the subjective and the psychological already referred to which leads us to believe that, when we strip away from those states which we call feelings any cognitive overlay – the knowledge that an observer or the person whose feeling it is can have of what is going on – what we are left with is a bare sensory *quale*, the 'feel' of the operating of the sense organs, or those states, such as pains and itches which, *faute de mieux*, we treat analogously. There is the further possibility, exemplified here, of feelings being the affect in us of the operation of the understanding. And since it is the nature of the understanding to be applied ('All we can do with concepts is judge by means of them'), awareness of the external world is part of the affect.

It is such a feeling we express, according to Kant, when we say 'That's marvellous!' and this is his answer to my question of how a feeling can contain within itself a reference to an object. The further question of how the feeling can be communicable and of how, therefore, questions about whether it is correct can arise, can be dealt with quickly. We have seen that, for Kant, communicability in the ordinary case is a matter of engaging in the same conceptual procedures, and that no such procedures are engaged in when one finds an object beautiful. That this does not happen is the proper reason, Kant insists, for saying that we are dealing with a feeling here, and not a knowing. But the distinctive property of this feeling which I have been at pains to describe – that it involves awareness of the object – gives rise to a further possibility: namely that it can be what Kant calls exemplary. His point is this. When I have reflective knowledge of the fact that I'm in pain, the state of affairs I know about is something of which I know, not just that it obtains in that part of the world that is myself, but that its obtaining has depended on properties of myself which are peculiar to myself – I happened to be where the brick landed, the inflamed joint is in my body. But when I confront an object which causes in me the feeling of its beauty, that feeling does not depend on properties peculiar to myself in this way. Of course, I have to be in the presence of the object and I have to be in a receptive mood if the feeling is to occur. But this

----

[2] See *The Metaphysics of Morals*, introduction to 'The Metaphysical Principles of Right', 211, 212 (particularly the footnote).

is analogous to the fact that if I am to know that something is a book, I have to be suitably placed sensorily and I have to have suitable conceptual resources for coping with the sensory events. If those conditions are met, I can enter a communicable belief state. Likewise, when I feel my understanding to be in that state which is indicative of its ability to operate successfully in the world, although it is a state of my own understanding that I feel, its being in that state is not dependent on any features peculiar to itself. What I feel is a way of relating to the world that any understanding like my own can exhibit, and so I can take my state to be exemplary and therefore communicable. It will not always be correct to do this, since, without my realizing it, personal distortions may have occurred. But the important thing is that the claim to exemplariness will make sense.

This is the merest sketch of Kant's theory; but I have said enough, I hope, to reveal its strategy. What I propose to do now is take a perfectly commonplace feeling – I shall deal for the most part with a case of pity – and argue for its communicability, making use of ideas closely analogous to Kant's 'exemplariness' and allied thoughts about the special role of the self in this area of experience. I shall thus be abandoning Kant's idea that 'pathological' feelings are not communicable. I shall discard too the abstract and, as I believe, wholly intractable account of the mechanism of cognition within which Kant frames his theory. Some diagnosis of why Kant insisted on such a framework will emerge from what I say.

II

(i)

Suppose I encounter a man who is old, infirm, obviously wretched, and that I feel pity for him. How are we to describe my pity? Clearly, my state must involve awareness of his infirmity – the effortfulness of his walk, his downcast eyes and so on; but equally clearly, that is not enough, for I could notice these things with indifference. We should not suppose too quickly, however, that in the latter case there is mere noticing, while, in the pitying case, there is noticing plus an affective element. For what is there to be noticed is, in one sense, merely a series of bodily movements. To ascribe a state of wretchedness to the man on this basis involves both background assumptions and imaginative projection from what I see; or, as I should prefer to say, it involves the occurrence of a cluster of thoughts associated with what I see. Noticing the man's walk, for example, I will realize that this is someone for whom movement has become a burden and this will induce further thoughts about the many pleasures his life must therefore lack. Seeing his eyes, I will note that he seems to have turned away already from anything there might be to encounter; and this will induce some such further thought as that he no longer expects to see anything pleasing or friendly. The occurrence of such a cluster of thoughts is necessary, it seems, for the ascription of wretchedness, whether that ascription is accompanied by pity or not.[3] It might seem plausible, therefore, to suppose that the difference between the pitying and the non-pitying state is to be sought in differences in the way in which the perceiver relates to these associated thoughts. The pitying observer will be held, or absorbed, by thoughts about what he sees; whereas in the dispassionate case, although the thoughts will occur, one's mind will quickly move on to other matters.

But this cannot be right; or, anyway, it cannot be enough. Certainly, one is absorbed, for the duration of the pity, by the pitied object. But to suppose that that is all we need to say ignores two things. It is possible, in the first place, to have a sudden and fleeting sense of pity. If all we can say about absorption is that it involves prolonged attention, we should have to say, implausibly, that such events are not genuine cases of pity. Secondly, and more importantly, it ignores the fact that it is possible to be absorbed by some situation in a wholly dispassionate way. I could, after all, be curious about what it is like to be old and infirm, my curiosity, while it lasts, involving just the sort of absorption I have described.

We need, then, further differentiation within the phenomenon of absorption. Two features which it may possess are of particular relevance. First, there is what might be called the resonance of the thoughts which occur in the absorbed state. By this I mean a certain power which these thoughts may have to modify one's current conative state. Suppose, for instance, that when I saw the old man, I was on my way to buy paint and brushes, having noticed that morning the shabbiness of my room. The state which the sight of the old man has induced in me might then be described as one of pity insofar as it destroys the power which awareness of that fact had to serve as a spring of action. This is not just to say that, for the duration of the pity, thoughts about the shabbiness of my room do not occur to me. That would follow merely from the fact that I am absorbed by what I see and would describe the state of the idly curious observer. My conative state would be altered as a result of a temporary forgetting. The point is, rather, that even if thoughts about these other matters were to occur while I was pityingly absorbed, they would no longer be thoughts about things that concerned me: in the face of a life as bereft of pleasure as this, the decorative state of my room, it would seem to me, no longer matters.

To talk of resonance in this way is of course to suppose that, when the

---

[3] This cluster of thoughts need not be conscious. For a discussion of some of the complexities involved in the notion of unconscious association, see my 'What Are We Frightened Of?', *Inquiry*, xxv (1982), 165–98.

associated thoughts constitute an emotional absorption, they have a conative force. I have spoken obliquely, nonetheless, only of their power to modify one's conative state, since I want to emphasize that this force is not a matter of their causing me (to be disposed) to act in any particular way. It is a matter, rather, of which facts I know about the world they allow me to continue to contemplate as concerns. To contemplate a fact as a concern is, I take it, for one's thought about it to be accompanied, because of the fact's relevance to some goal one has, by a growth of energy – I mean the process, which occurs as the prelude to action, of increasingly detailed and rapid thoughts about what movements need to be made, or the occurrence of anticipatory thoughts about what one will want to do in a world appropriately modified by one's action. When an emotion such as my pity for the old man occurs, its typical effect, I am claiming, is to interfere with processes such as these. And so its power consists not in its providing one with some specifiable goal, having an unexplained compellingness which gives it precedence over other goals, but in its weakening one's conative ties with the rest of the world. Our talk of pity as a state which can have degrees of depth can be understood, I believe, in this way: how deep the pity goes is to be measured by the range and degree of entrenchment within one's life of the concerns it negates.

The second feature of pitying absorption which I want to emphasize, closely related to its resonance, is the fact that it involves attributing a certain salience to the pitied object. It is a point that applies quite generally to the emotions. Suppose someone insults me, calls me a fool. I might register his contempt quite dispassionately: here is someone who despises me, I will note, in which respect he differs from many other people I know who respect me. I will wonder further, perhaps, what his contempt reveals about him. But to be hurt by the insult is to be unable to locate the contempt in this way, as just one feature of the world among others. That there are people elsewhere who respect me will not only be something that is literally less immediately evident to me than this man's contempt: it is something which will have no power to modify the desire to hide myself, or whatever, which the insult has induced. The salience of the insult, then, is, again, not a matter of my attending to it and therefore necessarily not attending to other things: it is a matter of its resonance causing me to believe that there is nowhere in the world which is not like this. Likewise in the case of the old man. I will know that there are happy people. I will know perhaps that he was himself once happy and that this is just one stage of his life among others. But this knowledge will not change my belief that *this* – his looking at me in that frightened way, his having to drag himself along – is what the world is like, in the sense that it is this which resonates through all my thoughts about what, in that world, is worth doing.

66

A feature of our psychology which contributes importantly to our ability to attach salience to particular situations is the immense ingenuity of our associative powers and the fluidity of the connections they make. Noticing that there are lots of cheerful people on the street around the old man, I can easily see this as exhibiting how wretchedness is ignored and therefore exacerbated; noticing, perhaps, that the man has a rather fine walking stick, I will think not that he has good as well as bad things in his life, but only that his life is such that the possession of fine objects is of no help. In this way, facts which would not, independently observed, be reasons for pity, can be incorporated into a current pity and even reinforce it. We shall hear more of this later.

(ii)

These features of resonance and salience are not intended as an exhaustive account of what it is to relate to a situation emotionally: only as intuitively acceptable necessary conditions of there being such a relationship. And the rough description I have offered of them is sufficient for me to be able to pose the question I now want to turn to, namely whether, and in what sense, a state having these features is communicable. I shall argue in this section that an examination of the way in which we experience our emotions suggests that we do take some of them to be communicable. In sub-section (iii), I shall argue that it is not, as some would claim, incoherent of us to do so.

But first, two preliminary remarks about the nature and significance of the communicability that is in question. Following Kant, I shall take it that it is the *subjective* states the communicability of which is of interest. That is to say, my knowledge that the old man is having a certain effect on me – making me unconcerned with the decorative state of my room – is uncontroversially and uninterestingly a knowledge which others can have. But our question concerns the state of *finding* that I cannot care about these things, given that life can be reduced to what I now see before me. I follow Kant also in supposing that to say the state is communicable is to say that its proper description transcends reference merely to events occurring within me; and that this transcendence involves the applicability of questions of correctness or truth. Recall that communicability is most commonly secured, according to Kant, by conceptualization. What makes conceptualization more than a mere ordering of sensory materials occurring in each individual is that the ordering is done according to rules; so that the state of having got the rules right is something that can be realized in many discrete states of myself and others.[4] In the case of finding something beautiful, what replaces the occurrence of rule-guided ordering is the exemplariness of what happens to me: the fact that the feelings I have result not from contingent features of my own personality, but from a part of human nature which is common to all. And so, again, a proper description of what has occurred must transcend reference just to me: we must talk of my having felt what it is like for all of us to be in the world. I shall not, in what follows, make use of the notion of a common human nature. But the claim I *will* defend involves transcendence and truth in just the way Kant supposed.

So, let me turn to my claim that, as a matter of fact, we do regard some of our emotional states as communicable. I shall begin with a case where we don't do this.

I mentioned the possibility of my having set out, before encountering the old man, to buy paints and brushes. Suppose that my goal is uninterrupted and I arrive at the shop only to find that they have a poor selection of paints and badly run-down stocks. Anger or contempt might then ensue, the thoughts constituting the anger having to do with the provincialness of small towns, the unimaginativeness of the people and so on. To the extent that there is anger here, there will be the resonance and salience I have spoken of; and while the anger lasts, I will therefore be quite unmoved by someone who points to the town's compensating virtues of peacefulness, friendliness and so on. But when it wanes and I reflect on my feelings, I will usually be quite prepared to acknowledge that the features of the town I focussed on in my anger were just one lot of features among others and have no greater significance than the rest.

There are several things to notice about this. First, those characteristics of the town and ways of seeing characteristics of the town – the poor stocks, the way in which friendliness can serve as a disguise for inefficiency – on which I concentrated in my anger are accessible to me, and to others, even when I am not angry. Secondly, it is reasonable to infer from this that the salience these characteristics have when I am angry does not differ, except by addition, from the centrality which any noticed item has, in virtue of being noticed. Suppose, for instance, that I'm looking for a flower of a certain kind. When I come to a place where one is growing, my goal, in combination with the recognitional capacity which having the concept of the flower typically involves, will cause me to articulate the scene visually in a certain way: the blossom, leaves etc. will stand out as a whole against the irrelevant background of grasses and other vegetation. A different

---

[4] This doesn't mean that mistaken beliefs are not communicable. The only requirement is that they occur as a result of following rules, even if the rules are the wrong ones. It may be that not all mistakes are of this sort; but some certainly are.

interest, in characteristic combinations of vegetation perhaps, would cause a different articulation. In just this way, it seems, my goal of buying some decent paints causes me to attend to those aspects of the scene which are relevant to that goal, by way of determining how it should be pursued or by frustrating it. What gives these features, in my anger, a salience, as opposed to mere centrality, is their resonance: that is to say, the power of my goal, as modified by what I perceive, either to make me immune to the conative appeal of other features of the scene or to cause me to see aspects of these other features that are equally frustrating.

The third, and most important point, is as follows. If it is right to see my anger or frustration in this situation as involving the interplay of goal and perception that I have described, we can see further that the question which is often raised, of whether the feeling is justified, is one that can arise on different levels and can receive different answers according to the level. It can, on one level, be the question whether the circumstance that arouses one really does have the relevance to one's goals that being aroused by it presupposes. Thus, the relaxed friendliness of the shop assistants really can be seen as causally related to their inefficiency; being jostled in a crowd really does show disregard for one's desire for privacy. In contrast, it would be unjustified to be angry at having to wait in the shop when all the assistants are attending to someone who has fainted; or at being banged into by someone who has stumbled. This is not because, in such cases, one's goals are not frustrated, but because one fails to realize that the frustration is fortuitous – these events provide no evidence of something in the world which systematically frustrates one's goals. We should talk in such cases of a childish anger.

But the question whether a feeling is justified can concern the quite different matter of whether the interest, to which the circumstance on which one focusses may or may not be appropriately related, is itself a justified interest. Or, a variant of this, whether the interest, though a justified one, is proper in present circumstances. Thus, the desire to buy decent paints and the desire to remain reasonably physically aloof from strangers are not desires for anything unreasonable or peculiarly hard to obtain, and so would be judged justified; whereas anger at their frustration when there is a crisis and even food is hard to obtain or when there is a rush from a burning building would clearly be absurd. To say that a feeling is or is not justified in this sense is to appeal, I take it, to social and psychological norms.

The point I wish to make is that none of these ways of assessing an emotion shows a concern with whether that emotion is correct, in any but the trivial sense of whether the emotion is a fairly standard one in the circumstances. As we have seen, there is the question whether I am correct in believing that some fact systematically frustrates a reasonable goal. But that that belief is correct does not mean that the feeling is correct, for of course I only have the feeling if I have the interest which the circumstance frustrates. And *whether* I have that interest remains, stubbornly, merely a fact about me. Others may resemble me in having the interest; and it may be a justified one, in the second sense. But having the interest (and therefore, in suitable circumstances, a feeling) is not a communicable state. It does not arise out of my following any correct procedures or out of a nature which I share with all other men. It is not therefore something which transcends me, something whose proper description involves reference to something more than my own psychological states. To suppose that such a state could be correct would be like supposing, absurdly, that to notice the flower, against an irrelevant background of vegetation, is, absolutely, the correct thing to notice about the scene.

This conclusion accords with a common view of how we understand our emotions and it is, I have argued, a correct account of our reflective experience of some of them. But it is not how we experience them all and, in particular, it is not what happens in the case of pity which I have been describing. To that I now turn.

Let me begin with a negative contrast. The most obvious point to make is that my pity is not the result of some antecedently operative interest, interacting with what I perceive. Certainly, we suppose it occurs because I'm in a certain mood, or have a certain temperament. This is something I shall say more about below, but it will suffice here to point out that an obvious way to understand moods and temperaments is as tendencies to have certain feelings; and these, clearly, do not explain those feelings in the way that identifiable and antecedently operative interests do. Certainly also, in describing my case, I supposed for expository reasons that certain interests were present. But it is not the frustration of those interests that causes the pity: on the contrary, the pity, I claimed, eliminates those interests. It seems, therefore, that I cannot justify or rationalize my pity by alluding to some interest which is itself a rational one. It follows from this that I cannot, either, justify the selective attention I give to the scene. In the anger case, we may suppose that there were many features of the shop which were not reasons for anger and to which, therefore, I did not attend. This does not mean, however, that I simply *sought out* those features of the scene which would serve as reasons for being annoyed and ignored the others. For in this case, there is a publicly recognizable set of facts which do indeed bear on the desire to buy paints; having that desire alerted me to this set of facts and justifies my concentration on them. (Though it does not, remember, make that concentration 'correct'.) But no such move is possible in the case of pity. There were lots of cheerful people around the old man whom I ignored and what made me ignore them can only be, it seems, that I did not find them pitiful. There is nothing true of those features of the scene I concentrate on which is independent of my finding them pitiful and which, therefore, given that I am feeling pity, makes it understandable and proper of me to concentrate on them.[5] There is only the brute, not further to be explained, fact that certain things elicit a pitying attention from me and others do not. It follows, finally, from the absence of an antecedently operative interest, that the situation arousing my pity is not one that is accessible to those who do not feel the pity. Of course, they will see the man's downcast eyes, his laborious walk, the evident fact that he derives no pleasure from the appearance of his stick. But, unlike the cluttered state of the shop and the casual friendliness of the assistants, which really are connected as part of that system which prevents one from getting decent service and are *therefore* annoying if that is something one wants, the various features of the old man constitute a whole, standing out against an irrelevant background, only to someone in whom they evoke pity.

The immediate conclusion which one might be inclined to draw from this contrast is that, since such rationality or justification as is attributable to emotions is given by their being interest-dependent, this justification is lacking in those cases where there is no such interest. Although, while the emotion persists, I will point in justification to those features of the world I am attending to, reflection will cause me to see that what I attend to and the salience I attribute to it has no more significance, no more call on others' attention, than, say, the attitude I have to things when I have a hangover. The disposition to see the world in this way will pass, as an ache might.

In some cases that is our reflective assessment of a feeling. But it isn't the only possibility. In other cases, reflecting on the feeling and noticing that there are those who do not share it, I shall suppose, not that they lack an interest which I have, nor that they differ from me in some blank, mood-like affective state, but that they differ from me in sensitivity, using that term in its full perceptual sense. These others have failed to see, I will claim, what is the case. I will suppose also that when my own feeling wanes, as it undoubtedly will, that will mark a failure

---

[5] I take it for granted here that there are no basic objects of pity. A favourite candidate for such a role is the state of suffering which we may observe in another. But we should note, first, that such states are not exclusively the objects of our pity. And we should note, secondly, that there is nothing incorrect in responding to another's suffering with indifference, though it may be improper in various ways to do so. If one does feel pity for someone in such a state, therefore, more must be said in explanation of the occurrence of pity than that it's the feeling we have when confronted by another's suffering. For more on this topic, see my 'What Are We Frightened Of?'.

to sustain that sensitivity.

Now everything turns here on what I can suppose myself to be sensitive *to*. That is a matter I shall take up in the next sub-section. But before doing that, it is important to emphasize how radically this new perspective differs from the one we have been describing.

The claim that an interest is itself a justified one is used, I have argued, to substantiate the claim that, in certain contexts, we are justified in attending to certain aspects of a situation and in attributing salience to those aspects. However, it is important to emphasize that the mere noticing of an aspect, as opposed to thinking that it is the important one, is something that neither requires nor can receive justification. Speaking very roughly, to try to justify something (a belief or action) is to allude to other facts (the evidence, one's having reasonable goals, considerations of morality) and to claim that they have been brought to bear on the present case in a legitimate way. But consider my perception, in circumstances which I rightly take to be normal, of a yellow trumpeted flower. This does not justify the belief I form that the flower is a daffodil. For there is no *way* in which being a yellow, trumpeted flower is relevant to its being a daffodil, a way I might have got wrong: yellow, trumpeted flowers growing in Spring, in England, are things it is right to think of as daffodils. If someone should ask me, in these circumstances, to justify my belief, and if I have ascertained that he does not believe that the situation is in any way abnormal, I will be at a loss. Since it is not being doubted that I have perceived what is there, have conceptualized my sensory intake in a legitimate way, no further thoughts or interests that *I* have are relevant to the propriety of what I have done. We try to justify an action or the forming of a belief by showing that it is the proper thing to have done in the circumstances. But our notion of propriety is such that when it is acknowledged that I have done the proper thing, because it is the proper thing, the question of my being justified in doing it cannot arise.

Returning now to our case of pity, we can see the contrast between that and interest-dependent emotions in a quite different way. Certainly the selectiveness of what I attend to and the salience I attribute to it cannot be justified by alluding to some further (justified) interest which I have. That is to say, however, not that such emotions lack the only kind of legitimacy that is available in this area, but that they do not depend for their legitimacy on the higher-level arbitrariness of what interests I happen to have. All that has been required of me is the ability to perceive pitifulness when it is there. And when, in such a situation, I do feel pity, the feeling will therefore be the proper one, no more in need of justification than my belief, in appropriate circumstances, that there is a daffodil before me. The feeling is something that happens in me, certainly; but so are those events which constitute my perceiving the daffodil. If the feeling is right, my state will be a communicable one, its proper description transcending reference merely to events occurring within a discrete subject of sensory and affective states.

No less a claim than this must be presupposed by our belief that some of our emotions, though not a result of special interests, are, nonetheless, something more than arbitrary impositions of significance upon what we encounter. We must suppose, as the alternative, that in these cases we contribute a special sensitivity to a significance that is there. We do suppose that, I have claimed; not just in the rather dramatic sort of case I've been describing, but in quite everyday situations, where, for example, I suddenly discover a charming whimsicality in the conversation of someone I've hitherto found dull. The problem, however, is whether the claim makes sense.

(iii)

The crucial question, I have suggested, is what we can suppose ourselves to be sensitive to. As we've seen, someone else could be aware of the old man's feebleness, his fear, the preoccupation with other things of the people around him, and have no feelings about them. How, he will ask me, are these quite disparate facts supposed to be connected? Certainly, the old man *can* be seen as pitiful and the preoccupation of the other people *can* be seen as contributing to that pitifulness; but they need not be seen in that way and as therefore forming a significant whole, in the light of which the decorative state of one's room is not a thing one could care about. What makes me see them in that way is that I impose a sad significance upon them. And that is perfectly all right, this man will continue; but I cannot then argue that my pity is a result of an awareness of that whole. There is no such whole – only those features of the scene which are alike in arousing my pity.

The challenge, then, is to show that there is such a connection among these features and that, although it is apparent only to one who finds them pitiful, the connection is not wholly constituted by his finding them so. We need something analogous to the fact that my perception of the daffodil can be said to be correct, even though it consists of an articulating of my visual field which occurs wholly within me.

Recall, to begin with, how Kant tried to tackle this problem. We saw that the rightness of the lake's position, the way in which it is connected with other features of the garden, is not something that follows from there being some rule to which its position conforms. The rightness is not therefore something which I can notice in any ordinary sense and to which I can bring a variety of attitudes. Finding it right is for it to be the case that when I see the lake, I feel myself coping with the world; I feel, as I put it, the reciprocity between myself and the world. So here, according to this theory, is something – the rightness of the lake's position – which I can only feel, but which can yet be said to be an awareness of a fact. For the feeling is an awareness of how the various features of the garden actually do relate, not to my present situation, but to my powers of cognition generally. Now Kant is concerned here with aesthetics, and he supposes that this feeling is necessarily one of pleasure. That is not a matter I shall take up. And also, as I've said, I want nothing to do with this talk of the nature of our cognitive powers. But Kant's thought that the facts which our feelings are awarenesses of are facts about our general situation in the world *as revealed by* awareness of facts about our specific states, is, I believe, correct. Detached from an exclusive concern with aesthetics and from other unacceptable features of his theory, it will help us answer the challenge I have posed.

I argued earlier that a feature of any emotional response, interest-dependent or not, is that we attribute a salience to the object of that response. To be hurt by the insult is not just to attend to the fact that the other despises me: it is for other facts I know, such as that others think well of me, to lose their power to modify the conative state, of wanting to hide or whatever, which the insult has induced in me; or for these other facts to be so interpreted as to reinforce that conative state. A way of describing that phenomenon, which I now want to press, is that the fact that I am despised becomes, not a fact about how the world is here and now, how I appear to those eyes in particular, but a fact about what the *world as such* is like. The phrase is perhaps grandiose; but it captures accurately, I believe, the state of believing that there is nothing, anywhere, capable of arousing in me goals which are stronger than my present desire to hide. The insult is what the world as such is like, inasmuch as it is exemplary, in Kant's sense, of how, as an agent, I engage with any part of it.

If this is right, we can immediately give a cogent sense to the superficially puzzling idea that there can be beliefs about how things are which take the form of feeling. The beliefs in question are not about how I am situated here and now, but about how my being situated thus and so here and now bears on how I relate to the world as such. And these are beliefs that take the form of feeling since it is feeling, construed as the bestowing of resonance and salience on a present situation, which *is* the relating of a present situation to myself in this way. As we have seen, I can have reflective knowledge that a situation is having this effect on me; but its actually having the effect is, itself, a way of understanding, of being aware of, the situation.

But what, it will quickly be asked, does this way of describing the matter achieve? Certainly, relating myself to the insult in this way is for me to be taking the insult as exemplary of what the world as such is like. But reflection will reveal what it was about myself – the desire to be thought well of, or something of the sort – that caused the relating. A natural way of describing the episode, thus understood, in my new terms, would be as an experience of what the world as such *seems* like, to one with that kind of interest, confronted by that kind of event. I will understand it as being, at most, a case of sensitivity in the colloquial sense – as exhibiting a tendency to bring a certain affective response to situations of a certain sort. The price my argument has paid, it will seem, for bringing together what I feel and what I am aware of is that the awareness in question has quite lost its cognitive sense – we are talking only of 'ways' of being aware of things, ways of responding, which are nothing more than psychological states of the perceiver.

The above is, I think, a fair account of how my talk of the world as such would apply to cases of that sort. But in other cases, where there is no interest to explain the relating, another possibility presents itself. Some of these cases, certainly, will appear on reflection to be mere manifestations of moods, of the world as such having appeared, for no particular reason, to have a certain character. But in others, I claim, we can suppose, on Kantian lines, that the relatings that occur are themselves exemplary and are therefore indicative of how the world as such actually is.

What we need to justify this presumption is the thought that there is operative in us a capacity to relate to situations in the way I have described, which is a product, not of the bearing which particular situations may have on particular interests we may have, but only of the bearing which certain situations may have on any creatures that are self-conscious occupiers of the world. And to suppose that there are occasions when such a capacity is operative means that, although the relating which occurs on such an occasion is something that is going on in me, it is not to be construed merely as that. Just as those connectings of sensory material that occur in me when I confront the daffodil are the connectings that *should* occur in a creature with my conceptual training in that situation, and therefore constitute an awareness of what is the case; so, to relate what I see, in the way I do, to thoughts about what is and what is not worth doing, is what any self-conscious occupant of the world should do. My feelings about the old man, I will suppose, are the feelings I should have.

As I've indicated, this move is analogous to the argument I have attributed to Kant: to the thought that feeling the rightness of the lake's position is an exemplary and therefore correct feeling, inasmuch as it is an awareness of how the lake's position, relative to other things, appeals to the nature of human cognition. It is crucial to see, however, that my argument differs. I am *not* claiming, as Kant does, that we know certain facts about the structure of the human mind, that certain ways of relating affectively to situations depend only on that structure and that *therefore* the feelings constituted by those relatings are exemplary. My claim is only that we *think* of ourselves as being such that, sometimes, how the world seems to us manifests not just how, because of some interest or mood, it seems to us but isn't; but how it seems, in the sense of what it is indeed like, for all of us. On this view, no thoughts about what we are like or what it is like to be in the world have a place in the *argument* for the claim that some particular occurrence of feeling is exemplary. On the contrary, it is merely the thought that there is in us the possibility of exemplary feeling which allows us to treat some particular occurrence of feeling as a candidate for that exemplariness.

And so, to answer the question I put to my argument at the beginning of this section, it is true that, when I look at the old man, I can see no connection exhibited by his gait, his eyes, his broken shoes, etc., except that they are pitiful; no way in which just these facts stand out from the surrounding world, except in their having a certain effect on me. We do not feel, however, on reflection, that such cases exhibit a mere imposition of significance. But what is the alternative, if not the even more unattractive one of supposing that the pitifulness is something that resides quite unproblematically in the world and may therefore be present even if no one could ever detect it? There is an alternative, I have argued. It is to suppose that the seemingly random operation of my psychology is a medium in which what the world is like for all of us can become apparent; and that this state of having related to what is before me in a certain way – excluding some elements, connecting and associating with others – is, insofar as it is a state of such a medium, a candidate for being an awareness of what is the case.

Why should we not think of ourselves as being capable, in this way, of exemplary affectability? As far as I can see, two things make it difficult for us to do so: first, a certain philosophical prejudice; and secondly, a misunderstanding of the fact that there is a variety of things the world can simultaneously be like.

The prejudice is a deep and highly ramified one: there is space here only for a very brief description. What I have in mind is the tacit adherence to the limits on the kind of self-awareness we are capable of which Kant imposed in the First Critique. Assigning any awareness we have of ourselves as representers of the world to a transcendental self which can only be thought and not known, Kant then supposed that any *experience* we have of ourselves can only be of a phenomenal self, of an object in the world. Thus, we know ourselves as the occupiers of a series of spatiotemporal places and, in addition to that, as things that bear, in our trajectory through the world, certain attitudes (pathological tendencies) which manifest themselves either as systematic modes of response to the things we encounter or as isolated sensations, having their place in the temporal order. As we have seen, Kant had to abandon this picture to account for aesthetic experience; he saw that here we encounter an object in a way that involves its relation to one, not as situated thus and so and as having certain attitudes, but merely as a knowing, acting occupant of the world. He tried to cope with the phenomenon by, as it were, dissecting the cognitive mechanism and elevating to the status of what is experienced the supposed meshing of its parts. I have argued that this story is unnecessary, quite apart from being implausible. For insofar as I experience some of my feelings as not having their source in anything peculiar to myself, I suppose that I can excogitate, from the endlessly complex play of my desires and experiences, from my pathology itself, an awareness of what it is like for all of us to be in the world. To have such awareness need not be thought of, in Kantian fashion, as some strange state of transcendental stasis. It consists of perfectly ordinary empirical events, subjective experiences of such and such activity seeming absurd in the light of such and such facts, which are then thought of as the becoming apparent to me of what the world is like.[6]

The second difficulty we have, I suggested, in recognizing the possibility of thinking of ourselves in this way, stems from a misreading of the fact that we can bring a great variety of non-interest-dependent responses to the same object. Others, clearly, can have quite different feelings about the old man; and although, while I am immersed in my own feelings, it would be natural to regard these others as mistaken, it would surely be an implausible consequence of my account if, even on reflection, I had to regard all responses except my own as due to imperceptiveness. On the

---

[6] There are many reasons why Kant could not have accepted this. The most important, I think, is that my account naturalizes processes which Kant insisted were transcendental. On my account, there are empirical events – our awarenesses of what the world is like – which cannot be given a place in a world which is, in principle, exhaustively describable in terms of socially acquired concepts. That was precisely what Kant tried to block by transcendentalizing the human perspective: allowing, in his epistemology, only the *empty* perspectives of discrete transcendental egos; and in his aesthetics, a stipulated content to that perspective, with an authority derived from a non-empirical source.

This is to broach the topic, much discussed recently (see, for example, David Wiggins' 'Truth, Invention and The Meaning of Life', *Proceedings of the British Academy*, LXII (1976), 331–78) of whether, in Wiggins' terms, the outer perspective can give a good account of the inner perspective. I have not addressed this topic here (though it will be easily surmised that I think it can't); my concern has been with what account a reflective inner perspective – one that knows that it *is* a perspective – can give of itself. I might mention too, that my idea of what the world is like is quite different from Thomas Nagel's belief that there is something it is indescribably like to have experiences – a notion of which I'm sceptical. If the world is experienced as like something in my sense, there would still be the question, for Nagel, of what it is like in *his* sense to experience it as like that.

other hand, if I don't do this, it seems we must retreat once more to the idea that, if the variety of response is not a result of a variety of interests, it is at least the result of a variety of ... what? Something like temperaments: a vague notion, everyone would admit, but clearly the notion of something whose manifestations would not be states transcending the psychology of discrete experiencers.

The situation, however, is more complex than that. It should be pointed out, first, that in some cases we do want to say that a response is a result of imperceptiveness; and we can substantiate such claims by talking of the sort of experiences the other could have which would make him understand more clearly the way in which the present object relates to him. This is surely how we would treat a child's frightened response to the old man, when we see that the fear results from his not having received the adult's customary fond gaze. The child does not yet understand the possibility of an isolatedness which precludes easy kindness.

But there are other possibilities, more interesting and more revealing than that. Suppose I notice someone responding to the old man with a kind of tense indifference. The tension will alert me to the fact that this is not just a case of imperceptiveness. He is as susceptible as I am, I will see, to the dispiriting resonance of old age and infirmity, but, evidently, he finds it necessary to fight that resonance. There are various ways in which I might deal with this realization. I might decide that it is a case of the other trying to block his sensitivity, of trying to produce an ignorance in himself. Another possibility, however, and the important one, is that I should try to *absorb* his response. I mean not that I abandon my own and adopt his, assuming that he is right; but that I realize that his response is another way of being right. That there are people in the world we cannot help is indeed a reason, I will continue to think, for coming to doubt that unthinking pride we often take in our lives as the manifestation of our will; but it is also a reason for steeling the will. Being in the world is like many things and it is like them simultaneously.[7] Which of them different people tend to be aware

---

[7] A case that nicely illustrates the point is that of Gulliver, who, it will be remembered, was appalled by the pitted and fissured complexions of the fine ladies of Brobdingnag. Swift has much malicious fun in depicting the pride of creatures who, in Gulliver's perspective (and the reader's), are hideous. But, supposing they became aware of Gulliver's perspective, what should these ladies have done? Ignore it, and insist that the ugliness was not apparent to them? – But a *simple* vanity can hardly sustain itself, once it knows it depends upon a resolute narrowing of vision. Adopt it, and abandon their pride? – But why? Gulliver's perspective has no more authority than theirs. Or should they have claimed, with Berkeley (First Dialogue between Hylas and Philonous), that what mites perceive is their business, what we perceive, ours, and that no perspective has access to anything outside itself? – We are familiar with the consequences of that, for the natural world itself, as well as for value. Should they not, rather, have absorbed Gulliver's perspective (though not perhaps the mites') and recognized that the physical delight we take in one another can only be

of and which of them one is oneself aware of at different times is no doubt a matter of temperament and mood. But these, we should now see, can sometimes be understood not as a kind of hidden interest, causing a wholly personal significance to attach to certain situations, but as exemplary sensitivities to certain truths about what it is like to be alive.

III

(i)

One of the things that gives emotional experience its importance is that it marks the point where we make contact with the value that the world has for us. Necessarily, we cannot be indifferent to the world when we are having a feeling about some part of it: what matters is, for the duration of the feeling, wholly apparent, even if what matters is only being aware of the world's intolerableness. And if my arguments have been right, some of these experiences are taken as marking points where we have encountered what truly matters. But since awareness of such truths lies in our subjective states – in our *finding* it impossible in such and such circumstances to care about certain matters, and not in our knowledge that we find things so – our grasp on these truths is unstable. My having related to the sight of the old man in a certain way has not been governed by socially entrenched conceptual or evidential norms; and therefore, when the feeling goes, there is no way of recovering it analogous to the way in which I might re-examine the facts to recover a forgotten conclusion. Nor can I appeal to the propriety of a procedure I have followed in order to get another to share my feeling and help confirm its truth. We tend to think that, although our knowings and believings belong to the psychological flux of our lives, *what* is known transcends that flux – this is what is normally thought to be involved in the notion of communicability we have been dealing with. But feelings, which are things that happen to us and which do not consist in following entrenched procedures, belong wholly to the flux; and therefore, if we take ourselves to be, in our feelings, in possession of truths, they too will belong to it. They are, necessarily, truths that matter to us; but they constantly escape us. The poignancy of emotional experience lies in this.

Kant only half accepts this point. Certainly, an object's beauty is, for him, a thing that can only be felt. But since the beauty involves the object's relation to a part of us which transcends nature, the beauty itself, in an odd way, is transcendent: it exists independently of those events in time which

sustained, with opened eyes, as long as it can persist alongside the knowledge that each of us is an amorphous lump of teeming, alien matter? The perspectives, if this were achieved, would not conflict, in the sense that each could be maintained only by denying the other. On the contrary, by becoming components of a single attitude, each perspective would lend to the other, precisely because of the felt danger of reciprocal destruction, an added urgency and force.

are our experiences of it. On my account, however, the point is wholly accepted. The transcendence involved in taking oneself to have perceived a truth of this sort amounts only to the presumed exemplariness of the relatings that have occurred in one. The pitifulness of the life I see just is the stilling of the will or whatever, presumed to be exemplary, which the sight of that life has induced in me. The experiential flux creates these truths and is not merely something through which they can sometimes be glimpsed.

The final point I want to argue in this paper is that one characteristically human activity, the creation of art, is in part a response to the poignancy which truths of this sort possess. In particular, the central demand in art for form can illuminatingly be seen as an attempt to cope with it.

(ii)

Suppose I try to write a short story, depicting a single episode which will convey, as we say, my feeling of pity. I'll have the man seated alone in a bleak café. A woman, evidently not troubled by his air of irascibility, sits beside him and starts to talk. The man realizes, after some moments of unresponsiveness, that he is not being talked to out of pity; the woman simply felt like talking and came to his table quite casually. The man is tempted. He could emerge from the isolation which he defends by irascibility and listen to what she is saying. But the temptation isn't strong enough. To listen to what she says would involve trying to understand another person. The quality of his understanding would then become relevant to someone else and, in thus allowing himself to be assessed by another, he would have to resume the task, long abandoned, of assessing himself. The man leaves.

Now, if I were to make anything of this story, the episode itself and all its details would have to meet two demands – for plausibility and for meaningfulness. The demands can only be understood as operating in combination. Suppose that when the man begins effortfully to reach towards the next table for sugar, the woman reaches out too and passes him the bowl. This would be perfectly plausible, but there would be no reason for its inclusion. The story I want to tell involves the woman's taking no notice of the man's infirmity; and to make her help him would therefore suggest that she has a thought which I do not want her to have. Alternatively, and supposing that the event is not mentioned again, it would distort my presentation of the man; for it is one of the cluster of my thoughts about him that he would respond aggressively to the merest hint of kindness. So, that the event could plausibly occur and that the man could plausibly ignore it as the most commonplace of civilities is not sufficient justification for its presence in the story. It would not, as we say, be integrated into it. On the other hand, if some event were included only because it served as a vehicle for one of the thoughts constituting my pity, it would be unintegrated in another way. If I made the woman talk of nothing but complicated family affairs, that would certainly be relevant, by contrast, to my theme of the man's isolation. But the meeting of a man wholly without social ties and a woman wholly immersed in them would be too implausibly neat – the story would seem to be set up merely to bear its meaning. What we demand then, of a successful story, is that there should be no event in it which is not plausible; but that each of the events be also meaningful, that is, each be a vehicle for a thought which is a member of the cluster constituting my pity.

In choosing a short story as my example, I have, of course, taken an easy case; and I've simplified, to the point of caricature, the sort of thinking that is likely to accompany its composition. But I believe that the duality of demand, in this case of plausibility and meaningfulness, is present in other guises in all art forms. And I believe that the case, artificial as it is, will enable me to justify a claim that works of art can express our subjectivity and help to cope with the poignancy I have alluded to.

I have already suggested that the events depicted in a successful story are related in the way in which the thoughts constituting my pity are related. They are not inferentially tied, nor do they jointly legitimize the application of some concept; but they are thought of, even so, as forming a whole. The collection of events in the story, however, unlike the collection of thoughts in my mind, has the further property of being plausible. The importance of this is that, insofar as it is plausible, the collection ceases to be something which, were it not for the feeling or insistence to the contrary, would be a quite arbitrary concatenation of events. The thoughts, it will be recalled, are conceived as a whole insofar as they justify my conative state. But that cannot mean that thoughts about what would be reasons for pitying someone serve to determine which features of the scene I dwell on or which associated thoughts I have. That would be a state of wanting to have none but gloomy thoughts and not a state of finding myself in possession of a truth about what the world is like. I must therefore suppose that the things which, *as it happens*, I notice, constitute a whole – and hence the instability and poignancy. But the constraint of plausibility on what events I include in the story means that I do exercise some control over them. The control is not an arbitrary imposition, however, as wanting to have none but gloomy thoughts would be; for although I choose to meet that constraint, I do not *choose* what can plausibly follow from what. Plausibility is something to which I submit. (In non-narrative art forms, it cannot of course be plausibility to which I submit. Here, such things as the nature of the material being worked or tradition become relevant.)

81

(iii)

If this were all that reference to the plausibility constraint achieved, however, it would not give us very much. The plausibility of the collection of events would, to some degree, rescue it from the fugitiveness of items in the experiential flux, but only at the cost, it would seem, of robbing it of its status as a truth that matters. It will no longer have anything analogous to that feature I attributed to the experience of pity – that, while it lasts, the world has meaning for me. For the fact that a sequence of events is a plausible one does not give it any interest. Since we do not choose what is plausible, combining events according to that constraint is analogous to combining items in accordance with some particular concept; and, as we have seen, one can be aware of the applicability of a concept in some situation without being interested in the fact.

But this is to forget that plausibility operates in combination with the constraint of meaningfulness. We need to be careful, however, about what this involves. Although I have spoken of what justifies an event's presence in the story, of what is relevant to my theme, we should not suppose that 'themes' are simply available as ways of combining events, as plausibilities are. We should not suppose, that is to say, that I might choose the theme of sadness or gaiety and then set about choosing, from among the class of sequences of events that are plausible, one that is also sad or gay. If that were what happened, then both the purpose and potency of art would be incomprehensible. For then a sequence of events which satisfied both constraints would be no less inane than one which merely satisfied the constraint of plausibility. To be presented with a plausible, though meaningless, sequence, would be like being in a room with someone in perfectly normal circumstances who suddenly announced, for no reason at all, that there was a window. But to be presented with a plausible sequence, each of the items of which was also clearly designed to exhibit sadness or whatever, would be equally baffling – though such objects are common enough. Are we supposed not to know that people can be sad? And if that is not being supposed, why is this particular passage of sadness being brought to our attention? It would have no more claim to be thought of as true in the way that interests us than, reverting to an earlier example, an interest that causes one to attend to the luxuriance of a plant's flower can be thought of as a true interest.

But the meaningfulness constraint is subtler than that. The sequence of events which I depict in the story is, it is important to admit, merely one plausible sequence among others. The woman could have succeeded in befriending the man and his life have been quite changed. Even if the story I tell is more likely, the other is perfectly possible; so that my having chosen to tell this one will seem to be merely an arbitrary choice of what aspect of the world to attend to, with no particular claim on others' attention. But of course, in writing the story, I do not suppose this. I suppose, in a way with which we are now familiar, that the other possibilities are irrelevant. The sequence of events which I depict, I will insist, is not just one plausible sequence in the world among others: it is a salient fact about the world as such, in the sense of being the epistemic component of an exemplary conative state which knowledge of the occasional piece of good fortune has no power to modify.

But if the non-arbitrariness of the collection of events I depict is only a matter of my taking it to be non-arbitrary, just as in the emotional case I take the cluster of my thoughts to be non-arbitrary, what does the production of the story achieve? If the events in the story which, I am assuming, mirror the cluster of thoughts, require just the same *ascription* of wholeness for them to be taken as a representation of what the world is like, there is surely no sense in which art could demonstrate the truth of the feeling. I am sure that this is true. Art could not do this, since nothing could. But there is something else it achieves.

Consider a different kind of case. There is the familiar human habit of marking hilltops with monuments or cairns. There is a complex psychology behind it; but one thread running through it is of particular relevance here. The pleasure of walking across moorland, as anyone who does it knows, involves not just an awareness of the space and silence, but an awareness of oneself as present in it. One looks around, engaged not in acquiring knowledge of how things are, but in savouring one's presence. Now, in such a place and in such a state, some high point will have a special significance: it will draw the eyes; one will want to climb to it; it will seem the natural place from which to survey where one is. (It will be possible to see more from there too, someone might say – deflatingly, as he hopes. But that won't explain one's climbing there unless we already know why one should want to survey the extent of the moors, which is different from wanting to discover how extensive they are.) And then one is pleased to find the spot marked, or to mark it oneself. But why should that be so? In the sort of case I'm considering, there is no purpose being served by the cairn such that its being in a particularly visible place is of relevance. And since hilltops are no more there than valleys and since piles of stones can be put anywhere, singling out the hilltop in this way cannot be understood, from the outside, as a means of achieving some known human purpose. But it is that which gives the cairn its meaning. Precisely because it serves no further purpose, it can only be understood by one who realizes that someone could have wished to leave a trace of his having been present in the place and that, since he wanted to do this, *that* was the place that had to be marked. The observer's only access to the non-arbitrary nature of the act and to the sense in which the hilltop is the centre of the scene is that that is where he too would have wanted to place the cairn.

There is a good deal more to say about this, but that will do for my present purposes. My point, applied to the story, is that the meaningfulness of presenting a sad sequence of events is not something that can have an external source. Sad events are merely things that happen, like happy ones. If, therefore, my depiction of the sad sequence is to be something more than an arbitrary choice of what to concentrate on, there must be something internal to the story which justifies the exclusion of happy possibilities. And all I can do is make an object, show how a sequence of events can be plausibly concatenated and be of such a kind as I *find* makes the possibility of happy resolutions of no help. And then I must simply offer this object as non-arbitrary.

Sometimes it works. Suppose we have been to see a film, depicting the sort of episode I have been talking about. I might say, as we come out of the cinema, that there was that moment where the man's eyes seemed to lose their focus and you will agree that that was good and mention some other, equally fragmentary, event. Such an exchange is typical and indicates a shared and enthusiastic response to the film. But how does it achieve this? We are not saying that eyes going out of focus is interesting; it isn't, any more than eyes glaring. We have not agreed that some directorial purpose, known about independently, has been skilfully achieved; we know of no such purposes. We pick out, it seems, for special attention, a number of events from a plausible sequence in order to ascertain that we have both found them central. But central to what? If the film was bad, in either of the ways I've schematically depicted, this question would be unanswerable. If, that is to say, the film was a plausible but meaningless sequence, then for us to have picked admiringly on one event would indicate only that we agreed in finding that event interesting, what interest it aroused in each of us remaining undetermined. If the film failed in the other way, that is if it was a sequence of implausibly concatenated but evocative images, then again, our agreeing that a certain image was good would indicate only a fortuitous coincidence of affectability at that point. If however, in adducing as central this or that event, we take one another to be indicating which points in the film have been relevant to our understanding the sequence as a non-arbitrary one, we communicate thereby our having felt (more or less) the same thing: we exhibit the fact that, while watching the film, we have felt that it depicted what the world is like.

This is merely to skim the surface of the psychology of making art objects. My purpose here, however, has been a limited one. The artist, I have suggested, manipulates the material of the world (in our case, in the form of plausible sequences of events) and produces an object which will only seem non-arbitrary to one who finds in his own feelings what will make sense of it – what justifies its exclusions, the specific connections it makes, and so on. In producing it, he therefore tries to rescue the truths he takes to reside in his feelings from the time-ridden medium of his own mind and lodge them in the world. That is only a part of what he does. But if the description I have offered of that part of his activity is plausible, that plausibility will accrue, I hope, to the account of feeling from which I have derived the description.

Solid joys or fading pleasures

R. A. SHARPE

I

Towards the end of his travels, Candide meets a wealthy Venetian connoisseur of the arts, Count Pococurante. Candide admires two Raphaels in the Count's possession, but the Count takes no pleasure in them; they are insufficiently accurate imitations of Nature. The concerto which is performed as they wait for dinner Candide finds enchanting; the Count merely concedes that the 'noise' is agreeable for half an hour or so but then, he avers, it becomes boring. Opera is dismissed as a wretched entertainment, Homer as tedious and Milton as a barbarian. The Count does allow some merit in a few books of the *Aeneid* and a few maxims of Horace. '"What a superior man", murmured Candide, "what a genius this Pococurante is! Nothing can please him."'

Pococurante is not quite as discriminating as Candide implies. A few works please him. I shall not try in this paper to justify the ways of Pococurante. It is not the connoisseur whom little pleases that I defend as the ideal aesthete but, to exaggerate a little, the connoisseur who is, perhaps, pleased by much but despises himself for being pleased by most of it. What I am interested in is the way in which the critic – and by 'critic' I mean not only the professional but the serious amateur – judges and values the pleasure that art gives him.

The concept of pleasure has played two roles in the philosophy of art. It has been thought to be the reason for the cultivating of art; since seeking pleasure has not usually been thought to require any justification, a concern for the arts can be founded on the desire for pleasure without further questions being asked. Secondly, pleasure has been thought to be the criterion which enables us to distinguish good and bad art; put so crudely the doctrine would have few supporters, but many writers on aesthetics favour taking the pleasure of the qualified as a guide to comparative evaluation.

Both these views are mistaken. Behind both lies the assumption that the art which connoisseurs cultivate is art which gives us pleasure. But a great deal of art is uncomfortable, upsetting or even horrifying, and is not valued any the less on that account. Dedicated lovers of the arts have to be stoical at least some of the time. So in order to substantiate either of these theses, we should have to construe 'pleasure' so widely that the thesis became trivially true: a corollary of 'Everything we do, we do for pleasure', a hypothesis with about as much charm and about as many advantages as universal egoism. Only by oscillating between this trivial sense of pleasure and the more substantial concept normally current, could the question of what pleasure we find in tragedy be a problem at all. Once we understand that the minimum claim we make of art is that it should not bore us,[1] we see that the problem of what drives us to see tragedies is a non-problem, if not a trivial non-problem (trivialised by a broad definition of pleasure which makes pleasure the end of all our actions). In many arts such as music, architecture and lyric verse, what is interesting is usually pleasurable, but that is not always the case; tragedy provides, of course, the paradigm example of art which exemplifies the distinction between the two. Indeed in any art, the finding of a particular episode pleasurable or interesting frequently provides us with what we might call the entry point into it. Pleasure is often, though by no means always, a link in the aetiology of our experience of a work of art, leading us to investigate it further. We may then find it right to say that we enjoy the work as a whole on the basis of the pleasures we take in different sections of it. Our enjoyment may be thought of as composed of pleasure taken in various episodes at various times; it is certainly compatible with a work having its *longueurs*.

However, in this paper I propose to narrow the inquiry. I am first of all interested in the pleasure we take in art rather than in the broader question of what motivates our cultivation of the arts. In particular, I am concerned with what is perhaps best called the 'pathology' of our experience of art. Even the cultivated critic can be misled by the pleasure he takes in art. How can things go wrong? Reflection on this leads to the problems of false pleasure, and thereby to a discussion of the rôle of judgement in pleasure, to the extent to which pleasure is properly classified as emotion, and thus, by degrees, to what will certainly be an incomplete taxonomy of critical failures. I shall not say too much about the distinction between enjoyment and pleasure. As Bernard Williams and Terence Penelhum both observe,[2] pleasure is like a passion in being something which comes upon us, whereas when we speak of enjoyment, we speak of enjoying activities. The Aristotle–Ryle tradition which treats pleasure as a form of heed or

---

[1] Not a very original observation. T. S. Eliot is only one of many authors who have made the point.

[2] Bernard Williams, 'Pleasure and Belief', I, *Proceedings of the Aristotelian Society*, supp. vol. 1959, 57–72. Terence Penelhum, 'Pleasure and Falsity', in T. Penelhum, W. E. Kennick, A. I. Isenberg, 'Symposium: Pleasure and Falsity', *American Philosophical Quarterly*, 1964, 81–91.

attention in the doing of a certain activity in a certain way is more appropriate to enjoyment than to pleasure.

II

One important task for the critic is that of ensuring that his reaction to a work of art is 'genuine', that is, that it is not conditioned by extraneous and non-aesthetic factors but by the work of art itself. In the case of pleasure, we need to ensure that the pleasure was caused by the work of art itself and not by some other factor, and that it was caused by those features of the work of art that we think it was caused by and not by some others. Although sentimentality is not in every way typical of the forms of response to art I wish to study, it is certainly the most familiar of what I have called 'pathological' reactions to art. A work of art may be sentimental, a performer's interpretation of a work of art may sentimentalise it, and a reader or listener may react in a sentimental way to a work or the performance of a work which does not deserve that reaction. The first two hardly need exemplifying. It is the last that we need to consider. Sentimentality in the arts does seem to be bound up with the idea that the purpose of art must be to give pleasure to its audience; the corollary is that the audience is entitled to hunt the work for features which it enjoys at the expense, perhaps, of a balanced view of the work. Perhaps it is a misconception which we lay ultimately at the door of Utilitarianism; certainly it is an accusation we make against art of the fairly recent past.[3]

What characterises a sentimental response to art is characteristic of sentimentality elsewhere; we take pleasure in the kitten's large appealing eyes and playful ways whilst setting aside the way it prolongs the agony of a dying mouse by tossing it in the air before dismembering it. We do not relish the play of the young rat or the young wart-hog whose behaviour and needs are not, I imagine, very different. Puccini presents us with the cliché of the lovers reunited just in time for the heroine to die of that romantic disease, consumption. The soprano lead will manage a discreet little cough but producers never give us blood and phlegm. We dodge realism by selecting carefully. *The Merry Widow* is sentimental because it presents intrigues amongst the privileged with no hint of the exploitation needed to preserve that society, or even of its darker side. *The Marriage of Figaro* is unsentimental because it does not duck that issue; we see the depth of corruption that power creates in the privileged. Compare again the anthropomorphised treatment of animals in any British film or novel with the witty but clear-eyed picture in Janáček's *Cunning Little Vixen*. Perhaps a producer could do something with *La Bohème* despite the rather sugary

[3] See Michael Tanner, 'Sentimentality', *Proceedings of the Aristotelian Society*, 1976–7, 130.

music, but *The Merry Widow* is surely beyond redemption.

Now the selectivity which the sentimentalist thus displays suggests that sentimentality might profitably be compared with self-deception. Imagine a self-deceiver who refuses to admit to himself that his son is a criminal; thus he withholds from himself certain information which would normally lead to that judgement. Paradoxically, we want to say that he both knows and does not know that his son is a criminal; he half sees it and turns aside. Now the reason why we should not want to say that the sentimentalist is a self-deceiver is that no comparable suppression of evidence in judgement is being made. If I am sentimental about kittens, I can admit their peccadilloes without ceasing to be sentimental; I do not deny that they are messy and cruel in their destruction of their prey. I simply do not pay attention to that side of their behaviour. I gloat over or relish their attractive characteristics whilst steering clear of their more anti-social behaviour. I join the cat in playing with a ping-pong ball but not with an injured mouse. Now, if I admit to self-deception, I admit to it retrospectively, for I cannot simultaneously deceive myself and know that I am deceiving myself. But I might acquiesce in the convention that consumptive heroines are sweet of breath and free of mucus without asserting that that is the case or even consciously considering whether it is. For his part the librettist or composer also uses these conventions. But none of us denies the facts. So although sentimentality may be cousin to self-deception, the two are no more closely related.

If then sentimentality involves the taking of pleasure in an object without attending to the object in its comprehensive character, what about the possibility of unjustifiable pleasure which lies, as it were, on the other side of self-deception – pleasure, that is, where a judgement is made but where that judgement is false without there being any suspicion of self-deception? (See again n. 2.) This possibility is, of course, considered by Plato under the heading of 'false pleasure' (*Philebus* 36c–41a). I am not qualified to comment on the immense amount of scholarly work on this topic; I introduce it as a stepping-stone to a more general discussion of the nature of mistaken or unjustified pleasure. Plato has in mind the matter of anticipatory pleasures. An example which seems to fit the bill is the story of the American visitor to London who started to do the pools and, finding his forecast agreed with the results, threw a very expensive party in celebration. Dividends were low that week. Assuming that he took great pleasure in the anticipation of his fortune, his pleasure was false because it was based on a judgement that was untrue.

Now, there are perhaps two interesting features in the idea of false pleasure. Firstly, our American's pleasure was real enough. Had he known what he later discovered, of course, then his pleasure would not have survived that knowledge. 'Unjustified pleasure' would be a better term than 'false pleasure' here. The second point is that this suggests an analogy with emotions. Anger or jealousy can be unjustified if the person with whom we are angry or of whom we are jealous is not guilty of the alleged offence. It is essential, it seems, to such an account of pleasure, the account that allows us to speak of unjustified pleasures, that pleasures connect with a proposition which asserts of the object that it has certain properties in virtue of which it is pleasure giving. Peters speaks of the 'cognitive core'.[4] The case is analogous to emotion; if x fears y then he attributes to y, by implication, certain dangerous features. Secondly, it is usual to draw a distinction between the cause and the object of emotion. I cannot cite my death as the cause of my fear of my death since it has yet to occur, whereas my death is certainly the object of my fear. The fear of the thought of death is, of course, different. If I take various measures to avoid the object of my fear, the measures will be different in the two cases. I might give up smoking and driving fast cars in the first case in an effort to put off the evil day, and make sure that I do not have too much time to sit about and muse in the second.

Bernard Williams argues that pleasure, like emotion, takes an intentional object as distinct from a cause. The distinction may become clear if one thinks of having a hallucination, say, of elves dancing. If the hallucinated person takes pleasure in that, the object of his pleasure is the dancing of the elves (which does not really occur) and not the thought of the elves dancing. He might plausibly take pleasure in that afterwards, or even in the course of day-dreaming. The distinction between the object and the cause of the pleasure is plain, because what does not exist cannot cause pleasure; the dancing of the elves, whilst an object of pleasure, cannot be the cause.

Are these various considerations sufficient for us to conclude, with Penelhum, that pleasure is a species of emotion? Despite appearances, anticipatory pleasures do not offer any special difficulties for Penelhum. Certainly our American took pleasure in the anticipation of his pools win. What caused his (present) pleasure was his present (false) belief that he would come into some money. It makes no sense to speak of my now enjoying my (future) fortune or my now taking pleasure in my future visit to the theatre. I may, however, take pleasure in the thought of the visit just as the American took pleasure in the thought of the money. Although the analogy with fear fails here since I can, and do, fear future occasions in the present, there are other emotions such as love and jealousy neither of which takes future objects.

[4] R. S. Peters and C. A. Mace, 'Emotions and the Category of Passivity', *Proceedings of the Aristotelian Society*, 1961–2, 118.

A more significant difference between pleasure and emotion is that the behaviour which is thought characteristic of a man who is jealous or envious or fearful is produced in answer to those emotions. It is because he is fearful that he flees. The emotion is causally prior to the characteristic behaviour. But behaviour which is comparably related to pleasure is the behaviour which intends to secure pleasure. Indeed, it has not been thought implausible to suppose that the end of all our action is pleasure. Pleasure generally succeeds rather than precedes the behaviour which it governs. Cases in which a person acts so as to prevent the present pleasure coming to an end are no exception to this rule, for it is clear that he here acts so as to secure even more pleasure in the future.

If I am correct in placing the weight of the concept of pleasure in its causal liaisons, then we shall also need to consider the rôle played by standing conditions. In the analysis of causal contexts we can identify the event which brings the effect about and the conditions without which it would not be operative. For the spark to cause the explosion the presence of oxygen is needed. That is one standing condition. Later we shall examine the standing conditions peculiar to the causation of pleasure by aesthetic objects.

Both Penelhum and Williams, in my view, fail to see the importance of the concept of cause in understanding pleasure, disregarding it in favour of the idea that pleasures have objects. Certainly there are cases where it seems proper to speak of pleasure as having an intentional object – the pleasure taken in hallucinations is an example – but the distinction between object and cause is not, as I have argued, required to understand the nature of anticipatory pleasures. What I take anticipatory pleasure in is the thought of what is to come and not in the actual event which is to come; thus the pleasure is contemporaneous with the object of pleasure. Furthermore, the cases of mistaken pleasure which I shall consider in the latter part of my paper are not cases which can be comfortably analysed in terms of the object–cause distinction, although Penelhum erroneously chooses to discuss some quite similar examples employing the concept of an object of pleasure. The cases of mistaken pleasure which I consider are cases where the critic misidentifies those features of the object or of the total situation which give him pleasure. They are not cases where the pleasure derives from either a non-existent object or from features of the object which do not exist. Now to speak, as Penelhum tends to do, of the misapprehended origin of pleasure as the object of pleasure gives the concept of object no other rôle than that of standing for the mistaken cause of the pleasure.

I have spoken quite freely of 'cause' in these contexts. Williams objects to its introduction on very general grounds such as that it is hard to see what causal law could govern the relationships. To defend my use of it here would require another paper, but perhaps it ought to be said that I cannot see how to make many important distinctions within the philosophy of mind without a concept of cause; the distinction between available reasons and the particular reason on which I act is an obvious example. It may well be, of course, that 'cause' or whatever other synonym we use is not identical with the sense of 'cause' that we employ in explaining relations between physical bodies.

III

The beliefs one has about the causes of pleasure may change the situation in one of two ways. Firstly, they may actually dissolve the pleasure. The film *King Rat* is the story of how certain criminal prisoners of war in a Japanese camp bred rats which they sold to the officers' compound as chicken. Now the officers' pleasure in eating chicken substitute which they believed to be the genuine article would not have survived the belief that what they were eating was Rat suprême. Secondly, and this situation is common in the arts, a change of belief will lead the critic to discount any pleasure he takes in the work as a basis for judgement. Let us consider some of the ways in which this may occur.

Firstly, let us set aside the point that the audience for a work of art may be unqualified to judge its merits. Given that they have a fairly narrow acquaintance with the art in question, their pleasure is not likely to be discriminating. Such readers, viewers or listeners do not count as critics in the sense I give to the word. Not having read Dickens, Hardy, Conrad or James, they may be too easily impressed by Hemingway and their pleasure in his work – of little account in an estimate of a novel's merits. I am not here arguing that they may not take the same sort of pleasure that an educated reader would take, and that the pleasure might be both of a similar intensity and caused by the same features; the difference then might be that the tyro does not discount his pleasure as might the thoughtful and widely read connoisseur. This is certainly possible and I shall have more to say about it in a moment. It is rather that the pleasure he does take may exceed the pleasure of a more experienced reader just because the latter has seen these particular tricks for engaging the reader's sympathy before, and that his pleasure is modified by his knowledge of the work's weakness. In this case the pleasure of the educated reader is actually less intense.

The unsophisticated reader may also take pleasure in the wrong things. *Hamlet* is something more than a ghost story enlivened by murders and sword fights. It is not that the play does not contain these elements. It is rather that it contains so much more, and a failure to respond to the play in at least much of its variety is comparable to the sentimentalist's failure to comprehend the full nature of the object to which he responds. The pleasure our imaginary tyro takes does not incorporate a judgement that the features he enjoys are the major features of the play. If it did, then it would come close to false pleasure but without the element of anticipation which Plato seems to have in mind.

A third and more interesting case may occur where someone misjudges the cause of his pleasure. This may happen in one of two ways; he may think his pleasure is caused by the work of art whereas in fact it is caused by some other extraneous fact not only not relevant to the aesthetic merits or demerits of the work, but perhaps having nothing much to do with the work at all. Suppose he enjoys the concert not because of the merits of the music but because he has the company of a pretty girl, or because he met the President of the Rotary Club during the interval. Now contrary to what is sometimes proposed, the cause of pleasure can sometimes be discovered by the application of inductive methods. After a few concerts when he has fewer social opportunities, the truth dawns. A more significant case is that in which a critic listens, say, to some new music by Boulez, Maxwell Davies or Stockhausen. May he not find it difficult to distinguish between the case in which his pleasure is caused by the qualities of the music and that in which it is caused by the music but amplified by the pleasure of being in the same fold as the *cognoscenti*? He catches something that he finds interesting; in his anxiety to get to grips with the music he mistakes his enthusiasm for the daybreak with pleasure owing no more to outside factors than does his pleasure in Mozart. Incidentally, this is not to say that pleasure in the classics may not also be enhanced by a feeling that your taste at last is maturing. The laughs at a Shakespeare comedy are usually forced. ('Methinks you do laugh too much.') But for the experienced critic that is less of a danger. The problem in my example is that he has an interest in enjoying the work; since critics cannot be eagles they hope to be cuckoos. The kudos of recognising a new talent is much prized, and the critic's pleasure may be created or enhanced by his anxiety to enjoy the work.

An analogous phenomenon will be familiar to philosophers. How often has one wrestled with some mannered writing only to find that what one took to be the pleasure of illumination was really only the pleasure of solving the problem of what the author is trying to say? The thesis turns out to be some rash generalisation or some triviality dressed in fine language. In the arts, we may mistake the pleasure of recognising some (any) landmark for the pleasure that is due to the work itself.

Parenthetically, a close relative of this case is where the reader, listener or viewer finds a work interesting not because of its qualities but because he wants to see what the creator makes of the work. I might read John Fowles's latest novel with pleasure not because the novel is interesting but because John Fowles is (on account of his *oeuvre*). So I want to see what he is writing now. It is easy to mistake the two, particularly, as my examples indicate, in the case of a new work by an established figure. But there is a crucial distinction between being interested in a work for reasons which pre-date the work and finding the work interesting because of the features that the work possesses. Penelhum argues that whenever we are mistaken over the nature of the pleasure we take or about its object, then the error must involve self-deception. He agrees that we can be mistaken about the nature of the object and think that it has properties which it does not, but in his view we cannot mistake the object itself without self-deception. My third case falls fairly squarely into this category; my examples were of enjoying a concert because of the company and enjoying a work because or partly because of the feeling of being 'in' with the real experts. Now no doubt self-deception could be involved here; it might reveal itself if the critic refused to acknowledge the real grounds of his pleasure despite having the evidence put in front of his nose. But it does not have to be self-deception. The problem is that Penelhum has a rather defective notion of self-deception, and consequently cannot distinguish it from inconsistency or simple error. In part it stems from his failure to see that a motive for believing something is more than a contingent feature of self-deception. Perhaps such a motive exists in the case under consideration, but for it to be self-deception rather than simple error, the motive would have to play a part in the coming into existence of the beliefs about the pleasure.

Perhaps Penelhum has been misled by use of the object-terminology here. As Williams remarks, there is a strong temptation to believe that the object of one's thought is not a matter about which one can be mistaken. In as much as pleasure too has a cognitive core, the same goes. Yet since we are obviously often mistaken about the object of our pleasures, there must presumably be some strong if unacknowledged reasons why the mistake occurs. Self-deception would be one plausible account. But in order to make room for self-deception here, Penelhum has to deny one of its salient features, the presence of an interest in believing what one believes. However that may be, it is not clear that it makes sense to say that the object as opposed to the cause of the pleasure in our third example is the company, the kudos of discovery or the *oeuvre* or, on the other hand, the work of art.

Conscious reflection on his own reaction is an important part of the critic's armoury. It is not all the critic does, of course; it has nothing to do with the scholarly business of establishing an uncorrupt text, and its relation to literary and artistic interpretation is important, but to some extent peripheral. An interpretation should be consistent with a structuring of the work which gives due place to those episodes which the critic finds the most striking, and these may very well be those which give him most pleasure. For this reason he must avoid two further pitfalls. He must not give due weight to his reaction to one part of a lengthy work whilst over-valuing others. He ought not to prize the first book of *Tom Jones* for the pleasure it gives him and give less weight to the denouement. You may wonder how he could do this. Well, he might very well pay less attention to his reactions because he is in the grip of a certain interpretation which places the weight of the novel in the first book. A consequence of this might be that he represents his enjoyment of the first book to himself as greater than it really is. Finally, even when all the conditions have been met and there is no reason to suppose that the critic is misleading himself about the causes of his enjoyment, he may reject his pleasure as grounds for thinking the work to be good. I may enjoy a second-rate play, but I do not place any great importance upon the pleasure it gives me. It might be, of course, that my pleasure is based upon rather special circumstances such as the associations which the play has through my previously seeing it in such circumstances. But then my pleasure will not be caused by the features of the play itself so much as by other memories which the play recalls.

Perhaps the most important reason for discounting pleasure is the most familiar; and it is echoed in my title. We assume that the pleasures of art ought to last. A great novel will repay re-readings and we may recapture not only the old pleasures but acquire new ones as well. The good critic guides us to those works. An *éducation sentimentale* in the arts is essentially concerned with the evaluation and the discounting where necessary of our pleasure. As Ortega y Gasset remarked, 'an aesthetic pleasure must be a seeing pleasure'. I have argued that many of the more important ways in which pleasure is judged to be irrelevant to questions of aesthetic worth are those in which we believe the critic has misidentified the cause of his pleasure or misidentified the features which cause the pleasure.

This paper has been largely concerned with deviant causation. What then would be non-deviant causation of pleasure? I have characterised non-deviant pleasure as deriving from those features of a work of art which are acknowledged as being central to it. Thus if my pleasure in *Macbeth* is non-deviant, then it derives from an experience of the play in which the soliloquies and the murder scene rather than the Porter's scene are foregrounded, to use the terminology of the Czech structuralists. But, it will be asked, what justification have we for picking out these sections as central to the play and therefore as central to a 'normal' reading of the play? The switch to an evaluative assessment of causation is accomplished, I think, through our seeing what critics of experience and discrimination pick out as central; we rely, in other words, on the consensus of connoisseurs. I have argued elsewhere that this is by no means an uncomplex or pellucid notion.[5] Nevertheless, as Hume and Kant saw in their different ways, it is crucial to an understanding of aesthetic judgement.

But suppose that the majority of qualified critics all 'happened' to obtain their pleasure from a work of art by a route which was more or less devious. Suppose that instead of taking their pleasure straight, caused by the work of art and it alone (as far as possible), it reached them via common associations and circumstances that encouraged their response to the work. The overtones a certain image has might be so general as to produce a chain of associations which most of the readers enjoyed, so that their pleasure in the work was thereby enhanced rather along the lines I described earlier. Alternatively, a certain setting might be necessary for a work to have its full effect. Thus a friend declined to borrow a record of the church music of Lassus on the grounds that it could not properly be enjoyed outside a great church. A large room rather than a concert hall might be the proper place for listening to chamber music. Suppose some such conditions are universal, their form varying from art to art ... It will then be argued that the normal and accepted response of a qualified critic is in fact deviant on my criterion because the pleasure he obtains from the work of art arrives via a route which is more or less circuitous. It approximates to the third case I discussed above where the pleasure, though certainly caused by the work of art, is amplified by standing conditions. None of these people is attending to the work of art in its pristine purity. For all of them it is coloured by fortuity.

In fact, I am happy to concede that the resonances of a particular image may be part of our culture and that the community of culture is a condition which makes a convergence of judgement upon what is central to a work of art possible. Equally, there is a proper place for appreciating art, and this partly defines the conditions for the optimum discrimination of a work of art. There are, after all, bound to be standing conditions of some sort or another. The idea of deviance is not wholly defined in terms of the forms I listed earlier. It depends also on an ideal of critical normality rather than solely on any single accredited causal route from work of art to critic. Unsurprisingly, then, we cannot give an analysis in purely causal terms of the conditions under which the pleasure one takes in it is a ground for esteeming a work of art. Nevertheless, in cases where the pleasure is a

[5] 'Transformations of a Structuralist Theme', *British Journal of Aesthetics*, 1978, 155–71.

relevant consideration in the assessment, the estimate of the causes of the pleasure is integral to critical judgement.

I referred to the possibility that the significance of an image, an idea or a symbol assumes a background of common culture between the author, painter or film maker and his public and that the pleasure taken by the audience will be mediated via such common ground. This is sufficiently obvious not to need exemplifying. Equally obvious is the fact that our culture is not monolithic; there are Christian, Freudian and Marxist approaches to literature, amongst many others. Though I cannot defend it here, the basis for choice between alternative accounts of the significance of a work lies in the continuity of the intellectual milieu of the audience with that of the culture of its origin. Consequently, there may well be cultural traditions so disparate from our own that there can be no standing conditions under which the pleasure we feel in the work can attest to the work's value. Musicians sometimes speak of an interpretative tradition's being lost or, in cases such as Debussy's *Jeux*, of no interpretative tradition having existed: so any attempt at a performance has to begin *ab initio*. A parallel situation to the first in the case of other arts is that we may not have any idea how to read a certain poem, because no guide to the reading of such verse either currently exists or is recoverable.

IV

Few philosophers nowadays find much time for the idea that there is a specifically aesthetic pleasure, a pleasure which is uniquely obtained from works of art or objects of aesthetic merit. In part, this is because we resist the thought that there could be different types of pleasure, different species of the same genus. Such musings too frequently lead to the conclusion that pleasure is some sort of sensation, and the difficulties of that theory are familiar from Ryle's criticisms. But the remark by Ortega y Gasset that I quoted above gives support to the idea that aesthetic pleasure is marked out by something other than the triviality that it is pleasure taken in the aesthetic features of objects; aesthetic pleasure in works of arts, if it can be marked out at all, is marked out by reference to certain failings to which it is heir. Aesthetic pleasure is that form of pleasure whose relationship with the evaluation of the object is conditional on its passing the sort of tests I discussed in the latter part of this paper.

The importance of these matters lies in the importance of aesthetic pleasure. I began by rejecting some of the more exaggerated claims made on behalf of pleasure in the arts. I shall end by stressing its importance. Ideally, the interpretation of a critic or a performer should reflect in its structure what he finds pleasurable or exciting or interesting in the work. To use the expression of the Czech structuralists again, he foregrounds

97

certain elements in a work. For most of us the soliloquies in *Hamlet* are outstanding in our experience of the work; perhaps they give us a special *frisson*. Most musicians will remember the moment when the main theme, with its giant, measured, even strides, enters in the last movement of Schubert's Ninth Symphony. This is one of the highlights of the work. The interpreter, if he takes the same view, will ensure that they are foregrounded and that they dominate the production. There is an anecdote about an inconsolable Rachmaninov saying after a concert, 'I threw it away' (referring to the climax of the work). Now, views of a work will differ from interpreter to interpreter, and it is by no means unusual for one critic's assessment of the centre of a work to differ from another's. But what one foregrounds is properly given a leading rôle in an interpretation; I imagine that it was because Claudius's speeches struck Wilson Knight as poignant that he gave them a leading rôle in his discussion of the play, with the consequence that Hamlet appears, not as the one sane and healthy individual at Elsinore, but as the disruptive influence in an ordered society. A more complicated case occurs where the overall structure of a work dictates a climax which most of us find less impressive than some of the detail; the fault may lie with the work or with ourselves.

These are fascinating issues which are crucial to an understanding of what critics do and much more could be said about them. For our purposes it is sufficient to note the importance of getting clear about the precise causes of our pleasure in works of art; otherwise we risk building our elaborate interpretative structures on false foundations.

This paper has been improved by the suggestions and criticism of several other philosophers including David Cockburn and Richard Rockingham Gill who took an early version in hand, Tom Roberts, Don Evans, Ross Harrison and William Charlton.

Beauty and attachment

ANTHONY SAVILE

Why are we devotedly attached to what we find beautiful? Is it possible to appreciate beauty in art or in nature without being deeply attached to it? Why do we think it important to cultivate this attachment? Why do we expect it to endure over time? These are difficult questions, and we shall want a philosophically satisfactory account of beauty not just to let us raise them but also to suggest how they might be intelligibly answered. Certainly the claims to acceptance of any proposed elucidation of the concept of beauty will be severely tested by the plausibility of the responses to these questions that it generates, and my aim here is to ask how well one particular account of it fares by this test. Only I shall limit my attention to the theory as it applies to beauty that we find in representational art and say nothing much about its application to music and abstract painting or to the natural world.

I

It is indisputable that our understanding of beauty cannot be correct unless it explicates the idea in terms of some experiential response.[1] In the mid-eighteenth century and for some time thereafter it also went unquestioned that the response in question was that of pleasure. What motivated that choice was only in part the facts of experience. It derived also from a right-minded desire to ensure that the claims upon us of the aesthetic were suitably autonomous and not legitimated only by its moral or didactic effects.[2] But whatever its success here, the choice of pleasure for the analysing response cannot be right, because the answers that it must give to our four initial questions are untenable.

At first glance things might not look too bad. The source of attachment

---

[1] A truth most famously put by Kant at the start of the *Critique of Judgment*: 'In order to distinguish whether anything is beautiful or not, we refer the representation, not by the understanding to the object for cognition, but by the imagination (perhaps in conjunction with the understanding) to the subject and its feeling of pleasure and pain' (§ 1, trans. J. H. Bernard (New York, 1951) p. 37).

[2] A particularly clear statement of this motivation is given by Schiller in his essay 'Über den Grund des Vergnügens an Tragischen Gegenständen'.

to the beautiful is unequivocally located in the allegedly constitutive response itself. Pleasure is unquestionably attaching. Indeed, as candidates for analyticity go, that statement seemed to be a pretty good one. Since another was that beauty provides the man who recognises it with pleasure, the second of our four questions got as straightforward an answer as the first. Not only does our attachment arise out of the analysing response, but it is also an analytic truth that it does so. Only both answers are over-simple.

In the first place, to say that beautiful art is pleasing does nothing at all to account for the *depth* of our attachment to it. When this is marked by speaking of it, as I have done, in terms of devotion, there can be no question of deriving that from considerations of meaning alone. Nor will it help to drop the idea of analyticity and replace it by the supposedly less obscure notion of conceptual elucidation. For if depth of attachment is to be accounted for by elucidation of the response that is partially constitutive of beauty, that response still cannot be the response of pleasure. Despite a long tradition in the empiricist philosophy of mind and in the absence of any decent specification of its internal objects, simple pleasure cannot have that reach.[3] So the obvious traditional choice of response must be abandoned. Doing that, we also abandon whatever serious hope there was of making it an analytic matter that beauty is attaching. This, of course, is not to give up the thought that beauty is *necessarily* attaching, only now we shall need to offer a substantive explanation of why it is so.

While we are about it, we should also notice that another defect in the choice of pleasure is that it makes it difficult to acknowledge the fact that there are occasions in the experience of each of us when although the beauty of some work of art is directly recognised, it is nonetheless found either to repel or else to leave us quite indifferent. Whatever attitude we may in the end take to this phenomenon, we must allow for its existence. So we do well to wonder at the start whether the occurrence of such experience will make it as simple to secure the necessarily attaching nature of beauty as is often assumed.

The two remaining questions are equally ill served by the eighteenth-century tradition. Until we know why our attachment to beauty is a deep one, we cannot begin to explain why it is one that is rational to cultivate. And once we recognise that we may occasionally want to stand off from what we recognise to be of beauty, there is little of an informative nature that can immediately be said about the claim that presently attaching

---

[3] It is interesting to see how the kind of pleasure that Schiller thinks is crucial is one that has the experience of order as its internal object. And the depth of our attachment to it is then explained via the 'taste for order which appeals to our understanding'. Cf. *Schillers Werke*, Nationalausgabe (Weimar, 1962), xx, 135.

beauties will claim our devotion in the future. Why may we not come in future to stand off from what in the present we love, even while continuing to recognise its beautiful character? On all four counts we have some cause for dissatisfaction.

II

Although the philosopher most obviously responsible for fixation with pleasure has been Kant, we owe it to him to acknowledge that the *Critique of Judgment* is largely constructed around quite a different response. It is the response of harmony or good match, which sometimes he regrettably dressed up in the cumbersome expression 'purposiveness without purpose'. That idea and its relation to pleasure is perhaps more clearly expressed by Kant's disciple Schiller than it is by Kant himself in a passage in which he explains what the pleasure is which is most relevant to aesthetic experience:

Pleasure is free when in representation we make purposiveness manifest and find the accompanying experience pleasant; so all representations in which we experience harmony and purposiveness are sources of free pleasure, and capable of service in art for this end.[4]

Leaving on one side the idea of purposiveness itself, we see here that aesthetic pleasure (free pleasure) is one we take in the occurrence of a different experience. And it is that *other* experiential response, not pleasure in it, which constitutively enters into our understanding of beauty. For Schiller, to say that we take pleasure in it is no more than the assertion that we do find beauty attaching, and that is something that he recognises is capable of substantive explanation (cf. n. 3). As to what purposiveness is, we shall have to go beyond what Kant and Schiller had in mind. For they both wanted to explain it in terms of a certain kind of fit between the renderings of sense (imagination) and our thought about what is sensibly presented (understanding), and without elaboration that means nothing very much to the modern ear.

If we concentrate on the idea of harmony, or match, and fix our attention firmly on works of art, it is not difficult to make a suggestion which has a discernible affinity with this obscure suggestion. We might crudely think that in our judgment of a picture or a sculpture as beautiful we shall in some way want to match the material constitution of the object to a certain idea that the artist seeks to realise. And we may feel that when the material constitution of the work is found to be fitting or just right to this idea then it is a beautiful work of its kind. If we now key the material constitution of the work to the function of the Kantian imagination, and the realisation of the

---

[4] *Werke*, xx, 136 (my translations unless otherwise stated).

artist's idea or project to that of the understanding, then we should have the beginning of an intelligible interpretation of the Kantian view that beauty is elucidated by a harmony of the faculties of imagination and understanding. Moreover with a bit of elaboration it provides us with an understanding of beauty in art which does perhaps have a power to give illuminating answers to the four questions that I set out at the start.

Before turning to them I need to say a bit more about what I take the proposal under test to be. I should also say that the elaboration is not explicitly offered in the name of either Kant or Schiller, though I hope it is one with which both thinkers might find themselves in close sympathy. The idea, then, is that a work of art is beautiful of its kind if it provokes in those who understand it a response of good fit or match to what I shall blandly call its 'project'. Under the head of project a number of things are comprised – and maybe even an indefinitely large number; but at the very least we can say that we shall not make a sound judgment of fit about representational art unless we take into account how the material constitution of the work meets, first, the (often indefinitely specifiable) representational demands upon it, and then, secondly, whether it does that in ways that satisfy the stylistic canons in play. In a word, the beautiful work is one that enough of us who understand it find just right according to these demands. It is with this response of good fit that we find the harmony (of imagination and understanding) in terms of which Kant and Schiller cast their theories.

Lest the suggestion seem too uninviting and not worth testing against our initial questions, let me note briefly a number of virtues that it offers.

(a) There is absolutely nothing about it that smacks of unacceptable subjectivity.[5] Just as with any other kind of judgment, we train ourselves to make estimates of good fit congruent with those of others, and over a period of training our experience in these matters comes to be tempered by our sensibility to theirs. Then, concerning the arts at least, we write it into our understanding of the beautiful that it is the artist who is to specify the parameters (of project and style) within which our commonly evolved powers of discrimination and judgment are to be exercised. So in no way have we scope for elucidating the beauty of art in terms of some dubiously private 'beauty-for-me'.

(b) It makes aesthetic judgment an active matter for the spectator rather than the passive one that empiricism customarily represented it as

---

[5] Kant's own position notwithstanding, I have tried to say what is wrong with his view that on his account of it aesthetic judgment is 'subjectively valid only' in a notice on Eva Schaper's *Studies in Kant's Aesthetics* (Edinburgh, 1979) that appeared in the *British Journal of Aesthetics*, XXI, 1981, 363–9.

being, for the reason that appreciation is now firmly wedded to understanding. The spectator cannot appreciate the beauty of art if his response of fit is not based upon the discovery of what the artist's endeavour is and what are the relevant aesthetic canons according to which his sentiment of fit must be guided.

(c) Because objects of similar configuration can be devised in answer to different projects and in different styles, those very same material features of one work that may make it beautiful may well condemn another to be a dismal and ugly failure. This variability in what accounts for beauty has often seemed to present a stumbling-block to our understanding,[6] but the suggestion that turns on fit makes it quite unsurprising.

(d) Lastly, the proposal can accommodate that fact of our common experience already alluded to, the fact that on occasion we recognise the beauty of some art yet without feeling drawn to it. Recognition of fit of work to project is very plausibly no sure guarantee of attachment to the work, and certainly no guarantee of attachment that strikes deep. It must be plain that what we feel about particular examples of match or fit will depend on what it is that enters into the project that the artist has undertaken, and evident that in the case of some contrivances indifference or even repulsion may coexist with what the present proposal identifies as their beauty.

III

There is no prospect of our devotion to beauty falling directly out of the new elucidating response. At most it could be argued that we must quite generally expect to welcome what we recognise as examples of good fit, on the grounds that it is through fit that the arts achieve what they set out to achieve, and because it is to fit that we give our attention in the recognition of their success. So, it may be said, our attitude could scarcely be a neutral one. That is true enough, but it is not an observation that takes us very far. It does no more than point out that artistic success is what we desire to find in the art we view. This fact could not move us at all unless we found in examples of successful art some source of attachment that justified us in recording them as successes. Abstracting from all appeal to that, the satisfaction that we have in finding success in individual works carries no theoretical weight. It leaves everything to be explained.

An altogether more challenging approach is inspired by neo-Platonic

[6] And not only in philosophy. Witness the puzzlement of Paulina de Bassompierre in Charlotte Brontë's *Villette*: 'To me he seems now all sacred, his locks are inaccessible, and Lucy, I feel a sort of fear when I look at his firm, marble chin, at his straight Greek features. Women are called beautiful, Lucy; he is not like a woman, therefore I suppose he is not beautiful, but what is he, then?' (ch. 37, *init.*)

thought; and from a combination of that with a dash of Humean psychology we might construct one substantive attempt to ground and explain the satisfaction that the single beautiful work of art brings us. While I do not know of anyone who has in fact put forward the account of the matter I am about to propound, it or something like it may well constitute the model on which those many who view the artist as a man of danger and one to fear unavowedly build.[7] The view I have in mind can be set out in three stages.

(i) It is first supposed that the world in which we live is axiologically inert – it contains no value or sense, is *hyle* uninformed by *eidos*. In consequence, value and sense, where they are found at all, must be our contribution, projected by the mind upon dull matter. (Strictly speaking, for the neo-Platonist the *noeton kallon* is unrealisable in this world, and interestingly Schiller took the same view of the ideal of beauty, 'which can never be realised in actuality'.[8])

(ii) The beautiful image is no mere replica of what naturally exists. It is that whereby, in art, matter is given form. Thus Plotinus, replying to Platonic criticism, speaks of the artist as adding much to nature, where something is missing [for perfection] (*Ennead* V.8.1), and following him, Dante speaks of art being found in the material that receives its form from *arte* (*De Monarchia* 11.2).[9] Neither writer, of course, gives extensive consideration to the way in which significance enters the world itself, or has any a priori view that it must happen through art and not through some other activity. But again we may note that this strong position is taken up unequivocally by Schiller in the claim that the play-drive, whose internal object is the beautiful, is the *sole* a priori source of significance and freedom (cf. e.g. Letter XVIII: 'By means of beauty sensuous man is led to form and thought; by means of beauty spiritual man is brought back to matter and restored to the world of sense').

(iii) The first two stages take us no further than the location of form (and value) in art. They say nothing about how that process is thence extended into life itself. Yet any thinker who believes that the significance of art

---

[7] For instance, I doubt whether the view of Schiller's opponent in Letter x of *Letters on the Aesthetic Education of Mankind* could really be set up except on such a model. Certainly Schiller was clear about the importance of projection. In his development of the Kantian account of the judgment of taste it turns up crucially in uniting what is sensibly given with the understanding's contribution. Thus in *Anmut und Würde* he writes: 'There are two ways in which appearances become objects of the understanding and able to express Ideas. Understanding need not always draw ideas out of the appearances; it can also project ideas onto them' (*Werke*, xx, 259), and he goes on to explain the difference between representations of perfection (the basis of Kant's judgments of adherent beauty) and representations of (pure) beauty in just these terms.

[8] *Letters on the Aesthetic Education of Mankind*, Letter xvi (cf *Werke*, xx, 360).

[9] Cf. Erwin Panofsky, *Idea: A Concept in Art Theory* (Harper Row, 1968), pp. 26, 43.

extends further than its works must have some explanation ready for the way in which this is supposed to be achieved. And here it might appeal to a mind of empiricist inclination to enrich these neo-Platonic beginnings with a Humean continuation. From that point of view it would be natural to suggest that it is association that turns the trick. Men find it difficult to keep apart their recognition of art's beauty – which, recall, we are treating as a suitability or fit of work to project – from a different sort of fit, namely that between the world as represented in the beautiful work and ourselves who view it. Given the mind's inclination to spread itself over the objects of its gaze, we easily inject significance into the world about us through our recognition and enjoyment[10] of the beauties that the artist prepares, mistaking, so to speak, the one for the other. And it is this extension of attachment beyond the work of art that explains its peculiar depth.[11]

Even in this caricatured mould the neo-Platonic model has non-trivial answers to give to our initial questions. It will be apparent in the first place why our attachment to beauty in art is deep, and why it sounds natural to speak of our attitude to it in terms of devotion and not just pleasure or delight. For as set out, it extensively facilitates something that can make our actual lives wonderful, and it can endow the world with a radiance we yearn for it to possess and which otherwise would be far harder to come by than it is. Then too, since the outcome of the process is one that we understand we all desire, we have an easy explanation of why we should think that the attachment is one to cultivate; it fosters common and deep-seated ends which we could not seriously envisage giving up. Again, because on this account of the matter the world itself is no more intrinsically endowed with form at one time than it is at another, there is nothing in it which could be expected to render the beautiful art of one period less potent for us than the beautiful art of a later age. So once it is allowed that the art of one age has a power to attach us deeply to it, there is no evident reason to believe that it will not exercise a stable hold on us even at a temporal distance. Barring special explanations, we should expect that what once provided joy will continue to do so long after our first acquaintance with it.

There remains the issue of modality – whether beauty is necessarily attaching or just contingently so. The Humean element of the tale has the effect of making it a contingent psychological truth about men that they are attached to beauty in art. I suppose that if we did not make the associative

---

[10] We have to allow beauty some initial power of attachment on this model. For otherwise the mechanism of association could not start. Only its depth is explained via the associative mechanism and the importance of what it achieves. 'Enjoyment' is conceived of as a relatively weak notion here.

[11] Recall here too how unavoidable it has often seemed to theorists to explain the images of art in terms of illusion.

move I have described from fit of work to project to fit to ourselves of the represented or intimated world, that attachment would probably break down. But that would do nothing to minimise the importance to us of art on this view, for contingency and fortuitousness are worlds apart. Contingency at this point is quite compatible with the claim that the rationale for the existence of art might well depend on the associative link's being maintained. Once its value to us is accounted for in terms of the facilitation it provides for the projection of significance onto the world, and once the mechanism on which that process is supposed to rest is imagined as ceasing to operate, art loses its point. So while it need not be held that art's beauty is necessarily attaching, we should only expect to find it existing in the world as long as it is attaching.

IV

I should expect reaction to this child of Plotinus and Hume to be mixed. True, it does offer direct answers to our questions; and true, too, sometimes our attachment to beauty may get explained in this way. Nevertheless, there are at least three reasons for thinking that, as a general answer to the problem, it will not do.

The first is this. While the artist is here represented as having the power to enlarge the spirit, so too he is given extensive power to wreak havoc in the soul. As the neo-Platonic situation is described, the audience or spectator has no means of resisting corruption through misguided attachment. It thus looks as if the artist is made a far more dubious figure than we of later date are inclined to allow him to be, and as if we might find ourselves sympathising with the man whom Schiller presented as the opponent of aesthetic education:

> It cannot be denied ... that the delights of beautiful art can, in the right hands, be made to serve laudable ends. But it is by no means contrary to its nature to have in the wrong hands quite the opposite effect, and to put its soul-seducing power at the service of error and injustice. Taste induces in the mind a dangerous tendency to neglect reality altogether and to sacrifice truth and morality to the alluring dress in which they appear.[12]

Since our attachment to beauty is, on the neo-Platonic story, indirect and gains its depth from its effects, and since we are represented as being powerless before its suggestion (the association taking place willy nilly), the indeterminacy of this view of beauty between good and ill will lead us to wonder whether we can be sure that its cultivation is generally desirable.

Secondly, the position is open to the criticism that the Humean

---

[12] *Letters on the Aesthetic Education of Mankind*, Letter x (trans. E. M. Wilkinson and L. A. Willoughby (Oxford, 1958), 65); *Werke*, xx, 338.

association on which it depends is not one that we have any independent reason to believe ourselves regularly to make – independent, that is, of the power that the supposition that we do make it gives us to answer the original questions. Once we disregard that power and look to our actual experience, we may doubt whether we find cases of the sort described. It might even be said that given the very neutral terms in which the beauty-characterising fit has been described – simply as fit of work to project – it is hard to understand why we should expect to project that fit into the world in such a way as to encourage us to find it directly and deeply engaging our affections. At most we might perhaps associatively project *coherence* into the world at several actual or possible points as a result of finding order in beautiful art, but coherence is neither identical with, nor a sufficient condition for, attachment to what displays it. As we have already seen, it may even be experienced as alienating rather than attaching; and when this is remembered, it may well look as if attachment has simply been smuggled in through the back door after our direct concern for beauty has been written down. The more firmly resolved we are to minimise that direct concern, the less surely we can hope to make good the resulting gap by appeal to any doctrine of association that is remotely plausible.

Thirdly and most seriously, an effect of the proposal is to make our attachment to the beautiful irrational. For either it rests on a mistake – that of taking fit of work to project as the very same thing as fit between ourselves and the world as represented; or it rests on the very assumption that the appeal to association sees itself as denying, namely that there is an internal route from one to the other. In either case, it would have to be acknowledged that the attachment that is formed on the basis of attention given to beautiful works of art is flawed in the justifications we are able to give for it. In consequence, it would be impossible for us to explain why that attachment is one to be encouraged and developed, and a rationally devised programme of aesthetic education – such as envisaged by Schiller – would be unrealisable. This is not of course to deny that we might often expect benefits to accrue from unreason; but once we became self-consciously aware of the way in which they had come about, they would surely dissipate their strength.

I dare say that an ingenious person might hope to find ways of meeting the first two of these objections. In trying to meet the first, he could argue that various concealed factors are there to prevent beautiful art from corrupting us; to the second, he could say more to link our perception of coherence with our finding it attaching. But it will not be necessary to follow him along either path, for whether he succeeds or not, the third objection is not to be met. And as long as we look for answers to the original questions which do not suppose our attachment to beauty to be irrational, a different approach is called for.

V

This failure does not of itself reflect on the account of beauty under scrutiny. It would do that only if there were no other way in which it could proceed than that just rejected. And we might think that there is one alternative ready to hand the working of which turns less on the power of beauty to *import* into life a radiance that it would otherwise lack than on its ability to *reveal* a radiance which the world we know already and independently contains. If, on the view rejected, we were supposing ourselves to love the beautiful in art for its power to invent significance, we might now do better instead to suppose our attachment to be rooted in its power to discover it.

The new view is very different from that just set aside, and the three criticisms that forced the change no longer arise. Fundamentally, this is because we no longer think of ourselves as having to appeal to factitious association to do the work. Instead we see ourselves able to recognise the world as having a power of answering to our needs and concerns and of accepting anthropocentric thoughts about it independently of the projections of order generated in art, where these ways of thought are most clearly set out and exemplified in the beautiful art we construct. Our attachment, then, is to what enables us to make these valuable discoveries; and because they are valuable, our devotion is in no way irrational. By it we properly honour what renders special service.

Thus irrationality yields to soundly based feeling. And as the most damning objection to the Humean story is avoided, so are the others. Replacing association by discovery we make it possible to resist the power the artist has to corrupt, for when the world he represents is untoward, we do not discover something which would, by the mechanism of gratitude, rationalise attachment. Unless we had simply made a mistake – and then it would be a mistake that we could correct – these would very likely be cases where we find beauty to which we are unresponsive. And detachment would not be at all mysterious, mediated by the action of 'hidden variables', but would rest on our uncontroversial ability sturdily to criticise and stand off from crippling forms of thought that art can sometimes offer in coherent guise.

Nor does altering the story in this apparently beneficial way detract from our ability to give informative answers to the original questions. (i) The source of our devotion remains located in the sense and value that through our exploration of art, we find a place for in the world; then, (ii) our cultivation of a sense of beauty is rational because through its development we come to find clear expression of those values and prepare the way for their understanding and, in consequent action, for their actualisation. (iii) Thirdly, the devotion that thus arises remains contingent in that (a) there are allowed to be non-attaching beauties and (b) it is taken as a psychological fact about men that they adopt aesthetic means to fill out the sort of understanding just described. Lastly (iv), the attachments that we form are likely to be long lasting for the same reason as before[13] – we see little prospect of giving up those values and concerns delineated in beautiful art, and unless there were good reason to do so we should not expect to detach ourselves from what mediates their discovery and understanding.

It must be confessed that the last of these responses is now less plainly assured than seemed previously. For here we can, as we could not before, ask the question why what exemplifies a value that we build into our lives should over a long period be thought of as a *vivid* exemplification of it. On the earlier account, that followed simply from the supposedly unvarying mechanism of association, which ensured that the mere understanding of a representation as beautiful would lead us to project into the world something that we cared about; and there the cultural or temporal provenance of the work that achieved this feat was supposed to make no difference to its power. By contrast, we can now ask whether at different times we might not find different means of rendering constant values that make them more or less accessible. If we answer 'yes', our attention might be thought likely to wander and be less firmly fixed, and in consequence attachment to be more changeable than stable. And this reflection could be reinforced by the further thought that at different times we find different aspects of our humanity to demand expression. Then we should expect those forms through which the values of different ages have been expressed to change their appeal to us. Certainly these doubts may be answered; but only when we know just how important it may be to acknowledge the labile aspects of our nature. So on the revised way of seeing the matter, the certainty with which we think a thing of beauty is a joy for ever is imperfectly founded.

This issue is one to which I shall return. For the moment, however, it is not one to pursue, because whatever we might say about it two objections to the revised scheme force us to set it aside. The first is that the connection between the beauty of beautiful art and its ability to discover ways in which

---

[13] But of course there is a different *explanation* suggested as to why we shall not give them up. The thought formerly was simply that they admitted of no criticism and that reason could not be brought to bear. Now the assumption is that they are well rooted in a stable set of relations in which we stand to the world and that there is no reason to expect that set of relations to change.

the world is amenable to our concerns is made no more than rhetorically and cannot be substantiated by detailed elaboration of the proposal. The second is that the importance of beautiful art is made subservient to apparently non-aesthetic considerations and hence denuded of its vaunted and desired autonomy. The effect of the first is to show that the proposal cannot do what it sets out to do – to answer questions that are specifically about beauty, taken as one particular feature that successful art can display. The effect of the second is to call in doubt the importance of aesthetic values except as means to non-aesthetic ends.

Of these, only the first needs any elaboration; and that can be quickly given. Having proposed that we conceive of beauty as just fit of work to project it must be unclear why the art which achieves that goal should well exemplify our discoveries of sense and value in the world. The connection between beauty and the clarity of understanding that it purportedly mediates is unacceptably obscure. After all, one wonders, why should clarity of this kind not result from something quite different from this artistic fit? There just is nothing yet visible in the very indeterminate idea of 'fit to project' that makes it compelling to say that fit does make a notable contribution to the discovery (or for that matter the invention) of ways in which the world may be found amenable to our ways of thought.

These difficulties are severe. But what they suggest to me is that something has again gone wrong with the way in which the Schillerian conception of beauty is being handled, rather than that the conception is itself untenable. This diagnosis receives some confirmation when it is noticed how both this version and its neo-Platonic predecessor conform to a common, yet unacceptable, model. The crucial assumption that they both make is best displayed by showing how a simple simile, distorting in its consequences, fits each of the two options so far discussed, and it may turn out that by shedding the assumption that makes the simile applicable, a way around the difficulties that have arisen can be found.

VI

The delusive image I have in mind is one that represents the beautiful work of art as a window through which something distinct is perceived as having a worth of its own. In both attempts on the problem it has been the nature of the something else that founds the depth of our attachment to the analogue of the window. So in the first case, while we could assume ourselves to have a certain immediate and bland affection for the window, that affection was only reinforced in the requisite degree as it allowed us to project onto the world beyond a vision that is deeply attaching. In the second, the window is appealing because it permits the view of a good that the world contains; even if it is not a good that can easily be discerned except from this particular vantage point (this work of art), its actual existence is not dependent on the placing of the window.

What is central to the simile in both applications is the idea that the window and what is seen through it are two distinct things, and that it makes good sense to identify the window independently of our sense of what we come to see beyond it. When we think of a window as an architectural detail of a building, that assumption is quite correct; but when we insist on this division to make the simile work in the aesthetic domain, it is apparent why the autonomy of the aesthetic is inevitably cast away and how tenuous the relationship becomes between beauty itself and what makes it of interest.

We have reason, then, to doubt the possibility of separating the two, the beauty of art and the good that it invents or discovers; and this doubt can be strengthened if we try to describe rather more fully than I have yet done that very thinly characterised idea of harmony or fit that lies at the heart of the Kantian-cum-Schillerian view under scrutiny. All that has been said so far is that our experience of beauty is a recognition of match between the material constitution of the work and the representational task that it undertakes within its chosen framework of aesthetic and stylistic constraints – which before I called its project. But what compels the response or the judgment of fit is quite ignored, and somewhat disingenuously I have left it to be assumed that that is a matter that cannot be further described at this very high level of generality and that everything else we shall want to say will be provided by discussion of the individual case.

However, there is one good reason why that assumption cannot be accepted. It is that unless something more is said at this still quite abstract point, the proposal with which I am concerned will find it difficult to distinguish at all surely between a beautiful work of art and one which is merely a good (successful) example of an attempt on a particular representational task within a particular style but which nevertheless fails of beauty. For it might appear that a successful example is precisely one which we recognise as such by consideration of fit of the work to what it attempts representationally and stylistically. If that is the case then clearly a mistake has been made, for distinct things, the good and the beautiful, are then being treated as one. We need to know how they are to be kept apart. An attractive suggestion of a still rather vague kind, though one that will receive a determinate content in the individual case, is this. In judging ourselves to have before us a case of beauty-constituting good fit, we cannot ignore whether the represented world is shown as having a measure of understandable coherence. And according to both the intensity and extensity of this coherence, so we assess the beauty of the work. Whatever is meant by 'understandable coherence', we should note that appeal to it in no way replaces the demands of task and style. On the contrary, it is meant to tell us something more specific about what those demands come to and what it is that compels the relevant feeling of fit that they generate. The world that is represented is one that is presented as coherent under the values of the style in point and the artist's work is only judged to be beautiful insofar as under these values it is experienced as compelling and making sense. Unless we feel that the whole comes out right, match of work to style and project will be found jarring or insipid, and in speaking of 'the whole' here we cannot avoid involving ourselves in an intellectual and emotional order that we find exemplified in the work before us.[14]

The effect of this move is to make it impossible for us now to do what was assumed to be necessary before. That is, we can no longer detach the significance or sense that previously we attempted to project or discover *beyond* the beauty of the work from our judgment that the work is a beautiful one. This significance turns up in the very assessment of the work as matching its project, and it is internal, not external, to the work's beauty. Thus all reliance on the simile of window and what is viewed through it is cast aside. Having jettisoned that, we are free to meet the objections that were last raised, and, it may be hoped, to preserve the virtues that the earlier schemes enjoyed.

In essence, the virtues are preserved because recognition of beauty has now become undetachable from finding a way of thinking about the world as coherent and from understanding how the values that it embodies may be exemplified. In the picture or the sculpture we effectively see them spread over a small portion of the world; and understanding them in it, we grasp how on occasion we might see more of the world in that same light or understand what others are doing when they see it so. What is important is

---

[14] With the introduction of this coherence we can explain how Schiller's claim that the understanding imports ideas into the beautiful appearance might really work. Schiller is trying to apply Kant's doctrine of aesthetic Ideas (which Kant restricted to beauty found in art) to natural beauty. For both writers the importance of the beautiful had sometimes to be explained in terms of ideas that the beautiful appearance symbolised. They were somehow suggested to us by the artist, and the spectator explores them in ways not strictly determined by the beautiful object itself. Now if, in art, beauty cannot be understood except by reference to a judgment of coherence about the represented world, this judgment will rest on what the spectator finds on dwelling with the work before him. Beyond a certain point the artist is quite powerless to control the way in which he comes to feel as he does. Yet without giving the spectator the impetus to explore and judge the represented world quite extensively the artist would not be able to produce those beautiful works to which we are most passionately devoted. (The importance of the imaginative component in appreciation is no stranger to the scene. Classically, we see it in Lessing's *Laokoon* (especially Chapter III); more recently, the theme is explored by R. K. Elliott in 'Imagination in the Experience of Art', *Royal Institute of Philosophy Lectures*, VI (London, 1973), 88–105.)

that we think of the representations we view not as displaying actual states of a possible world distinct from this one – for then we should not understand why our thought about them had any importance – but that we see our art as showing us possible ways of finding order in our own world (or imagined extensions of it). Then insofar as we can extend these ways of thought beyond the samples found in the work before us, we see why they matter to us: they discover possible projections of sense for us and test them against the resources of our imagination. Thereby we come to a feeling for the world's ability to sustain order of the kinds these works envisage. Elements both of invention and of discovery have their place. As for the objections, the embarrassment that the connection between beauty and the ground of our attachment to it was quite rhetorical seems now to dissolve. The two are fastened together, since it is suggested that we cannot make a correct judgment of beauty unless in so doing we make the experiential judgment of coherence or sense. A contingent connection does not have to be found; the one and the other are of a piece. Subject to the provisions of the next section, that directly makes way for attachment.

Secondly, it should be clear now that the charge of having made our interest in aesthetic matters heteronomous can be rejected.

We have explained what it is that underlies our devotion to beauty neither via an irrational projection from the recognition of good fit nor as a discovery to which that recognition might lead, but ultimately in terms of the beautiful itself.

At the same time, this is not to claim that we could understand the importance of the beautiful to us except in terms of connections it makes with our wider intellectual, practical and emotional concerns. On the supposition that having aesthetic interests does involve these things, we shall not be explaining its worth independently of them. Autonomy, one needs to remember, does not mean locating the value of the arts by reference to concerns that are unconnected with the rest of our lives. If it did then their value would be minimal. It insists only that it be one that is not explained in terms of the non-aesthetic.

VII

At this point I envisage a critic raising the following doubt. Noticing that I have already insisted on the existence of repelling, or at least, non-attaching beauties, beauties to which we respond in those ways while still recognising their beauty, he may object that no real room has been left in the newly amplified description of fit for fit to underpin attachment. The mere experiential recognition of coherence in a displayed way of thought does not apparently carry with it any presumption that we shall actually adopt those ways of thought or find what they offer us attractive. This defect, he may say, was somewhat obscured by my speaking of the 'understandable coherence' of the pictured world, for that may seem to carry with it the suggestion that in our understanding of the beautiful picture we see the world under the aspect of the good. And if we did make use of that assumption to secure attachment, more would have been read into the proposal than I have any right to put there, for then the alienating cases would be assumed to be impossible. If this is acknowledged, where are we to locate the ground of attachment? Has that not been thrown away?

The answer is that it has not. While there may be cases in which we find the coherence of the represented world alienating and the order of the picture one from which we detach ourselves, there are other cases in which the order in question is undoubtedly experienced as benign. It will be an adequate reply to this critic to say that because devotion and attachment are inseparable from coherence that we experience as benign, his objection will be met providing that the benignly coherent constitutes the norm. If it can be shown that it does, the effect will be to allow us to see non-attaching beauties as abnormal deviations for whose existence space has to be made. We shall also see that the standard case is one that does, as we expect, generate devotion. With this issue so construed, we shall finally have the answer to the modal question about beauty and *necessity* of attachment that appeared on my initial list.

I have already rejected the view that it is an analytic matter that beauty attracts devotion. The non-empty distinction just drawn between order that we experience as benign and that which we find alienating seems to rule out any straightforward linkage between the two ideas. However, that is not to say that there is only a contingent connection between them. If there were, we should scarcely know what to say to the artist who reckoned his task was complete with the delineation in his work of coherent fit of undetermined type, or to the man who thought that beyond that fit the addition of benignity is merely a matter of good luck. Yet we must have something to say here not just because our prejudices point in that direction, but because unless we do we shall find that we have no reason to suppose it important for the future that our successors be educated in matters of taste. In the absence of anything at this point, we should have no ground to project into the future what has in the past made our commerce with art so fruitful, and then no reason to think that preparation for that same future possibility was at all urgent.

One suggestion sometimes canvassed is that while there can be beauty that is unattaching, unless it were sometimes found attaching we should not be able to say that a man had any aesthetic experience at all.[15] But this

[15] E.g. Roger Scruton's *The Aesthetics of Architecture* (London, 1979), 112.

way with the problem does not seem immediately compelling to me. As long as we exercise the aesthetic sense in the discernment of order, I can see little reason for thinking that we could only do that if sometimes the order we discern (or project) is of a benign kind. As far as concept acquisition goes, at least, there seems to be no logical dependence of the right sort, and what else the argument might rest on is obscure. However, there is an argument rather different from this that turns on the notion of art itself, and with its help I suggest that our imagined critic can be answered.

Art, let us agree, has to be thought of as a public matter. Outside the institutional setting it would scarcely have a history, and without a history we should not be able to see its works as exhibiting sufficient richness of style to generate those constraints within which sharp experience of fit is possible.[16] Now, when we ask what it is that makes it possible for an institution of art to arise, we have to assume that its doing so answers to desires we have for what the institution can provide. What is produced under its sign must therefore be thought of as having a sense and importance for us. And while this reflection cannot be used to guarantee that what is made as art does actually achieve such a goal, we can say that it constitutes a theoretical norm towards which what we make as art must strive. Here, with what Schiller calls 'the ideal of beauty' or its 'pure rational concept', benignity must reign. Unless it did, the institution of art could not get off the ground.

It might perhaps be contended that such an argument can only work as long as we ask about the generation of the institution of art, but that once it has become established, there is no longer any reason to insist that the norm should be attaching. This is mistaken; for we shall have no easily explicable reason to want what is made to belong to the institution once that is established *unless* we think of these things as aiming at what might be taken as a publicly recognised good, *scilicet* aiming at a display of coherence by which people are neither repelled nor left indifferent. So both the generation and the survival of art suppose it to be normal that beauty be attaching, even though we often find cases that do not live up to the norm and which sometimes even appear to repudiate it.

VIII

The elaboration of the Schillerian view of beauty that has dominated the last two sections makes it necessary now to return to the last question of my quartet, about which doubts had begun to arise in section v. How should we respond to the critic who sees the beauties of the past as evanescent? What are we to say to the reasoning on which he builds his anti-Keatsian

[16] This suggests that the beauty of nature is conceptually parasitic on that of art. I do not find that implication repugnant or surprising.

view, reasoning which suggests that the benign beauties of one age may not be seen as benign by another, and that even if they are, their old vivacity may fade with time and no longer speak to us with its once familiar but now lost directness?

These are queries of uncertain weight which need to be discussed separately. The burden of the first is to suggest that at a distance we may recognise clearly enough the beauties of the past, but that nothing can ensure that a coherence which was once benign will preserve that character over time. So that what once was a source of joy may cease to compel our love. It will go a long way to answering this question if we are sure-footed in avoiding one mistake in our thought about benignity that it is very easy to make. This is the mistake of assuming that the judgment of benignity is one that is made from an egocentric viewpoint. We need to recognise that those beauties are attaching not merely which display an order which we find warming for ourselves, but which we can see are so for others too. And a reason why we are forced to extend the perception of benignity beyond the self in this way is that unless we did so it would be hard to see how art could offer anything to the spectator other than a replica of his own actual conception of the world. For if he could only recognise as benign a kind of coherence that struck *him* that way, so in all consistency we should acknowledge that he could only recognise as benign at a given time what struck him so *at that time*. Thus deprived of the exercise of his imagination, his art would be restricted to representing the world as he actually saw it.[17] What is more, since we are now talking about the norm of beauty, and because that could and would differ from person to person, it is also hard to see how it could be something that is sufficiently common to form the basis of a public institution. So on the egocentric supposition not only would art merely aim at replicating the vision of the world each of us has; it would also be exposed to the risk of solipsistic collapse.

To prevent this defect arising, we need first to extend what we see as benign beyond what we recognise to be benign for ourselves in the present to what *might* be benign for us – that is to what we recognise as a benign *possibility* for ourselves. And immediately we take that step we should see that we cannot stop there. For moving beyond the actual for ourselves we shall immediately want to step beyond the representation of possibilities for *ourselves*. There is no such thing in art as seeing a world representing a benign possibility for me rather than for another, and no such thing as recognising a representation as offering a benign order other than one which is benign for someone whom we might understand or sympathise with. So even in our reflections about contemporary art we see that our

---

[17] Assuming of course that he sees benign order in it at all. If he doesn't, I suppose he lacks the motivation even for solipsistic art.

concerns extend beyond the self. And this is something which we should have no trouble applying immediately to the art of the past as easily as we do to the art of the present.

The effect of this is clear. It is that when we reflect that the beautiful art of the past embodies representations we recognise as coherent, it will be irrelevant to our recognition of them as benign that they no longer (if once they did) set out benign possibilities for ourselves. All that is necessary is that we should be able to understand their character as benign for people with whom we can see ourselves sympathising and whose forms of life we can comprehend. That our concerns are not the same as theirs can have absolutely no bearing on the issue, though of course, that is not to say that we may not find their forms of order hard to understand.

The reason then for thinking that a thing of beauty is a joy for ever is this. What is perceived as benignly coherent or fitting at one time will in all likelihood still be something the coherence of which can, at later times, be seen as and sympathetically experienced as possibly benign. To suggest that it might not be is a quite comprehensible suggestion, but we must not be mistaken about what would make it correct. It is not that the possibility it offers for thought about how to see the world is a possibility we could not realise. Rather it is that it should cease to be one that we could even understand as suiting men. This could come about if we found that we could no longer understand as non-alienating what was once taken as a viable model for thought about the world. When this is insisted on, we see how hard it would be to take away the understanding that once was achieved. For even if we did not manage to secure it for a while, we should have very good reason to expect that with an effort we might once again come to do so. The reason is supplied simply by the thought that, *ex hypothesi*, we know that possibility is one which has been found to be benign by others – by our predecessors.

The other hesitation turned on the thought that in the future we might not find to be vivid what once had been found so. That is true enough – but we need to be cautious about what conclusions we draw. We need to distinguish as sharply as we can between no longer understanding and recognising the character of earlier art (which may easily happen) and thinking of its character as actually changing over time. Now it seems attractive to me to say that the beauty that a work of the past has it has by reference to contemporary standards, by those that set the parameters within which it is to be understood. By those standards it is and remains as beautiful in the future as it was in the past. The problem for the later generations is to recapture enough of the old ways of seeing to allow its excellence of fit to be recognised. Often, of course, we do not and cannot do so. But that is something that we have to acknowledge and make the best of. It only confuses the matter to say that the aged work is less vividly beautiful than once it was. We may find it less vivid – though often, happily, we do not – and when we do, the fault may lie in a remediable defect of our understanding. To think dogmatically that there is no remedy is to accept in blind faith the adage that we cannot return to the past. Where the mind is concerned, that strikes me as an empirical, not a metaphysical claim; and one that is very often false.

IX

Beyond recording how much of the phenomenology of our aesthetic experience the Schillerian conception of beauty can accommodate and explain, there is little one can do to persuade the sceptical of its correctness. Explanatory power is all there is to go by. But we should not underestimate the breadth of experience that calls for explanation. One feature of recurrent force that has often struck those who love the arts is the peculiar melancholy with which so much that is beautiful is charged. Where, one wants to know, does that stem from?

While there may be many different answers to this question, three sources of the sadness are suggested by the view I have been propounding.

(i) Sometimes what affects us is the thought that a certain recognisable possibility of human fullness is not a possibility for us. We have chosen different goals and different ways of finding ourselves at one with the world. That, however, does not stop us from seeing other ways as good ones and regretting that they are not open to us. Their beautiful presentation may be what brings it about that we are sharply aware of what we miss.

(ii) It may not be so much that we have turned our backs on something that we should dearly like to have (if only the cost were not so high) as that we can be brought to feel that a certain beautiful vision of the world is one we could not hope to achieve. The good that is shown us is perhaps one that we could not maintain; it is too fragile; and here at the source of our regret may lie our awareness of our impotence. We painfully see our own distance from that perfection, not, this time, by choice, but because of what Schiller calls our finitude.

(iii) Distinct from the regret that arises out of passing by a good we recognise, and distinct also from the sadness that roots in our imperfection, there is also the regret that what we see as having once been a benign possibility can no longer be so thought of. Perhaps our modes of thought cannot capture the simplicities that seemed so obvious to an earlier age. Were we to try to make them ours we should not find welcome stability but facile simplification. We recognise that we cannot step back except in imagination even if we want to, and the beautiful art that shows us this gives cause for melancholy by displaying an attaching possibility that no longer exists.

X

Removing the self from the centre of the stage, as I have done in section VIII, may appear to make it mysterious why we should care so much about the display in art of benign possibilities that are not so much for us as for those we can understand and with whom we can sympathise. It should not really do so. To notice that we do care in this way is to see that it is a capacity that humans have and one we also exercise. Furthermore it is a capacity that we easily understand the need to cultivate. As Schiller put it:

If we are to become compassionate, helpful and effective human beings, feeling and character must unite, even as wide open senses must combine with vigour of intellect if we are to acquire experience. How can we, however laudable our precepts, how can we be just, kindly and human towards others if we lack the power of receiving into ourselves faithfully and truly natures unlike ours, of feeling our way into the situation of others, of making other people's feelings our own? (*Letters on the Aesthetic Education of Mankind*, Letter XIII, footnote (trans. Wilkinson and Willoughby, pp. 89, 91); *Werke*, xx, 350)

Seeing this, we know our care is anything but irrational.

Jokes

TED COHEN

Liveliness is specially conveyed by metaphor, and by the further power of surprising the hearer; because the hearer expected something different, his acquisition of the new idea impresses him all the more. His mind seems to say, 'Yes, to be sure; I never thought of that' ... Well-constructed riddles are attractive for the same reason ... The effect is produced even by jokes depending upon changes of the letters of a word.
(Aristotle, the Stagirite)

The wise man made up his mind that he had to know the essence of the country. And how could he know the essence of the country? By the country's jokes. Because when one has to know something, one should know the jokes related to it.
(Nachman, the Bratslaver)

This is a wonderful topic for philosophy. Besides the indigenous questions which jokes raise they also afford new entries into some classical philosophical discussions, especially in aesthetics and ethics. This paper is a rehearsal of preliminaries, intended mainly to expose the subject. The expository character reflects my own first interest in jokes, when I began to see them as curiously like works of art. That led me to attempt to think about them in the way one might think about art, with a bias that comes from my conviction that metaphors are perhaps quintessentially works of art. That orientation is maintained in this paper, but because I should like to spark as much – and as broad – philosophical interest as I can, I have indulged myself in some other concerns not obviously those of standard aesthetics, introducing them wherever seemed appropriate.

The thesis of this paper is not that jokes are works of art, although I think that may be true, or at least that some of the value and significance of jokes and art may be the same. What I hope to show is that jokes and art have enough in common so that they might illuminate one another's most enigmatic characteristics. In particular, I shall begin to develop two subjects: (1) the relation of a joke to its proper effect, and (2) the question of why we occupy ourselves with jokes. The proper effect of a joke, in some sense, must be to amuse people, to make them laugh. My first question, then, is, What is the relation of the joke to the amusement? The second question is, Why do we care to amuse one another in this way?

I

> If you hear a joke, then you laugh.

Perhaps it should be,

> If you hear a good joke and understand it, then you laugh.

What relation is signaled by this 'If – then'? It certainly isn't implication, for you can understand a good joke but not laugh. You might be in a bad mood, or not like jokes of that kind, or not like the particular joke-teller. If we could rule out all these adversities we would have,

> If you understand a good joke and nothing militates against its humor, then you laugh.

Is that true? Probably not: it seems possible to comprehend a joke without prejudice and not find it funny. There is ambiguity, however, in the phrase 'find it funny'. It may be that failing to find it funny means only that you don't laugh, or that you are not amused.[1] But finding it funny can also mean finding the fun, in which case failing to find it funny means not detecting the funniness, and in that case it is a bit harder to credit you, after all, with comprehending the joke. If you don't find the fun, what reason have you for thinking it a joke? That someone told you it is a joke? That it is in a joke book? The issue surfaces, although not with perfect clarity, in the not uncommon complaint 'It is supposed to be a joke', which is not quite the same as 'It is supposed to be funny'.

Of course you might find the funniness and still not laugh. There is a difference between finding the funniness and sensing or feeling the funniness.[2] It is the latter which characteristically consists of laughter. What should we say about someone who didn't sense the fun, even when he could find it? It may help to turn to another kind of structure with a proper effect.

---

[1] These are certainly not the same: you can be amused without laughing, and you can laugh without being amused. I prefer not to make much of that in this paper, although I will say a bit about amusement without laughter when discussing fraudulence.

[2] There is a similar distinction to be made, vital but hard to formulate, in discussing responses to art. There is a difference between knowing or seeing that a work is good, and liking it. If we could explain, or even describe, the relation between understanding a work and responding to it (in some more or less specific way – say, by liking it), we would go far toward answering what ought to be an absolutely basic question in the philosophy of art: what is *appreciation*?

A DIGRESSION ON JOKES AND ARGUMENTS

> If you understand a sound argument, then you are persuaded of its conclusion.

That's not right, is it? It must be,

> If you understand a sound argument and take it to be sound, then you are persuaded of its conclusion.

Now what does the 'If – then' indicate? Still not implication, for it is *possible* for a person to digest a good argument and not be induced to believe the conclusion. But we are prepared to be harsh with this person, although we must be careful in describing his failure. If you aren't persuaded by a good argument, the breakdown may have come in two ways. Perhaps the argument is good but you don't see it. You don't detect the validity, or if the argument has premisses you don't believe them. But if you do see that the argument is good, do take it to be sound, then there is a real breakdown. It is this failure to be persuaded which is *like* the failure to be amused by a joke whose funniness you detect. With an argument this failure is called what? Irrationality? What else are we to say of someone who believes p and also believes that p implies q, but is not therein induced to believe q? Before trying to say what goes with the failure to laugh in the way that irrationality goes with the failure to believe, I should like to draw attention to some other comparisons of jokes with arguments.

What if an argument's conclusion, considered simply by itself, is plainly out of the question? Then the argument can't be good. If it is not possible to believe the conclusion – say, because it is inconsistent – then the argument cannot be sound: either a premiss or the argument form is bad. If all the premisses are true, then the argument isn't valid. There is more than a quibbler's sense in which an invalid argument isn't an argument. What if a joke couldn't make anyone laugh, not because it was too complicated to be followed, but just because it was hopelessly unfunny, with a punch line that could do nothing? Then would it be a joke? This is a troublesome question, with reasons for answering both ways.

What if, although an argument's conclusion is consistent, perhaps even true, its premisses don't *lead* to the conclusion, don't even come close? What about this:

> First premiss: There is no god but Allah.
> Second premiss: Every action has an equal and opposite reaction.
> Therefore: The square root of two is an irrational number.

Is that an argument? Would you be content to say, Yes, but it's an invalid one? That is a clumsy answer. It is a philosopher's answer. This is not so much an argument as a burlesque of an argument. There are comparable phenomena mixed in with jokes and with art works. Troubling art there is Dada. To vex joke appreciators is the shaggy dog story. Some Dadaists did things I think best described as going through the motions of making art. When telling a shaggy dog story one goes through the motions of telling a joke. From that it follows that putting a blank canvas up in a gallery, displaying a urinal in ways appropriate to fine sculpture, and telling an unbelievably long story about a dog who turns out to be not so shaggy, are all activities that derive their sense from presumed backgrounds of normal art-making and joke-telling. It does not follow that they are, therefore, themselves art works or jokes. What, then, are they? I don't know; but I know that the answer can't be simple or unproblematic.[3]

A final remark about arguments and jokes. When you finish your argument, when you give the final premiss, or if you're especially thorough, when you've given all the premisses and gone on to say 'therefore', and then recited the conclusion – when you've given the QED – what do you expect? Well, you expect your hearer to click into believing the conclusion. You expect the gap between your argument and his belief to be bridged. Compare that with finishing your joke, delivering the punch line. Now what do you expect? Laughter, of course. Your feeling when you finish the joke seems to me not unlike the feeling when you complete your argument. It is a sense of having done something meant to move your hearer, of having created a momentum which now moves to him. But there is a difference. In both cases there is your expectation: of assent to your argument's conclusion, of laughter at your joke's punch line; but for the argument your expectation is more a demand, while for the joke it is much less a demand and far more a hope. When you tell a joke you lose control in a way in which you don't when you tell a sound argument. You leave extra room for the hearer, and that is why it is harder to find what to say about him if he fails to come across – the point which began these ruminations about jokes and arguments.

*

If it is irrational to fail to be persuaded by a good argument, what is it to fail to be amused by a good joke? Not irrational, I think; certainly not in the same way. It is like being without taste. We will say 'irrational', I think, not only of someone unpersuaded by a good argument, but also of someone who is unable to see that it *is* a good argument if the form is plainly valid and the premisses obviously true. And we will, I think, deny a sense of

---

[3] If these things are essentially problematic, as some were surely intended to be, then there may be no canonical way to domesticate them. I suggested this in 'The Possibility of Art', *Philosophical Review*, 82, 1973, 69–82.

humor not only in someone who isn't amused by the funniness he sees, but also in someone who can't see the funniness when it is clearly there.[4]

What is a sense of humor? A capacity to be amused by the amusing, I suppose.[5] What makes this capacity remarkable is that it is not coerced into activity. You don't *have* to laugh. Your response is not compelled in the way that an argument compels belief. Your response is not arbitrary, however. We don't all just happen coincidentally to be laughing when we've heard a joke, as if we'd all simultaneously been tickled under the arms.

If I am correct, then the 'If – then' in 'If you hear a joke, then you laugh' stands for a relation we are poorly equipped to describe, for it is neither sternly logical nor merely contingent. Surely the joke must *cause* you to laugh, but it isn't the same as when tickling makes you laugh. It is exactly the relation Kant is ill-equipped to describe when he undertakes to analyze the judgment of taste. This judgment, he says, exhibits a response (to beauty) which is free but also somehow necessitated.[6]

What is wrong with you if you are not amused, if you are not reached by this non-necessary, non-contingent relation? In escaping the proper response you are not so much wrong as different. It is not a trivial difference. It is a difference which leaves you outside a vital community, the community of those who feel this fun. It is a community which creates and acknowledges itself in the moment, and is powerless to conscript its membership. To fail to laugh at a joke is to remain outside that community. But you cannot will yourself in, any more than you can will yourself out.

II

A point in telling a joke is the attainment of community. There is special intimacy in shared laughter, and a mastering aim of joke-telling is the purveyance of this intimacy. The intimacy is most purified, refined, and uncluttered when the laughter is bound to the joke by the relation I have

---

[4] Again there is a parallel with art, this time showing the difficulty in formulating the distinction mentioned earlier, the one between understanding and liking. What is a person of taste? Someone who discerns all that is there, or someone who reacts to what is there by exhibiting a preference? Both? Imagine a master wine-taster who infallibly identifies the date and source of what he tastes but himself is as happy with Ripple as with Château Rothschild. Would you say he has taste?

[5] It is, perhaps, just the kind of thing Aristotle calls a virtue in the *Nicomachean Ethics*, a 'settled capacity', a *hexis*.

[6] In the *Critique of Judgment*, where he discusses taste and judgments of beauty, I think Kant wears the apparatus of the *Critique of Pure Reason* like a millstone. Thus constrained, when he wants to describe the special character of this judgment Kant finds that the best he can do is to say that the judgment is both necessary and subjective – a grotesque formulation. This is not unlike our own options, forged of even cruder stuff, which permit us to say only logical or contingent even though we ought to be uncomfortable saying either.

just been worrying over, a relation in which the laughter is not exacted but is nonetheless rendered fit. There are derivative forms of intimacy, in which the laughter is not so absolutely free. These obtain when the joke calls upon the background of the audience and uses this as a material condition for securing the effect. I think there are two main forms.

In the first form the joke is *hermetic*. It really makes sense only to those with special information, and the intimacy brought to those who qualify is bound up with a recognition – or re-recognition – that they do constitute an audience more select than humanity in general. The joke occasions the reconstitution of that select community. For an hermetic joke the required background may be very specific and decisive.

> What is Sacramento?
> It is the stuffing in a Catholic olive.[7]

Either you know about pimento and the Church and its sacraments, and you get this joke, or you don't know these things and the joke is opaque. In America a very common device of this kind of joke is the incorporation of words or phrases in Yiddish. Appreciators of these jokes were once nearly restricted to certain Jews, but this has changed as an endless stream of Jewish comics forces more and more elements of Jewish humor, including vocabulary, on more and more of the general public.

Not every hermetic joke offers itself on this all-or-nothing basis. Some have depths which permit appreciation on different, if cumulative, levels.

> One day Toscanini was rehearsing the NBC Symphony. He stopped the playing to correct the trumpet line only to discover that the first-chair trumpet had intended exactly what he had played, and disagreed with Toscanini over how it should go. There ensued a heated argument which ended only when the trumpeter stalked angrily off the stage. As he reached the wings he turned to Toscanini and said 'Schmuck!' The maestro replied, 'It's-a too late to apologize.'

If you know only the word 'Schmuck' you can manage this joke. In fact even if you don't know what it means you can sense enough from its phonetic quality to salvage the joke. But the more you know of professional musicians in New York, of Toscanini's ego and his peculiar approach to non-Roman language, and so on, the more you will make of the joke.

Here is a more intricate example of an hermetic joke.

> A musician was performing a solo recital in Israel. When he ended the last selection, a thunderous response came from the audience, including many cries of 'Play it again.' He stepped

[7] For the provenance of this rare example see my 'Metaphor and the Cultivation of Intimacy', *Critical Inquiry*, vol. 5, no. 1, Autumn, 1978, 8 and n. 6.

forward, bowed, and said, 'What a wonderfully moving response. Of course I shall be delighted to play it again.' And he did. At the end, again there was a roar from the audience, and again many cries of 'Play it again.' This time the soloist came forward smiling and said, 'Thank you. I have never been so touched in all my concert career. I should love to play it again, but there is no time, for I must perform tonight in Tel Aviv. So, thank you from the bottom of my heart – and farewell.' Immediately a voice was heard from the back of the hall saying, 'You will stay here and play it again until you get it right.'[8]

This joke works with nearly any audience, but its total riches are available only to those who know the Jewish religious requirement that on certain occasions the appropriate portion of the Hebrew Bible be read out, that those present make known any errors they detect in the reading, and that the reader not only acknowledge these corrections but that he then go back and read out the text correctly. That audience – those entirely within the community of this joke – will not only be able to find this extra level, but they should also find it a better joke. For them there is a point in the story's being set in Israel, and if there were no point in that, the joke would do better to omit the geography altogether.

In the second derivative form of intimacy the joke is likely to be rather simple, although not necessarily, and the background required is not one of knowledge but one of attitude or prejudice. I call these *affective* jokes. The most common examples are probably what in America are called ethnic jokes. It is not necessary that one actually believe that Jews are immoral, or Poles inept, or Italians lascivious, or whatever: indeed, most appreciators known to me have the opposite beliefs.[9] What's needed is not a belief but a predisposition to enjoy situations in which Jews, Poles, Blacks, or whoever are singled out.[10]

A SPECIAL CASE: THE GENRE JOKE

Some of these, like the Irish jokes current in England, are both hermetic and affective. They are affective as all such 'ethnic' jokes are – Polish ones, Jewish ones, racist ones. The concern here, however, is with the respect in

[8] I owe the bases of both these musical jokes to Professor Peter Kivy, himself a New York musician as well as a scholar.

[9] Among studies this paper is meant to lead to is the question of when and why it is wrong to find things funny. Perhaps it is wrong to find negative ethnic jokes funny. But if it is wrong, it is for reasons far more subtle than that they play upon certain unpleasant beliefs. Except in the case of young children – and even there it is far from certain – it is not a matter of *belief*.

[10] Strictly speaking, of course, it is not the situation but a story of such a situation. What we have is not the thing but what Aristotle calls an imitation of the thing, and as he notes, a repellant thing may have a delightful imitation.

which they are hermetic. This respect is the need for prior acquaintance with jokes of the relevant type; that is, the need for an understanding of the form. Such a joke is hermetic because its full appreciation requires this understanding; but because that understanding is all that is required, the joke is marginally hermetic. We might say that it is intrinsically hermetic, and not extrinsically hermetic, because its requirement will be satisfied by the audience's exposure to jokes of the relevant type and no additional, extra information will be required. It is possible, of course, that any particular instance of the type will be extrinsically hermetic, but that is a different matter. It is a bit complicated to sort everything out, and it will help to have an example. Let us take as a genus, or genre or type, lightbulb-changing jokes.

If, say, lightbulb-changing jokes are good, and *J* is a lightbulb joke, then *J* will be a good, lightbulb joke; and that is a comma away from being a good lightbulb joke. There is also a kind of intermediate case likely to be missed. Suppose you like a joke which is a lightbulb joke, but you don't like it only because it's a lightbulb joke: you don't like all lightbulb jokes. It doesn't follow that your liking it and its being a lightbulb joke are unconnected. Its being a lightbulb joke might have almost everything to do with your liking it. You may well need considerable earlier acquaintance with lightbulb jokes in order to be able to find the humor in this one.

The first lightbulb joke I remember hearing was not really a lightbulb joke at all, at the time. It was one of a number of those dismal Polish jokes concerning how many Poles it takes to do this or that, and it was merely the one which happened to involve lightbulbs:

How many Poles does it take to change a lightbulb?

But by now the lightbulb motif is itself a form.

How many Southern Californians does it take to change a lightbulb?
Five. One to replace the bulb; four to share the experience.

How many WASPs does it take to change a lightbulb?
Two. One to mix martinis while the other calls the repairman.

How many psychiatrists does it take to change a lightbulb?
Variation 1: Only one; but he cannot do it until the lightbulb really wants to change.
Variation 2: It doesn't take any. The lightbulb must change itself, steadily but over a long time.

> How many Zen Buddhists does it take to change a lightbulb?
> Two. One to replace the bulb, and one not to replace the bulb.

The form acquires a second-stage development when the teller moves from questioning narrator to character himself.

> How many New Yorkers does it take to change a lightbulb?
> None of your damned business.

> How many feminists does it take to change a lightbulb?
> That's not funny.

A further possibility is that the answer come from a character who is not one of the maligned group.

> How many Jewish sons does it take to change a lightbulb?
> Only one. But it's all right; I can sit in the dark.

Each of these jokes is extrinsically hermetic, for one must be aware of commonplaces concerning Southern Californians, WASPs, feminists, *et al.* And some or all of them may be affective as well, for one may need something related to a prejudice in order to be amused by references to these commonplaces. But the only element with which I am concerned here is that special hermetic quality they possess as members of a genus. It adds considerably to the force of these jokes if they are grasped as instances of a type, for each has its *raison* in large part as a variation. This seems to me exactly how it is with art forms. The form itself induces particular expectations and forms of attention, and then the individual work moves with or against them. The work cannot get to you unless you can see it in its frame. In these jokes and in this art there operates a kind of principle which requires that the medium be exploited. In a very good joke every element in the story has a point. If the joke is of a type, then that generic feature is one of the elements most in need of being used, of being given a point. The lapse of most ethnic jokes consists exactly in the failure to *use* the ethnicity, to do anything with it besides using it as a code to establish a vague and general presumption that the main character is an oaf or ignoramus (as if Shylock were made a Jew only in order to signal that he will be mean and grasping).[11] Perfectly suited to explain this is one of Aristotle's sharpest insights. If you write a tragedy, you are stuck with having a plot. (It is, he says, the *only* thing you are stuck with.) You had therefore better do something with the plot: how good the plot is will have more than anything else to do with how good the whole tragedy is. If you want to tell a really

---

[11] Lightbulb jokes are designed expressly to succeed on this count, although they may lapse on others. The lightbulb joke is a kind of dual of the ethnic joke. It asks, How does P or Q or R do x?, while the ethnic joke asks, How does P do x or y or z?

good joke, then don't let it be a Polish joke unless you can really make the Polishness count for something.

*

THE UTILITY OF EXEGESIS

With hermetic jokes the question arises whether the teller could supply the necessary information along with the joke. While this may be possible after a fashion with some jokes, in all cases there seems bound to be a loss. What will be lost, specifically, is the special way in which the participants in a joke transaction acknowledge their mutual membership in a community. When your hermetic joke works with me, in that moment we attain the intimacy of community. If you *first* instruct me in the background, knowledge of which constitutes the community's membership conditions, then the joke itself cannot be the occasion of the uncovering of our mutuality. And that is a loss which deprives the joke of its characteristic humanizing force.

With jokes in general, as also with metaphors and works of art, the question arises whether they can be supplanted or augmented by their exegetical descriptions. We are virtually all agreed that no description or explanation of an art work will do in place of the work, but we find it very difficult to say exactly why not. Two things become more tractable if we turn to simple jokes. First, the structure of the thing is unlikely to be very complex. Second, a reason for thinking that art works and jokes have no exact equivalents is that only the original seems able to get the relevant effect; and it is, at least initially, much easier to say what that effect is if the object is a joke. It's the laughter. It is because of these two things that our intuition about the irreplaceability of things may become clearer if we turn to jokes.

Some jokes seem to work by delivering a composite effect, by bringing things together all at once. That's how it is with 'What is Sacramento?', and that is how it is with very many children's jokes.

> Where does the king keep his armies?
> Up his sleevies.
>
> Where does the Lone Ranger take his garbage?
> To the dump, to the dump, to the dump, dump, dump.[12]

These jokes, many of them riddles, are somewhat like simultaneous

---

[12] This was told to me in a bar in Tucson by Janet Casebier as she was recalling her days as a Girl Scout. Shoshannah Cohen, a person of exceptional wit, and the retailer of the first of these two jokes, has since persuaded me that every child in the world has either already heard the second joke or was born knowing it.

equations in algebra. The solution requires delivering something that can do more than one thing at once. The explanation of a joke will necessarily be discursive. It will give the solution discretely, and that will prevent the magical all-at-once click. That is like art, but now there is a puzzling difference. Although exegesis won't do in place of either an art work or a joke, it can augment appreciation of art while it seems to destroy a joke altogether. If I do not get your joke you can explain it to me and then I shall understand it, but I shall now 'get it' only in a severely attenuated sense, an academic sense indeed. It can now never jolt me, snap my sensibilities together. But if I do not appreciate some art, you may well explain and describe it to me, eventually equipping me to appreciate it profoundly. Why is there this difference? Would the difference disappear if we turned from simple stories and children's riddles to more elaborate jokes? Let us have an example.

> An old, childless, married couple live together in a tiny town so poverty-stricken, remote, and backward that no one in the town knows anything of modern conveniences. In fact no one has ever seen a mirror. One day the husband chances on a small piece of reflecting glass nearly buried in the dirt. He takes it home, carries it up to the attic loft in his cottage, and then cleans it and leans it against the wall. After looking into it intently for a long time he says 'Papa!' and then goes downstairs. During the next few weeks he takes every opportunity to go upstairs alone, where he spends long hours.
>
> His wife becomes concerned, and she begins to worry that her always devoted husband may have found someone else. She waits until one day she is left alone at home with enough time to investigate, and then she fearfully climbs the stairs. Once inside the loft she immediately sees the mirror, gazes into it briefly, and then goes downstairs cheerfully, saying aloud to herself, 'Oh, I am relieved. He couldn't possibly be interested in anyone so wrinkled and worn-out as that. She looks old enough to be my mother.'

That story will bear a lot of analysis, especially if you like it nearly as much as I do.[13] Its charm, its good humor, its bitter humor, have deep sources. And talking about them does not seem to obliterate the joke. We might even have discussed these things before hearing the joke and then still found the joke effective. Does this show that a joke can bear analysis just as

---

[13] I owe this marvelous joke/parable to Edward and Martha Snyder, but I received it at second hand and I have altered it still more, and so I am not sure what is the canonical version. In telling the story I have noticed an illustration of Hume's conviction that no standard of taste can eradicate differences owing to age. Younger audiences often think the couple benighted, and that either seems funny or not. Older hearers know that there is nothing whatever the couple needs to learn.

an art work can? I was once inclined to say that this joke just happens to be art as well, but now I think I missed the point. It is not a difference between jokes and art works, but a difference between a structure, joke or art, which can work only once, and one which can work again and again. If a joke or an art work can be truly effective only once, then it is smothered by its exegesis. The explanation seems to usurp the one chance the work had. But if the work has a multiple capacity, then exegesis can even be invigorating.

*

There is nothing whatever wrong with what we might call 'conditional' (or derivative) intimacy as such, in either of its two forms. Jokes which lead to it are among the finest ways we have of identifying others with whom we belong. You tell me such a joke in order to determine whether we have a sensibility in common, and when I work my way through, using my special background, which you are invoking, we earn the comfort of shared feeling. These jokes are the equivalent in mirth of what Kant calls the forms of dependent beauty. But there is also the joking relation I was working on earlier, and I think that is the hard one to understand. It is parallel to what Kant calls the relation between free beauty and the feeling to which it leads. In this relation the joke elicits the unconditioned intimacy of free community. You are expected to understand the language, but that is all. Nothing else is presupposed concerning what you know or what you find funny. You just find the particular joke funny. This kind of laughter, which makes us freely one with all others (who find the funniness) is, I think, a unique way of coming out of oneself. It takes you out of yourself and out of your groups and makes you one with everyone. It is worth study in its own right, and that study may well have other benefits, for I think that one of the only other available experiences very much like this is the shared experience of art.

III

The little schematism I've sketched divides jokes into two kinds, the pure ones and the conditional ones. The conditional ones, the ones the success of which requires a special background in the audience, are again divisible into two kinds: the hermetic ones, whose presumed background is one of knowlege or belief, and the affective ones, which require of the audience a particular prejudice, or feeling, or disposition, or inclination. (If you have a passion for this you might further divide the affective jokes into those for which the requisite predisposition is affirmative and those for which it is negative. In what Americans call a 'Polish' joke, the prejudice defames Poles. In Warsaw, however, a Polish joke is typically celebratory, and in the story a Pole subdues a Russian or a German or the Polish government.)

I am not saying that pure jokes are *better*. And they do not seem to be more interesting as a subject. Let me note two excellent topics associated with the complexity of conditional jokes.

First is the matter of active complicity. When your special background is called into play, your sensibility is galvanized. Something that sets you apart from just any person is brought into your apprehension and this adds to the quantity and alters the quality of the intimacy achieved. The point is like the one I think Aristotle has in mind when he declares the enthymeme the argument most suitable for certain kinds of persuasion. His idea is this: if you wish to set your audience in motion, especially with an eye toward provoking them to action, then you are well advised to induce them to supply the initial momentum themselves. You can do this by offering them an incomplete argument. They must then undertake a mental scramble in order to locate the premisses necessary to render the argument valid. This scramble is a motion of the mind undertaken *before* the legitimate arrival of the conclusion, and that motion augments the persuasion implicit in the validity of the completed argument. So it is, approximately, with conditional jokes. The requirement of a special background is not stated explicitly. The audience discovers that and it also discovers that it can supply what's needed. It is further aware that not everyone can supply the background (unlike an enthymeme's audience which potentially includes everyone because minimal logical acuity is enough to formulate the implicated missing premiss). In doing this the audience collaborates in the success of the joke – the constitution of intimacy – just as the audience for an enthymeme collaborates in the construction of a valid argument, with the difference that the audience of the joke derives additional intensity of feeling from knowing that the success is due to them specifically, that other groups would fail.

A second good topic concerning conditional jokes is the means they afford to a kind of fakery. A conditional joke demands a special contribution from the audience, either cognitive or affective. What if the joke-teller himself cannot supply this special constituent? In the first case, where the implicated background is cognitive, the teller is like a parrot, and he cannot himself know (find) what fun there is in the joke. This charlatan resembles a musician who doesn't divine the sense of a piece but nonetheless bangs it out note for note, or a religious practitioner who reads out texts or prayers in Latin or Hebrew, perhaps even 'with feeling', but doesn't know what the words mean.[14]

---

[14] None of these performances has to be contemptible. A person might, with a kind of integrity, tell such a joke, play such music, or recite such a text, and he might even invest it

In the second case, where the requisite special contribution is a matter of feeling, the teller is more like a liar. He can, typically, find the fun – recognize it or identify it – but he cannot feel it. Perhaps the plainest examples of this insincerity are jokes told to groups of (say, racially) prejudiced people – genuine bigots, that is – by one who does not share the true depths of the bigotry but means to ingratiate himself with the group. This is a kind of fraudulence, like that of the man who says 'I apologize' without feeling sorry, of the artist who mimics unfelt forms, and of the performer who does not feel the passion in the scores he plays with mindless virtuosity.[15]

The two kinds of fakery are different. The first is, mainly, simply bizarre. The second is more devious, even deceitful. In both, however, there is the fraudulence of emptiness, as both betray the commitment to intimacy I have characterized as a kind of generic aim of joke-telling. The teller of these jokes is inauthentic: he invites and even induces you into a putative community in which he himself has no place. Who is he to be issuing these invitations?

The difference between pure and conditional jokes corresponds to a difference in moral and religious conceptions. The idea of a pure joke rests on a conviction that at some level people are essentially the same and can all be reached by the same device. This is, perhaps, a fundamentally Christian idea. The denial of the possibility of a pure joke rests on a conviction that people are essentially different, or at least that they belong to essentially different groups. The idea that all jokes necessarily are conditional seems to me a kind of Jewish idea (not the only kind).

Those who believe only in conditional jokes will concede that it is possible to appreciate a joke whose community does not include oneself. How is this possible? It must be through an act of imagination which transports one into the relevant community. Thus I can appreciate jokes meant for women, Englishmen, and mathematicians, although I am none of those. There is a point, however, at which it becomes impossible for me to be amused. I reach that point sooner when the joke is anti-Jewish or anti-American than when it is anti-women or anti-English. And there is a point for any type of affective joke beyond which its instances are objectionable. They are in bad taste. If you think that lapses of 'taste' are always relatively innocuous, then I would insist that these jokes are in fact unacceptable – immoral. Why does this happen, and when?

with conviction, but, relative to the model of communities of intimacy, this achievement will be disjointed and indirect.

[15] A correlative fraud is the member of the audience who refuses to laugh although genuinely tickled, because he knows the joke is working on him in part because he possesses a disposition he pretends not to have. He wants not to be the kind of man who is amused by that kind of joke. But he is. Is he a better man for dissembling?

I cannot give a complete answer, even in outline, because there is a fundamental question I do not know how to answer. Suppose that x is some real event, and that it is (morally) unacceptable to laugh at x. The question I cannot answer is, under what conditions is it wrong to laugh at a fictional report of x, and why? It may be that a heavy traffic of amusement in x-jokes creates or reinforces beliefs or attitudes that are themselves objectionable or that lead to intolerable acts. That answer is insufficient, for two reasons. First, there is little evidence to show that it is always true, and some indication that it is sometimes false. Second, it doesn't get to the heart of the evil, even if it is true, for even if it could be demonstrated that these jokes lead to no bad ends the jokes themselves would still be offensive. With no good answer to the question of why (and when) it is wrong to laugh at a story of something you shouldn't laugh at, I shall nevertheless go on to suggest how an answer – if we had one – might lead to an understanding of the unacceptability of some jokes.

Suppose that prejudice against P's is a bad thing, and that to be amused by an x-joke requires a disposition which is related to anti-P prejudice, although that disposition is not itself a prejudice. The joke will be accessible only to those who either have the disposition or can, in imagination, respond as if they had it. The joke is obviously conditional – it is affective; but it will also be fundamentally parochial (essentially conditional, one might say) if there are people who cannot find it accessible. What people will be in this position? P's, I think. Even the imagined possession of the disposition is in conflict with what makes these people P's. To appreciate the joke a P must disfigure himself. He must forsake himself. He should not do that. In fact he cannot do that while remaining a P. The rest of us, who are not P's, *should* not appreciate the joke although we *can* in this sense in which a P cannot. The joke is viciously exclusionary, and it should be resisted.

What this implies depends upon exactly what people essentially are. Are they essentially men or women, of some race, of some age, of some religion, of some profession, of some size? That is a fine question in the metaphysics of morality, and one I do not care to answer here. I offer this account of a kind of unacceptable joke as an explanation and justification of why some people find some jokes intolerable. A currently common exchange begins with a man telling a joke (involving women, typically) which a woman finds offensive. She objects and is told she has no sense of humor. Her reply could be that she cannot bring her sense of humor to that joke without imaginatively taking on a disposition which is incompatible with her conception of herself as a woman or a certain kind of woman. And if she is essentially a woman or a certain kind of woman, then she cannot reach the joke without a hideous cost.

Although the basis for a pure joke has an obvious moral flavor, akin to the idea of a universal human sameness, conditional jokes are also congenial to the serious idea of morality. Conditional jokes are related to the idea that we can respect and even appreciate one another while remaining irreducibly different. They carry a danger, however, for their parochialism easily becomes unbearably sectarian.

A final note about pure jokes. The major question, I suppose, is whether there are any. If there are, they will be jokes whose presumptive success depends on nothing whatever. The audience need no special background. They bring to the joke only their humanity. Now the question is, When you tell such a joke, upon what basis do you expect anyone else to be moved? The answer must be, Upon the fact that the joke moves you, plus your estimate that it moves you simply as a person and without regard to any idiosyncrasy of yours. The logic here is exactly the same as that which Kant cites in answering the question, By what right do you judge anything to be beautiful (where this means, Upon what basis do you suppose that anyone else should take pleasure in this thing?)? Kant answers: Upon the fact that the object pleases you, plus your estimate that the pleasure is due to nothing about you beyond the fact that you are a person.

But now comes the nasty question, which Kant believes he can answer with regard to the beauty of things, and I am not so sure about with regard to the funniness of jokes. If a thing touches you, so to speak, only in the rudiments of your person – if ever such a thing happens, with all those things dormant which make you more than just a person; why should it be good as well for any other rudimentary person? Isn't there room within even the most elementary, stripped-down, homogenized human sensibility for variation? Couldn't you and I be mere men and nothing more, and yet be pleased by different beauties and laugh at different jokes? No, says Kant, in the first instance, for the capacity to feel this pleasure is identical with the capacity which makes knowledge possible (and knowledge *is* possible, he insists interminably). And so there is an argument, however good.[16]

Is there such an argument for the postulation of a universal sense of humor? I do not know. Is the capacity to find a joke funny a basic, essential feature of our sensibility? It needn't seem entirely implausible that it is if we suppose it to be, minimally – and it is only its minimal presence that matters – the capacity to feel simultaneously the appropriateness and the

---

[16] Appraising this argument is absolutely no part of this paper. I will note, however, that a just appraisal requires first assessing the argument for the possibility of knowledge in the *Critique of Pure Reason*, and then formulating the relation between that argument and the 'Deduction' of judgments of taste in the *Critique of Judgment*. A stupefying task. An outline of the argument and some critical interpretation may be found in *Essays in Kant's Aesthetics*, edited by Ted Cohen and Paul Guyer (Chicago, 1982).

absurdity of a punch line. It is like feeling the wonderful hopelessness of the world. (Or is it the hopeless wonder of the world?) But must every one of us have within himself the capacity for that feeling, however disfigured it may have become? God knows.

IV

The sudden click at the end of a certain kind of joke is its hallmark. There is an unexpected, an almost-but-not-quite-predicted coincidence of moments. And this is part of a marvelous reflexivity. Earlier I guessed that the whole joke relates to its effect in an enigmatic relation which renders that effect both unforced and fitting. The relation can be found again entirely within the joke. The joke itself has a beginning which leads to an end which is unforced (and so, unpredicted), but altogether right. In laughing we fit ourselves to a joke just as its punch line fits to its body, by this relation of self-warranting propriety. It is a kind of mirroring. We find ourselves reflected in a surface which mirrors our dearest and perhaps most human hope: to do well, but not under compulsion. A joke shows us that and shows us doing that. Anything which can show us that aspect of ourselves deserves fond and serious attention.

In the work of this essay I have been helped by many people. I should acknowledge the students at Augustana College and the philosophers at the University of Wisconsin, all of whom forced me to try to describe the offense in some jokes; and the marvelously cordial members of the Thyssen Philosophy Group (England) who made me rethink everything, and one of whom, Hidé Ishiguro, showed me that my first idea of fraudulence was too simple.

Belief and sincerity in poetry

MALCOLM BUDD

I

The common function of declarative sentences in poetry would be misunderstood if it was thought appropriate to object whenever such a sentence was not true. Someone for whom it was an invariable requirement that anything that is asserted in a poem should be true would be devoid of the idea of fiction. The fictional character of much poetic composition has indeed been considered by some theorists of poetry to be problematic; and puzzlement about the generally fictional nature of poetry has been reflected in a preoccupation with the correct characterisation of the state of mind of the reader of poetry. Coleridge produced some memorable formulations: 'that willing suspension of disbelief for the moment, which constitutes poetic faith', 'that negative faith ... without either denial or affirmation', 'a sort of temporary half-faith', 'this sort of negative belief'.[1] The fact is that we possess the capacity to entertain a thought without accepting it, the capacity to make believe, without believing, that some state of affairs obtains, and the capacity to imagine what we do not know to have happened. It is true that there are problems in giving an account of these capacities and in explaining the value of their exercise in the reading of poetry, but the possibly fictional nature of poetry in itself presents no obstacle to its appreciation. Nevertheless, not all poetry is intended to be understood as fiction and, even for poems where that is in fact the intention, there is a variety of ways in which poetry can present or give expression to beliefs; and these beliefs are either true or false. What significance should be attached to the acceptability, or the unacceptability, of any beliefs that a poem expresses?

II

The issue of the relevance of the truth of the beliefs that a poem may

[1] See *Biographia Literaria*, edited by J. Shawcross (Oxford, 1907), II, p. 6, II, p. 107, and *Coleridge's Shakespearean Criticism*, edited by T. M. Raysor (London, 1930) I, pp. 200–2. Whilst Coleridge's remarks were directed primarily at the drama and at poems which have supernatural subject matter he did not restrict their significance to these two kinds of art. See M. H. Abrams, *The Mirror and the Lamp* (Oxford, 1976), p. 324.

express faces in two directions: towards the poet and towards the reader. As it pertains to the poet, the question is whether there must be a particular connection, for example, coincidence, between the beliefs of the poet and the beliefs that the poem expresses if the poem is not to be thereby deficient in poetic value. This question may be re-expressed (in the subjective mode) as the question whether a reader's judgement as to whether the poet accepted or believed what his poem expresses is properly relevant to the reader's enjoyment of the poem and to his opinion of the poem's value. In this sense, the question concerns the relevance of the poet's sincerity. As the issue pertains specifically to the reader, the question is whether there must be a particular connection, again, perhaps, coincidence, between the beliefs expressed in the poem and the beliefs of the reader if the reader is to enjoy, to appreciate and to value the poem fully. It is the second question that is usually discussed under the heading 'The problem of belief'. This second question, concerning the match or mismatch between the beliefs expressed in the poem and those of the reader, is an instance of a more general issue: whether there must be a particular relationship, for example admiration or sympathy, between the reader and the various qualities of mind or character or the outlook or attitude or sentiment expressed in the poem, if the reader is not to regard the poem as flawed or defective.

III

Reference to the beliefs or the outlook that a poem expresses must be disambiguated; for it is necessary to distinguish between the imagined speaker of a poem and the poem's implied author, and reference might be to the beliefs or the outlook of the one or the other.[2] Characteristically, a poem has an implicit speaker (or more than one such speaker): the ostensible utterer of the lines of which the poem consists.[3] A poem of this kind has an implied narrator, speaker or thinker who utters the lines. He can be called the poem's persona.[4] But in composing the poem the poet will also create an image of himself as its author. The poem will give the impression of having been written by a person of a certain kind. The reader receives from it an impression of the person who was responsible for its composition. He is the poem's implied author. This self-image that the poet creates may reveal much, little or nothing of himself: it may be an accurate, distorted or unfaithful picture of himself. If there is no apparent sign in the poem itself of its having been composed by a particular kind of person, then its implied author is not a person of that kind even though its

[2] See Wayne C. Booth, *The Rhetoric of Fiction* (Chicago, 1973), pp. 70f.

[3] The words do not, of course, have to be imagined as being spoken aloud rather than internally.

[4] My use of this term diverges from the use that Booth favours. See *A Rhetoric of Irony* (Chicago, 1974), p. 181n.

actual author is such a person. A poem characteristically invites concurrence with the view of life that its imagined speaker, its persona, expresses; it invites sympathy or admiration for, it solicits approval of, the attitude expressed by the persona of the poem. In such cases the philosophy of the persona and the philosophy of the implied author are one. But it is possible to write poetry in such a style that there is a divorce between the beliefs, values and attitudes of the implied author of the poem and those of the poem's persona, so that the poem does not invite acquiescence in the speaker's beliefs, values and attitudes. The implied author sometimes has an ironical attitude towards his persona. He does not regard his persona altogether uncritically and he does not expect the reader to respond without reservations to the persona's thoughts and feelings. The response that the poem invites does not involve in this sense an identification of the reader's sympathies with the poem's persona. Instead, the poem invites ironical contemplation. The implicit creator of a poem speaks from a particular standpoint or mouthpiece, but it may be clear from the nature of the poem that the poem is not in fact the product of someone located at that point of view or of such a person, and it may be apparent that the implicit creator of the poem does not regard the imagined person whose words compose the lines of the poem with unqualified approval. We may recognise that the poem's persona is the assumed form of, for example, a more intelligent person.

The possibility of this kind of irony affects the form that the consideration of the different problems of belief should take. It matters little whether it is pursued in terms of the outlook of the implied author or of the persona when ironical distancing is not present in a poem. But when there is ironical distancing, the consideration must be directed towards the outlook of the implied author of the poem rather than that of its persona. A full identification between the reader and the philosophy of the poem may not be precluded by a disparity between the beliefs and attitudes that are held or expressed by the poem's persona and those of the reader if the beliefs and attitudes of the poem's implied author coincide with the reader's. Likewise, a poet's sincerity is not put in question by a clash between his own outlook and that of the persona of one of his poems, but only by a lack of harmony between his own outlook and that of the implied author of the poem.

IV

A poet's insincerity can take many forms. But if his insincerity is not manifest in the poems that he writes, it does not affect the value of his poems as poems. T. S. Eliot advanced the view that the suggestion that Lucretius did not believe the cosmology expounded in *On the Nature of*

Things, or that Dante did not believe the Aristotelian philosophy that is the material of some cantos of the *Purgatorio*, would necessitate the condemnation of the poems that they wrote. A poet must believe a philosophy or philosophical idea that he embodies in his verse on pain of insincerity; and insincerity would annihilate all poetic values except those of technical accomplishment.[5] But an argument can be a valid argument even though the person who advances it believes that it is not; and a system of beliefs is not rendered false by the fact that it is put forward for our acceptance by someone who rejects it. When Eliot says that a poet's insincerity would annihilate all poetic values except those of technical accomplishment, that is at most true for the poet's view of his own work. If he is not concerned that his poem should express an acceptable system of beliefs, and yet he wishes to compose a philosophical poem, his interest will be taken up entirely by the mode of expression into which his poem is to render a given philosophy. It is unclear why it should be thought that a poet's insincerity must affect the response of readers in the same way, and prevent us from attaching different values to poems of equal technical accomplishment. It would be open to us to assess a philosophical poem not solely by its manner of expression but also by the acceptability of the view of the world that it expresses. The fact that the poet did not hold the philosophy that his poem expresses does not imply that the philosophy is false, and it does not prevent the poem from being a good poem. It may be true that if we were to believe that a poet did not himself have the deep convictions that his poetry apparently evinces, our reaction would be undermined and we should feel ill at ease. But a poet's insincerity need not result in an unsatisfactory poem, and there is no compelling reason why we should not attempt to insulate our response to the poem from our knowledge of the poet's real beliefs.

It might be objected that a poem that is the creation of a poet who does not believe what his poem expresses should be criticised on the ground that it carries itself as though it were the expression of the poet's beliefs when it is not. For if the poet attempts to pass off the poem as the expression of his own beliefs, then he is behaving in a similar fashion to a poet who attempts to pass off a poem that he has written as the creation of another (possibly fictitious) poet, who supposedly wrote the poem at an earlier period and expressed in it the beliefs that he then held. And the misrepresentation of the poem's origins misleads readers about the poem's nature and so about the proper approach to the poem. If, on the other hand, the poet is not concerned to pass off the poem as the expression of his own beliefs – about which there may be no secrecy – even so he will be writing against a background where the normal expectation is that a philosophical poem

[5] T. S. Eliot, 'Goethe as the Sage' in *On Poetry and Poets* (London, 1957), pp. 207–77.

expresses the poet's philosophy. But this objection lacks force. For it counts in no way against the possibility that a non-believer might construct in poetic form a finer expression of a system of beliefs than a believer, and that readers can react to the poem as an expression of these beliefs without being concerned about the lack of fit between the beliefs of the poem and the beliefs of its author.

A poet can also be insincere in a poem which does not express a system of beliefs about the nature of the world. The poem may, for example, deliberately misrepresent his thoughts and feelings about a particular person. But if the poet's insincerity is not detectable in the poem itself, a reader may properly discount it and consider the poem only as the product of an implied author who is sincere in what he professes.[6]

V

I. A. Richards pointed out that one form of insincerity that a poet can practise is the deliberate attempt to produce effects in the reader that do not happen for him: he attempts to kid others. He is not moved by the sentiments that his poem expresses in the manner that he desires his readers to be moved. This kind of insincerity is closely connected with that involved in the issue Eliot raised about the relation between the philosophical beliefs expressed in a poem and those held by the poem's author. But, as Richards went on to say, a more important kind of insincerity, from a literary point of view, is the inability of the poet to be true to his own genuine feelings.[7] He may be unable to distinguish them from those that he merely would like to have, so that in his own thoughts he misrepresents his feelings, perhaps out of a desire to avoid acknowledging them, or in an effort to match up to an ideal; or he may be unable to distinguish his real feelings from those which he hopes will make a good, or an original, or a striking poem: he kids himself. This form of insincerity may be apparent in the poetry that he writes. The poem's persona and the poem's implied author may be insincere. If the poet identifies himself with the imagined speaker of his poem then the insincerity of the speaker will feed back to the poet. Indeed, a poet's insincerity may be precisely what leads him to write an unironical poem with an insincere persona. But it is the lack of sincerity of the persona that is directly our concern, for a poem with an insincere persona and insincere implied author may emerge – perhaps as an exercise – from a poet who does not identify himself with either. And here it is clear that the poetic merit of much poetry is bound up with the sincerity of the imagined speaker of the poem. It is often a poet's

[6] I am not suggesting that reference to the (real) author of a poem is always critically irrelevant. That, I am sure, is false.

[7] I. A. Richards, *Practical Criticism* (London, 1964), pp. 94–5, pp. 280f.

intention to compose a poem which has a persona whose thoughts and feelings are sincere; and if the persona's thoughts and feelings are insincere, the poem is a failure. As T. S. Eliot remarked, most religious verse is bad because of a pious insincerity.[8] It is the expression of ideals not truly felt.

The persona's sincerity is especially important in that form of poetry that consists in the representation from the standpoint of the first person of someone's outward verbal expression of his mental condition or of the internal counterpart to it; that is to say, in poetry that is the representation of a person expressing his thoughts and feelings in speech or that is the representation of his process of thought and feeling itself: in lyric poetry (in one sense of the term). In fact, there is a well-known problem about the evaluation of lyric poems by reference to their sincerity or lack of sincerity. For the following dilemma can be posed. Either the reference is to the poet's sincerity – to whether he agrees with the sentiment that the poem expresses – which is a fact that is external to the poem, and so irrelevant to the evaluation of the poem as a poem; or the notion of sincerity can have no application at all, for there is no reality that the lyric 'I' can either be misrepresenting or be representing aright. That is, the imagined person's thought or utterance cannot represent his emotion rightly or wrongly, cannot correspond or fail to correspond to his emotion, for the poem consists only of the representation of his thought or utterance, and this is the only reality that the imagined person, and so his supposed emotion, has: the sincerity of the thought or utterance cannot be ascertained by reference to its correctly representing the subject's emotion because, since the emotion is not otherwise represented, there is no sense to the idea of what the emotion really is, whether it matches or mismatches the thought or utterance. In short: a reference to sincerity in the evaluation of poetry is, from the literary point of view, either irrelevant or inapplicable.

The escape from this dilemma is not hard to find. It lies in a two-fold realisation: lack of sincerity need not involve a mismatch between a person's thought or utterance and his feeling, and defects in sincerity, or forms of insincerity, can properly be attributed on the basis of the manner in which a person expresses his feeling or the style of his self-communion. In the first place, the dilemma operates with an over-simple concept of sincerity.[9] The expression 'lack of sincerity' in fact ranges over a series of cases. At one end are various forms of insincerity – the deliberate misrepresentation to others of one's real feelings in order to deceive and

---

[8] T. S. Eliot, *After Strange Gods* (London, 1934), pp. 28–9.

[9] Some of the complexities in the notion of sincerity are explored interestingly by Stuart Hampshire in 'Sincerity and Single-Mindedness' in *Freedom of Mind* (Oxford, 1972), pp. 232–56.

self-deception; and the series moves through the attempt to feel differently from others for the sake of originality, the absence of self-examination to discover what are one's real feelings, the failure or inability to see lucidly and soberly into oneself and self-ignorance that derives from emotional and intellectual immaturity. Lack of (complete) sincerity, or insincerity, is not merely something that can be present in one's profession of feeling; it can infect the feeling itself.[10] Furthermore, the manner in which a person thinks, speaks or writes can be indicative of a lack of sincerity on his part. When we find certain kinds of thinking, speech or writing in poetry we therefore properly regard the poem as if it were the work of someone who is insincere in its production. It is part of the imaginative project involved in reading and understanding a lyric poem to form a conception of the poem's persona and implied author, and there are various features the presence of which in the poem may be explained for us by the recognition of what they are signs of: lack of sincerity. The failure by a poem's implied author to achieve complete imaginative integrity can be revealed by such features as the use of inflated language, vague emotive clichés, the lack of precision and the manner of the poem's indebtedness to other poetry. The implied author may be posing or striking an attitude; his feeling may be forced, or artificial, or merely superficial, and in these different ways lacking in sincerity. In consequence the poem is devalued. Hence reference to sincerity in the evaluation of poetry can be both relevant and applicable.

A justly celebrated and instructive attempt to rehabilitate the term 'sincerity' for criticism is F. R. Leavis's 'Reality and Sincerity'.[11] A cursory reading might leave the impression that when Leavis says that in postulating the situation of *Barbara* Alexander Smith is seeking a licence for an emotional debauch, and when he says that in *Cold in the Earth* Emily Brontë conceives a situation in order to have the satisfaction of a disciplined imaginative exercise – the satisfaction of dramatising herself in a tragic role, maintaining an attitude, nobly impressive, of sternly controlled passionate desolation – his judgements are essentially, and unacceptably from the poetic or critical point of view, about the poet. But Leavis was vividly aware of the need to provide reasons for his judgements that are internal to the poems, and his judgements are supported by descriptions of the poems and not the poets. *Barbara* is characterised as offering 'a luxurious enjoyment that, to be enjoyed, must be taken for the suffering of an unbearable sorrow', and it may therefore be said to be

[10] In 'The Autonomy of Art' in *Philosophy and the Arts, Royal Institute of Philosophy Lectures 1971–2* (London, 1973), 65–87, John Casey examines how the way in which one expresses one's feelings in words – to others or to oneself – may impose insincerity upon them; and how the inability to express one's feelings sincerely may carry with it an inability to feel sincerely.

[11] *Scrutiny*, XIX (1952–3), 90–8, reprinted in *A Selection from Scrutiny*, compiled by F. R. Leavis (Cambridge, 1968), Vol. I, pp. 248–57.

insincere. Someone who luxuriates in the poem, and this is true also of its imagined speaker in his thoughts, is deceiving himself, for he must take himself to be imagining an unbearably painful experience, whereas the experience is really an indulgence in the sweets of sorrow, an emotional or sentimental wallowing, the alleged situation only spuriously an excuse for the indulgence, which is in fact sought for its own sake. And in *Cold in the Earth* the imaginative self-projection is said to be insufficiently informed by experience of the imagined situation, as is evident from the paradoxically noble declamation and the accompanying generality, the imagery being in places essentially rhetorical, unable to sustain the claim to strength that it makes.

It is therefore not essential to the validity of this kind of account that, for example, in fact Emily Brontë did not have the experience of the type of situation that her poem expresses. She could have experienced in reality the kind of situation that she imagines in the poem and yet still have written the same poem. All that is necessary for her poem to be judged to be lacking in sincerity, or to be insincere, is for the represented thoughts, which purport to be those of someone who has undergone a particular experience, to be judged not to be the thoughts as of a deeply sincere person who has suffered that experience and is now being true to it in her thoughts. Hence judgements about the relation of the poem's persona and implied author to the experience that is presented or expressed may properly be made by features internal to the poem, and corresponding judgements about the poet as author of the poem derived from the empathic and uncritical identification of the poet with the implicit speaker of the poem. It is unsurprising that Leavis, having attempted to show that Hardy's *After a Journey* represents a profounder and more complete sincerity than *Cold in the Earth*, that it manifests a rare and subtle form of integrity, with no nobly imaginative self-deception or idealisation, explicitly makes the point that it could have been written only by a man who had the experience of a life to remember back through, and that we can be sure from the poem what personal qualities we should have found to admire in Hardy if we could have known him. But even if this last inference should be suspected, it is possible to agree with Leavis's account of the poem.

VI

A poem can be judged to be sentimental in a fashion similar to that in which it can be judged to be insincere. There is a variety of ways in which the idea of sentimentality can be understood, but one important conception of it ties it closely to a form of insincerity. A person's response can be sentimental in the sense that his emotion is something that is rewarding for him to feel and the existence or continuation of the emotion is motivated by the satisfaction experienced in feeling the emotion, so that in consequence he is unready to act from the emotion in an appropriate manner.[12] Whether sentimentality is construed in this fashion or whether it is taken to imply merely an excess of sentiment that is not occasioned by unmotivated error, a poem is sentimental if its persona and implied author are sentimental. I. A. Richards defined three senses of 'sentimentality', and he maintained that when a poem is said to be sentimental in his first or his second sense there are two possible locations for the sentimentality. When we call a poem sentimental in his first ('quantitative') sense we mean, Richards says, either

(i) that the poem was produced by someone who was too easily stirred to emotion: the author was sentimental; or

(ii) that we should be too easily moved if we responded highly emotionally to the poem: we should be sentimental.[13]

But if, when we say that a poem is sentimental, we mean to assert the first alternative, we are making an inference from the nature of the poem to the character of the poet himself, and this inference may not only be ill-founded but turns us from a consideration of the poem to a concern for the poem's author. We may instead mean that the poem's persona and its *implied* author are sentimental. Our concern remains bound up with the nature of the poem itself, and it continues to be critical rather than biographical.

VII

In Section II of his Dante essay, T. S. Eliot tentatively advanced the view that in order to understand and to appreciate the poetry of *The Divine Comedy* it is not necessary to believe what Dante, as poet, believed.[14] Rather, we should suspend both belief and disbelief in the philosophical and theological views that the poem expresses. And in talking of appreciation of the poetry as poetry Eliot is talking of enjoyment.[15] In the note to Section II Eliot puts forward the thesis as having general application: it is not necessary for the reader to share the beliefs of the poet

---

[12] See Michael Tanner, 'Sentimentality', *Proceedings of the Aristotelian Society* (1976–7), 127–47.

[13] See *Practical Criticism*, pp. 261–2.

[14] T. S. Eliot, 'Dante' in *Selected Essays* (London, 1934, 3rd edn, 1951), pp. 252–71.

[15] Eliot moves freely between talking of understanding or appreciation and talking of enjoyment because he takes understanding a poem to be enjoyment of it for the right reasons. One should not enjoy bad poems unless their badness is amusing. See *On Poetry and Poets*, p. 115.

in order to enjoy the poetry fully.[16]

When Eliot came to write his essay on Shelley and Keats a development in his thought had taken place.[17] In this essay Eliot begins by saying that where the poets are such as Dante and Lucretius his previous view that it is not necessary to accept the philosophy of the poet in order to enjoy the poetry still seems satisfactory. One may, he claims, share the essential beliefs of Dante and yet enjoy Lucretius to the full. But some of Shelley's views he positively dislikes, and that hampers his enjoyment of the poems in which they occur; and others seem to him so puerile that he cannot enjoy the poems in which they are to be found. Eliot suggests that it is not the presentation of beliefs which he does not hold or beliefs that excite his abhorrence that creates the difficulty for him. Instead he makes the following claim:

When the doctrine, theory, belief, or 'view of life' presented in a poem is one which the mind of the reader can accept as coherent, mature, and founded on the facts of experience, it interposes no obstacle to the reader's enjoyment, whether it be one that he accept or deny, approve or deprecate. When it is one which the reader rejects as childish or feeble, it may, for a reader of well-developed mind, set up an almost complete check.

Eliot is inclined to think that the reason why he was intoxicated by Shelley's poetry at the age of fifteen, and now finds it almost unreadable, is not so much that at that age he accepted his ideas, and has since come to reject them, as that at that age 'the question of belief or disbelief', in I. A. Richards's phrase, did not arise in reading the poetry. The young Eliot was in a much better position to read Shelley with enjoyment not because he was then under an illusion which experience has dissipated, but because the question of belief or disbelief did not present itself to him. Eliot quotes this passage from Richards with approval:

Coleridge, when he remarked that a 'willing suspension of disbelief' accompanied much poetry, was noting an important fact, but not in the quite happiest terms, for we are neither aware of a disbelief nor voluntarily suspending it in these cases. It is better to say that the question of belief and disbelief, in the intellectual sense, never arises when we are reading well. If unfortunately it does arise ... we have for the moment ceased to be reading and have become astronomers, or theologians, or moralists, persons engaged in quite a different type of activity.

Eliot's point therefore seems to be that he is no longer capable of reading Shelley well, as formerly he could, and that he can no longer derive

---

[16] Eliot expresses reservations about his position and in fact it contains inconsistencies. He says, for example, that Keats's line 'Beauty is truth, truth beauty...' strikes him as a serious blemish on a beautiful poem, and that the reason must be either that he fails to understand the line *or that it is a statement which is untrue.*

[17] T. S. Eliot, *The Use of Poetry and the Use of Criticism* (London, 1959), Chapter v.

enjoyment from his poetry, for the question of belief and disbelief does now arise ineluctably. And the reason for this is that Eliot regards the doctrines or view of life presented in much of Shelley's poetry as childish or feeble, rather than coherent, mature and founded on the facts of experience.

Eliot's position is, I believe, unsatisfactory. Firstly, it is difficult to reconcile with Eliot's admission that he can still enjoy Fitzgerald's *Omar Khayyám*, though he does not hold 'that rather smart and shallow view of life'. For it is hard to see that a shallow view of life is one that is mature and founded on the facts of experience; and a shallow view of life does not seem to differ in any relevant way from one that is childish or feeble: at most it differs in degree. A further inadequacy emerges if we ask whether the poems of Lucretius and Dante are supposed nowhere to be founded on anything that is not a fact of experience and not to be inconsistent with any facts of experience – in which case they could not present opposed philosophies; or whether they are supposed to be founded upon certain specially important facts, their inconsistency with other facts being of no poetic importance. Eliot is silent here.

In fact the question to which Eliot addresses himself, whether it is possible fully to enjoy a poem that expresses a philosophy that one does not accept, does not identify the real or most important issue from the critical point of view. It is necessary, first of all, to put aside the matter of the intensity of a person's enjoyment of a poem. Intensity of enjoyment is not denied necessarily to someone who rejects, or is unconvinced of, the philosophy that a poem expresses. In principle, he can derive as much enjoyment from a poem which advances a philosophy that he denies or about which he is agnostic as can someone who accepts the philosophy, whether or not the believer's enjoyment is in part founded upon the poem's expressing a philosophy that he considers to be true. But there is a kind of enjoyment that is open to the believer from which the unbeliever is debarred. A person who embraces the philosophy that the poem presents can enjoy the poem not only on account of the fineness of its expression, but also on account of the poem's expressing a philosophy that he believes. It is therefore the nature, rather than the intensity, of the enjoyment that is available to the believer that is different from that available to the unbeliever.

In the second place, if we are asked to discount that aspect of the enjoyment that is founded upon agreement between the beliefs of the poem and the beliefs of the reader, and to consider only that aspect of a believer's enjoyment of a poem that is not founded in the possession of a common philosophy, we will accede to this request only if we believe that there is adequate justification for regarding only this aspect as relevant to the appreciation and criticism of poetry. Furthermore, the question whether a person can fully enjoy a poem which expresses opinions that do not accord with his own is a psychological question and it can receive only a personal or a statistical answer. The ability to disconnect one's response to a poem from the attitude one has to the beliefs that it expresses varies from person to person and belief to belief. Different people have unequal capacities to derive pleasure from the imaginative experience of a philosophy that they do not embrace, and the ease with which any particular person can manage this will be dependent upon the nature of the specific philosophy in question. This issue is therefore not of immediate relevance to the question what should be the appropriate attitude of a reader to a poem that expresses a philosophy that he does not consider to be true, that perhaps he rejects. The question whether a reader's rejection of the philosophy that a poem presents should or may properly affect adversely his estimate of the poem's value – or whether the falsity of the philosophy that a poem presents is a defect in the poem – must not be run together with a question about people's ability to enjoy poems that present a philosophy to which they do not adhere. The one question is significant in the theory of poetry, the other is proper to psychology. It is clear that the rejection of the philosophy embodied in a poem is not always and to everyone an insuperable barrier to experiencing the poem with enjoyment. It may in a particular case prevent or detract from enjoyment. But even if no diminution of enjoyment is experienced by an unbeliever when he reads a poem, the question remains whether his estimate of the value of the experience may properly be qualified by virtue of his rejection of the philosophy that the poem embodies. Eliot, in his concern with enjoyment, does not engage with the question of the value of the enjoyment derived from Shelley's poetry by the not as yet well-developed mind of the fifteen-year-old Eliot, which enjoyment is unavailable to him as an adult. It therefore leaves untouched the question of the value of Shelley's poetry. But what is supposed to be the value of the enjoyment of the imaginative experience of the expression of a childish or feeble view of life, in which experience the question of belief or disbelief does not arise? Eliot gives the impression that it is a valuable experience, but one from which unfortunately he is debarred when grown up since the question of belief or disbelief will irresistibly arise for someone of mature mind. But this is not made out. In like fashion, even if it is possible for a mature person to enjoy a poem that expresses a view of life that he deprecates as long as the view is not childish or feeble, it is a separate matter whether a mature reader may or should properly devalue both the poem and his experience of it in virtue of the poem's expressing a view which is unacceptable to him.[18]

VIII

The truth of the matter is that Lucretius's *On the Nature of Things* is significantly different from most poems, and the particular nature of the poem invites special considerations. It is a doctrinal or didactic poem in the specific sense that it is explicitly concerned to expound, enforce and render attractive a philosophical, cosmological and physical system of beliefs: the Epicurean account of the nature of the universe, the origin of the world and of the various forms of life that inhabit it, the physical laws that govern matter, and the nature of the gods and their relevance to human life. The poem is in fact essentially a series of assertions and arguments. It consists in the main of a set of theses with supporting reasons. Furthermore, the ultimate object of the poem is to encourage the eradication of unnecessary fears – especially of the gods and of death – through understanding the true nature of reality. In consequence the poem, despite its imaginative grandeur, is defective or unsatisfactory wherever the arguments that it presents are fallacious or inconclusive. Lucretius's Epicurean arguments for the finite divisibility of matter (for the existence of indivisible and indestructible atoms), for the infinite extent of space, for the precise physical nature and bodily location of the mind, and for the irrationality of being concerned about the fact that we will die, are merely a few of the arguments that the discerning reader will properly fault and regard as blemishes on the poem.

It is perhaps possible to read *On the Nature of Things* without considering whether any of its arguments are compelling or whether the propositions that it advances are true; that is to say, without the thought ever crossing one's mind that or whether any argument is valid or invalid or a certain thesis is tenable or untenable. But the value of reading the poem in such a manner is questionable, and the view that it is the only proper way to read the poem as a work of literature has no adequate foundation.

It is also perhaps possible to read *On the Nature of Things* by making believe that one is a convinced or incipient Epicurean, and so making believe that the arguments that it contains are always valid and the propositions that it advances are true. Such activity would be less pointless, for it would enable us imaginatively to appropriate the experience of an adherent to the Epicurean philosophy. But it does not follow from this possibility that inadequacies in the account of the universe that the poem presents are irrelevant to the poem's value as a poem.

It is true that our response to *On the Nature of Things* is affected by the fact that it would not have been unreasonable for an intelligent and cultured

---

[18] Eliot returned to the problem of belief in 'Goethe as the Sage', but his treatment is unhelpful.

person of Lucretius's time and circumstances to accept the philosophy that the poem presents. Furthermore, the qualities of mind that the poem displays are of the highest order. Our rejection of the philosophy is compatible with unqualified admiration for the poem's author, and the greatness of Lucretius's accomplishment is secure. But our admiration for the poet is consistent with the opinion that the value of his creation, the poem, is lessened by the inadequacy of the system of beliefs that it expounds.

IX

Underlying the view that agreement with the philosophy that a poem expresses is properly irrelevant to a judgement as to its worth as a poem, and so to the poetic enjoyment of it – since the adequacy of the philosophy is irrelevant to the poem's value as a poem – are the related considerations:

(i) that only what is distinctive of poetry, and not what it has in common with (unpoetic) prose, can determine the poetic worth of a poem;

(ii) that two poems might make equally meritorious use of any distinctive or prominent features of poetry – such characteristics as versification and figurative uses of language – and if so would be equally fine poems because *as poetry* they are equally distinguished.

If the first consideration is understood as the claim that any features that can be possessed by both poetry and prose should be discounted in assessing the poetic value of a poem, then it undoubtedly secures the desired consequence that the nature, and so the truth, of a thought poetically expressed is irrelevant to the poetic worth of the poem. For prose and poetry share the capacity to express thoughts. But construed in this way the first consideration has the undesired and unacceptable consequence that not even the fact that the words of a poem are concatenated in such a manner as to form meaningful sequences is relevant to poetic merit. Indeed, there would appear to be nothing of substance in which poetic merit could reside.

If, alternatively, the first consideration is understood as the claim that any features that can be common to prose and poetry are insufficient to make something a fine poem, then it fails to secure the desired consequence, for it leaves open the possibility that the falsity of a thesis advanced by a poem is a defect in the poem.

The second consideration is based upon the assumption that the meritorious use of distinctive or prominent features of poetry is the sole determinant of poetic merit, and so the sole proper object of poetic enjoyment. This assumption is encouraged by the thought that a composition that is better (as) poetry than another poem is thereby a better poem. But this is false encouragement. One person might express his thoughts on a certain subject in better prose than does another person and yet the second person might write the better essay. If the thoughts of the first are untenable, the merits of their presentation are not enough fully to redeem the work. A work that is composed in better prose is not thereby the better composition (in prose): the better essay, the better story. There is a sense of 'better poetry' in which it refers to a judgement about only certain features of a poem. Just as one prose composition can be written in a clumsy style, lack economy and elegance and be in those respects inferior to another composition – which is therefore said to be written in better prose – so one poem can use language in a less felicitous manner than another poem and the superiority of the second work marked by calling it better poetry. But in each case our judgement overall may be that the less well-written work is the better work of literature: the better story, the better poem.

It is certainly true that a poet with a philosophy of life that we reject may present this view for our acceptance by making better use of any other features that are relevant to poetic merit than does another poet whose philosophy we find sympathetic. We may choose to put this by saying that the first poet writes better poetry than the second, just as he might express his objectionable view in better prose, and just as Schopenhauer better expresses an unacceptable philosophy than many capable of correctly criticising it. And this poetry might have such advantages as to outweigh the true but uninspired poem. But there remains the question whether the mistaken philosophy is a defect in the poem, as a silly thesis would flaw a song no matter how beautiful the melody is to which the words are set. It is, in itself, a matter of indifference how this defect is characterised. If the view of life is not said to detract from the poetic merit of the poem, or from the worth of the poem *as a poem*, there will still be the question whether it renders it a less valuable work of literature, and whether the unacceptability of the philosophy is properly held against the poem, as a deserved lack of interest in what a poem says is held against it. T. S. Eliot said of Akenside that he 'never says anything worth saying, but what is not worth saying he says well'.[19] A poet who has nothing worth saying may in one sense write better poetry than another who does have something interesting to say, but what he writes may be a poem of less value. If poetic merit is tied only to what are sometimes called 'purely literary values' then our interest should undergo a change of focus. There is no reason for our interest, in our experience of poetry, to be concentrated solely upon 'purely literary values', good writing for its own sake, for that has minimal value unless in conjunction with something worth saying.

[19] T. S. Eliot, *On Poetry and Poets*, p. 174.

X

The doctrinal nature of Lucretius's *On the Nature of Things* is shared by few poems. Many poems do not advance any arguments or theses that the reader is invited to accept. But the weakness created in a poem that presents a world view by inadequate arguments in support of that view arises equally in all poems which contain arguments the function of which is to establish a thesis that the poem invites us to accept. Furthermore, it is not merely that unsatisfactory arguments make a poem that proposes a thesis to that extent unsatisfactory. If a poem maintains a thesis that is unacceptable, then the poem is flawed even if it does not present inadequate arguments in support of the thesis.

The problem of belief, as considered so far, is only a minor issue in the theory of poetry. For there are many kinds of poetry, and openly didactic poems form a relatively small class. The scope of our concern has indeed been widened to include not only doctrinal poems of the order of Lucretius's *On the Nature of Things* but also such a poem as Johnson's *The Vanity of Human Wishes*, written in the mode of general statement and illustration. Most poems, however, fall outside the circle of those which in this sense lay a claim upon the reader's belief. Nevertheless, many poems have personae or implied authors whose philosophies of life may in various ways be unacceptable to a particular reader, and even if the intention of a poem is not to advance a thesis that the reader is asked to accept, but instead to give expression to some aspect of life as seen or experienced from a certain point of view, or to render dramatically the experience of a person of a given persuasion in a specific circumstance, there arises a question as to the relevance of the reader's closeness to or distance from this point of view to his evaluation of the poem. This question cannot be answered as it stands, or in the abstract, for how much that is distinctive of the point of view actually is expressed in the poem, its significance within the poem, and the extent to which the reader shares beliefs or values with the persona or with what is expressed of the alien philosophy will vary from poem to poem. The problem presented to the non-Christian by Nashe's 'Adieu, farewell earth's bliss', Ralegh's *The Passionate Man's Pilgrimage*, Donne's 'At the round earth's imagin'd corners' and Hopkins's *The Blessed Virgin compared to the Air we Breathe* is in each case different. But whilst it is indisputable that a non-Christian can assume the Christian standpoint imaginatively and that Christian belief is inessential to the full and perfect imaginative realisation of any one of these poems, this does not settle the question whether the non-Christian's interest in Hopkins's poem, for example, and his estimate of the value of the experience that it offers may properly be qualified precisely by his non-Christian point of view. If this is a non-Christian's attitude to Hopkins's poem, must he be failing to consider it solely as a poem, or from the point of view of literature, and applying to it inappropriate, because non-artistic, standards? Is he concerned with its value not as a work of art but as something else? I believe that he is not.[20]

XI

A person can value an object that is a work of art for many different kinds of reason. His reasons for valuing the work of art may or may not give him a reason to experience the work of art. If his reasons leave it always a matter of indifference to him whether, if he is to experience *a* work of art, he should experience *this* work of art in preference to at least certain other works of art, then he does not value the work of art as a work of art.[21] If his reasons give him a reason to experience this work of art amongst works of art, it may or may not be because he finds the experience of the work of art intrinsically rewarding. Only if he finds the experience of the work of art intrinsically rewarding does he value the work as a work of art. But a person can find the experience of a work of art intrinsically rewarding and yet not value it as a work of art. He might find it intrinsically rewarding because, for example, it conveys a message to which he is sympathetic and he enjoys the experience of just about anything that conveys that message: he is pleased to find something that conveys the message and derives enjoyment from experiencing its expression. If a particular moral is for him sufficient to make the experience of a work of art intrinsically rewarding and he is indifferent to the various possible realisations of the moral, then he does not value the work as a work of art. Also, a person can value a work of art only because he finds the experience of part of the work intrinsically rewarding: his attitude may not be one of unqualified admiration. He may experience the work as having a part which is both in itself unrewarding and inessential to the rewards of the experience of the complete work and

---

[20] The objection that the non-Christian is not concerned with a poem's value as a work of art (or as a poem) but as something else – as a reliable source of information about the world, perhaps – lapses unless there is a concept of valuing something as a work of art that is sufficiently precise to deliver a verdict on the issue whether the non-Christian's valuation, grounded as it is, can properly be said to evaluate a poem as a work of art. The objection fails unless there is a necessary condition of a person's valuing something as a work of art that the non-Christian cannot satisfy. But it is a further question whether the non-Christian's evaluation – if it can properly be said to evaluate a poem as a poem – is right or wrong. In the following section I begin to articulate the concept of valuing something as a work of art by attempting to specify an important necessary condition of someone's valuing something as a work of art. And I try to say what the value of a work of art as a work of art is.

[21] Someone can value something as a work of art without wanting to experience it if, for example, he is thoroughly familiar with it and he believes that time must elapse before he can again respond fully to it; or he considers the experience of the work to be extremely

these rewards may be enough to outweigh the lack of reward from the uninteresting or defective part. Unless this condition applies a person values a work of art as a work of art only if he finds the experience of the work of art intrinsically rewarding in such a manner that, or for such a reason that, nothing else that yields a different experience could reward him in the same way: nothing else could provide him with a different experience which he values for precisely the same reason, and only for the same reason, that he values the first experience.[22] The experience of the work of art must be for him irreplaceable. If the experience of the work of art were not to be available to him then, no matter what alternative experiences were to be available, something that is of value to him would be lost. In this sense the value of a work of art is autonomous for someone who values a work of art as a work of art.

Someone who values a work of art as a work of art must find the experience of the work intrinsically rewarding. Furthermore, he must value the work because he finds the experience intrinsically rewarding. The more valuable he finds the experience, the more valuable he finds the work. The degree and the nature of the rewards determine the degree and the kind of intrinsic value that he assigns to the work. But all that follows from this is that for a reader to evaluate a poem as a poem he must evaluate the experience that the poem invites the reader to have, the experience of the poem itself, and not something different. And it is what the reader considers to be the *intrinsic* value of this imaginative experience that determines for him the value of the poem as a poem. Someone who is interested in the value of a work of art as a work of art is concerned with the intrinsic value of the experience that it provides. For the value of a work of art as a work of art is the intrinsic value of the experience that it offers.[23] If the reader is concerned with the poem's instrumental value, its beneficial

demanding or distressing and he is not prepared to make the necessary effort; or he believes that it will have harmful effects on him. In the absence of such explanations someone who values an object as a work of art cannot be entirely indifferent to his experiencing it, if he values the experience of art. (Someone can find an experience intrinsically rewarding and yet not *value* it or the object of which it is the experience.)

[22] Even this criterion requires qualification. For two works of art might differ in their structural properties in such a way that none of their aesthetic features differ. And in at least some cases of this kind there is no requirement that someone who values one work as a work of art should regard this work of art as rewarding him differently from any other. He need not value artistic individuality of experience as such if he is to value something as a work of art. But nothing of substance in the argument that follows in the text turns on this qualification of (or other necessary requirements on) the criterion, or the extra necessary conditions needed to secure a set which is *sufficient* for someone's valuing a work of art as a work of art. For convincing arguments against and counter-examples to the view that works of art which differ structurally must differ in their aesthetic attributes see Jerrold Levinson, 'Aesthetic Uniqueness', *The Journal of Aesthetics and Art Criticism*, xxxviii (Summer 1980), 435–49.

[23] Someone who is radically hostile to art and who regards the experience of works of art as

or harmful, short- or long-term effects or influence, either on a given person or people in general – where the effects are consequences of the experience and not elements or aspects of the experience itself – then in that respect his concern is not with its value as a poem. The question whether a certain kind of experience is or is not worth having for its own sake is not the same question as the question whether the experience is beneficial or is harmful to those who, for example, find the experience enjoyable, exciting, or in some other way rewarding, even if in many cases the two questions may be answered in the same way; and it is the first issue that is of concern from the point of view of the evaluation of a poem as a poem.

The traditional defence of poetry has been founded on the consideration that the finest works of poetry can help us to better our lives. They provide us with a particularly important means of enriching our awareness of human experience, and they enable us to give to our feelings greater precision, purity, strength and depth. Poetry is a means of increasing our intelligence and strengthening our moral temper.[24] That kind of apology for poetry is not something that I wish to dispute. But it does not follow from it that a person should assess a poem's value as a poem by reference to the benefit that he believes his life will receive from it. And a poem's value as a poem does not reside in its actually accomplishing the desirable end of moral and intellectual improvement in the case of one, some or many of us. For what is achieved by reading a poem depends not only on it – on the experience that its appreciation involves – but on the character, attitude and will of each particular reader. The gratification that a person derives from poetry may in fact lead him only to devour more poetry. It may be in other ways sterile. Many people have a notable capacity to isolate or compartmentalise their appreciation of literature and of art in general. They are unconcerned that it should affect their lives in any manner that will be beneficial to themselves or to others. Their approach to art is unreflectively or determinedly 'aesthetic' or sentimental. And even those for whom this is not true often, when they return to a familiar work, merely find their deepest feelings reflected in the poetry rather than being induced by their experience of the poem to become better people. It is only if poetry is approached in a particular spirit that it is likely to bring about the end for which it can be a peculiarly suitable means. But even if poetry is approached in that spirit, it is the nature of the imaginative experience that a poem provides that determines its greatness as a work of literature and not the effects that its reading in fact brings about.

It might be thought that this is to depreciate the moral (or social) value

having no positive intrinsic value need not disagree that it is the intrinsic value of the experience that a work of art offers that determines its value as a work of art.

[24] See Yvor Winters, *In Defense of Reason* (London, 1960), p. 29.

of poetry: the value of a poem as a poem is being claimed to be more important than the moral value of the poem. But that is a misunderstanding. It is not a matter of weighing one kind of value against another, but of discriminating the one from the other.[25] If the moral value of a poem refers to the actual effects – beneficial or harmful – of the experience of the work on the minds, characters and behaviour of its readers, then the moral value of a poem is different for different readers, and the value of a poem as a poem is not determined by any individual moral value that it may have or by its overall moral consequences. These effects are certainly of great importance; but it is not the effects of the work's experience that determine the value of the poem as a work of literature. It is the character of the experience that the work offers – in conjunction with the nature of its readers – that determines what these effects are likely to be, and it is the character of that experience which determines the poetic value of the work. This is not to downgrade the moral value of literature. It is to insist that it is not the moral value – understood as the moral effects of the work – that determines its value as literature. If a poem invites us to relish the degradation of women, or to thrill to the glamorisation of brutality, the experience that it offers can be condemned independently of determining whether in any particular person's case it has further, undesirable effects. But the insistence that the value of a poem as a poem is determined by the nature of the experience that it offers rather than by any (separable) effects that it may have – its actual influence – can be tempered by the consideration that the experience of the poem, if it is intrinsically valuable, will be of such a nature as to render it suitable to bring about valuable effects in those who approach the poem in the right frame of mind.

It would be mistaken to think that this thesis about the evaluation of poetry is an unacceptable version of the equivocal doctrine of 'Art for Art's sake', for the thesis does not maintain the existence of a specifically aesthetic emotion which it is the aesthetic function of poetry to arouse, it does not allege the indifference of a poem's subject-matter, and it does not recommend that the reader's response to a poem should be disconnected from his attitude to the moral or other evaluative stance that the poem adopts. It is not necessary to accept the theory of a poem as a *sui generis* world, to be experienced and valued independently of whether it conflicts or accords with one's own beliefs and values, but only in terms of whether it creates a coherent and satisfying world of its own – the theory that was held up by adherents of the doctrine of 'Art for Art's sake' against the demands for truth and morality in art – in order to restrict what determines

[25] The value of a poem as a poem may not, all things considered, be the most important kind of value. But it *is* the value of a poem as a poem.

the poetic value of a poem to the nature of the experience in which the poem is realised, so as to exclude any further separable effect. It is not necessary to embrace the theory of a poem as an autonomous world in order to maintain the autonomy of poetry. The thesis that the value of a poem as a poem is determined by the intrinsic value of the experience that the poem offers is in fact one of the few acceptable forms of the doctrine of 'Art for Art's sake'.[26]

I do not think, therefore, that the non-Christian who values poetry less highly when it gives expression to Christian attitudes or beliefs that he does not share must be considering poems from some point of view other than their value as poems. He may instead be concerned with the intrinsic value of the experience of a poem, and his view may be that the intrinsic value of an imaginative experience can be adversely affected by the unreality or unacceptability of the outlook that it expresses. The reason he has to regret that much distinguished poetry – despite its manifest sincerity – is the expression of religious views of life that do not by his lights correspond to the true nature of reality may derive from his estimate of the poems' value as poems. If, indeed, this is his view, I do not believe that he can properly be said to be mistaken: even though in consequence he is led to fault *The Divine Comedy*.[27]

---

[26] Compare the first two implications that Bradley wished his formula 'Poetry for Poetry's sake' to carry. See A. C. Bradley, 'Poetry for Poetry's Sake' in *Oxford Lectures on Poetry* (London, 2nd edn, November 1909), pp. 3–34.

[27] I have not argued that it is mandatory to assess the intrinsic value of the imaginative experience that a poem offers by reference to the unreality or unacceptability of the view of the world to which it gives expression. My view is that it is not mistaken to proceed in this fashion. If there are no constraints on the proper assessment of the intrinsic value of experiences, then the non-Christian's position cannot be mistaken. If there are constraints the non-Christian does not appear to flout them.

I am grateful to David Landells for his extremely helpful comments on a previous version of this paper.

Autobiography and philosophical perplexity

J. M. CAMERON

Autobiography is today valued for the autopsychography woven into it. Much autobiography before Rousseau is history, with the 'I' having a privileged access to the material but with no attempt to give directly an account of the soul. Such an account may be *betrayed* to the modern reader, who, after reading Lord Herbert of Cherbury's autobiography, may apprehend a character quite other than the chaste, long-suffering, rationally pious character Herbert plainly wants to give us. My intention here, in emphasizing that modern autobiography is autopsychography, is to elucidate the connexion between the autobiographical intention and achievement and the inward account of the self. I am uncertain whether or not the connexion between the autobiographical enterprise and the range of philosophical problems – notably what I shall call the thesis of epistemological solitude – is necessary or contingent, a logical consequence of the nature of the task (to go through autobiography to autopsychography) or something that is just associated historically with the enterprise, as in the autobiographical fragment embodied in the *Discourse on Method*. My intention is to open up the argument rather than conclude it.

I give here three fragments to which I shall need to refer in what follows:

(1) ... not one of these philosophical theories held me so much as scepticism, which at one time brought me to the verge of insanity. I fancied that besides myself nobody and nothing existed in the universe, that objects were not real at all but images which appeared when I directed my attention to them, and that as soon as I stopped thinking of them these images immediately vanished. In short, I came to the same conclusion as Schelling, that objects do not exist but only my relation to them exists. There were moments when I became so deranged by this *idée fixe* that I would glance sharply round in some opposite direction, hoping to catch unawares the void (the *néant*) where I was not. (L. N. Tolstoy, *Childhood, Boyhood and Youth*, Translated and with an Introduction by Rosemary Edmonds, Harmondsworth, 1964, pp. 158, 159)

(2) I used to wish the Arabian tales were true: my imagination ran on unknown influences, on magical powers, and talismans.... I thought life might be a dream, or I an Angel, and all this world a deception, my fellow-angels by a

playful device concealing themselves from me, and deceiving me with the semblance of a material world. (John Henry Cardinal Newman, *Apologia pro Vita Sua*, Edited by Martin J. Svaglic, Oxford, 1967, pp. 15, 16)

(3) Longtemps, je me suis couché de bonne heure.... Je n'avais pas cessé en dormant de faire des réflexions sur ce qui je venais de lire, mais ces réflexions avaient pris un tour un peu particulier; il me semblait que j'étais moi-même ce dont parlait l'ouvrage; une église, un quatuor, la rivalité de François Ier et de Charles-Quint. (Marcel Proust, *Du Côté de Chez Swann*, in *A la Recherche du Temps Perdu*, Paris, 1968, Vol. 1, p. 3)

I think it is harmless to include the passage from Proust's novel; it is in the autobiographical mode and the question I shall want to raise is that of possibility. The passage by Tolstoy is also formally a fiction.

It seems to follow from the intelligibility and power of Tolstoy's and Newman's work here cited that how we think, feel, judge, even perhaps perceive is in part determined by our intellectual history, not so much our history as individuals as the history of our nurturing culture. We take a lot as intelligible and imaginable that to men of other times and places would seem queer or nonsensical; and other things that belong to our intellectual history in only a very remote way we have difficulty in grasping. Those who have discussed the *Poetics* with their pupils will have come across the difficulty – a difficulty for the teacher almost as much as for the pupil – presented by what Aristotle says about the connexion between character and action. Recent philosophical tradition, Cartesian and empiricist, has persuaded us to think of the human individual as a distinct, separate, idiosyncratic centre of consciousness provided with internal objects only contingently connected with the ends of action. It is possible to think this is the common sense of the matter, so difficult is it to distinguish what goes with a certain philosophical style from what would strike us as being the case if we could exist in a state of pre-philosophical naivety. It is possible that the work of Newman and Tolstoy does not represent the sad triumph of philosophy; it may be, though it seems unlikely, that the underlying picture is naturally constructed as a way of ordering our experience, the philosophy being simply a kind of varnish applied to an already established structure. Even if we allow this to be a possibility, a particular philosophical tradition still seems to provide the authoritative images, to tell us where the connexion with the world is firmly and unassailably established. But such a notion of a *connexion* carries with it a doctrine of two worlds: the world of immediate experience, perceptual, sensational, whatever; and that conjectured world which is related to the world of immediate experience as a hypothesis explaining and justifying the intentionality that marks the experience. Once this distinction is made, we are entitled to take as a possibly complete world that of perception, sensation, imaging, feeling, however much it may be shot through with an intentionality that seems to take us beyond the world of unchallengeable immediacy. Given this starting-point, the possibility of scepticism is there.

It seems a common view among philosophers that this (historically) influential picture is a mess; that it appears thinkable only because we take all well-formed sentences as having, in use, some semantic function; they stand in a semantic relation to some actual or possible state of affairs. It is argued that this is simple-minded; language here is going on a spree, conjuring up the ghosts of reference; we are mistaken in thinking that any given series of well-formed sentences represents what is thinkable. The task which the young Tolstoy sets himself, that of catching *le néant* if he turns round quickly enough, is neither possible nor thinkable. It appears to be a task – and this appearance of its being a task has consequences for feeling and action such as are here specified – but this appearance rests upon confusions of a kind that can be brought out by analysis. Analysis may effect less than may be hoped for. Universal doubt may have no sense; but the one who doubts the solidity of all bodies is not cured by argument. Even those who are by common standards psychologically healthy and live contentedly in the climate established by Moore and Wittgenstein understand what it would be like (though 'what it would be like' needs scrutiny) to take the world as Descartes did, or Hume. There is a sense in which we understand Tolstoy and Newman, just as we understand the strange transformations related by Proust. The state of mind expressed in and through a certain picture of the perceiving subject survives the dissolution of the underpinning philosophical argument. We are, for example, able to entertain a picture of the self as within a theatre in which some episodes of the play take place at an illuminated centre, with other – perhaps more important – episodes occurring in the darkness that surrounds the centre, such episodes manifesting themselves in noises and flashes of light; what goes on at the illuminated centre is not self-explanatory but seems to require as ground and cause what goes on in the darkness. This is one way of schematizing the Freudian theory, though the schematizing of repression seems to require us to frame a supplementary picture, political or mechanical.

We throw away false factual claims and bankrupt scientific theories without much regret, or rather with the kind of regret we feel when we come to know that factually the worlds of the old ballads and fairy tales do not exist. We may regret Izaak Walton's world: 'that eels may be bred as some worms and some kinds of bees and wasps are, either of dew or out of the corruption of the earth, seems to be made probable by the barnacles and young goslings bred by the sun's heat and the rotten planks of an old ship, and hatched of trees' (*The Compleat Angler*, ch. 13). But we cannot inhabit it. The status of those accounts of the self that arise out of epistemological theories seems quite different. We are able to repeat the pilgrimage of the *Discourse on Method*, beginning with the retirement to winter quarters and the solitary reflexions in the stove-heated room, not simply by reason of the affable, buttonholing, persuasive style of the account, but also because the difficulties thrown up by the argument are matters of such deep perplexity that we find our way through them, if we do, only after generations of reflexion. One philosophical generation may set aside a philosophical theory, and the next reinstate it, no doubt with variations and refinements. (We may recall the fortunes of the Ontological Argument from Anselm to Malcolm.) Epistemological theories are lived through; the history of philosophy is not optional in the full study of philosophy; Aristotle was right in the strategy he adopted at the beginning of the *Metaphysics*. To establish 'the state of the question' in physical theory one need not go back behind Newton – and perhaps not so far; but on an ethical or an aesthetic or an epistemological question it seems necessary to live again the experiences of Plato and Aristotle, Hume and Kant.

To live such experiences is to understand but not necessarily to accept the entailments which this or that philosopher saw as attached to his account. The force of the pictures given by philosophers (for example Plato's picture of the soul given in the *Phaedrus*) is closer to the various 'natural' pictures of human life than it is to the theory it is used to illustrate. It is close to our talk of 'within' and 'without', to our association of darkness with ignorance and vice, and of light with knowledge and virtue. *Such* associations can scarcely be arbitrary or conventional. Philosophical pictures are not quite like this. But I want to argue that the picture of the self 'environed with the deepest darkness', given to scepticism and reflexions on the strange experience of dreaming, inclined to slide into the position of supposing that the physical world is an explanatory construct that always has less authority than the primary given – that which sparkles for us through the darkness – gets its power from experience and not just from philosophical delusion. Without philosophers, we might not have had such pictures; it may also be true that few would ever have fallen in love without reading about the state of being in love in poems and novels.

The impulse to picture is at the source of the autobiographical enterprise. 'Je suis bien aise de faire voir, en ce discours, quels sont les chemins que j'ai suivis, et d'y représenter ma vie comme en un tableau.' Thus Descartes. Here the philosophical and the autobiographical task are one. The autobiography is aimed at the philosophical conversion of the reader. We are to repeat the steps set out in the account of methodical doubting and to interrogate our memories, our perceptions, and our dreams. It remains a question how far the picture of the life is sustainable apart from the philosophical argument. Emily Dickinson gives us an account which may be thought to show us that the picture, with its transitions between the within and the without, is – just – sustainable apart from the argument.[1]

> There's a certain Slant of light,
> Winter Afternoons –
> That oppresses, like the Heft
> Of Cathedral Tunes –
>
> Heavenly Hurt, it gives us –
> We can find no scar,
> But internal difference,
> Where the Meanings are –

This is an acute and subtle picture by one whose poetic enterprise was as a whole autobiographical.

When in a famous passage of the *Treatise* Hume tells us that he began to 'fancy [himself] in the most deplorable condition imaginable, environed with the deepest darkness, and utterly deprived of the use of every member and faculty', and then remarks that but for 'Nature' he would remain in a state of 'philosophical melancholy and delirium', we are inclined to find in it traces of affectation. It is hard to think that the good-natured and complacent philosopher is even momentarily in a state of dread. But it is clearly possible that another should take as substantial what in Hume is vividly depicted for dialectical purposes and to make a literary effect. Newman is a good example.

From Locke and Hume he collects some what seem to him philosophical truisms. He thinks we have privileged intuitive knowledge of ourselves, demonstrative knowledge only within logic and mathematics, opinion or probable knowledge in empirical matters. If there is to be philosophy, it is to be spun out of our inwardness. In his private philosophical notebooks: 'The soul would not think without some external stimulus [but] our experience is not so much of external things but of our own minds'; and: 'In most departments of writing to speak of self is egotistical: not so in metaphysics. In it the writer cannot propose to do more than record his own opinions, the phenomena to which he appeals and the principles which he assumes being within his own breast ... His hermit spirit dwells in his own sphere.' This seems almost to propose the strong thesis that philosophy is essentially an autobiographical enterprise.

(I use Newman simply as an illustration. A just exposition of his views would have to bring in the Christianized Platonism of some of the Fathers.

[1] *The Complete Poems of Emily Dickinson*, ed. Thomas A. Johnson, Boston, 1960, p. 118.

His mind was formed by the empiricists and the Fathers; there is no trace of medieval influence or of the influence of Aristotle, except the *Nicomachean Ethics*, which, with Locke and Butler, influenced all Tractarians.)

The general thesis to be found in the above philosophical fragments I shall call the principle of epistemological solitude. That the soul is better known than the body and that what we know about the body rests, if we are to justify it, upon what is given to the soul, is taken to be settled truth. It continues to be a truth that startles – as it had been startling in the work of Descartes and Hume – only because, it might be argued, the pre-critical consciousness has such rude life: perhaps, as Nietzsche supposed, it enables us to bear the heavy burdens of living and thus makes for survival.

There seem to be two ways in which we may take the saying that philosophy begins in or with wonder. First, we may wonder at existence, that there is something and not nothing. This I do not consider. The other way is to take things that are part of the world of common experience and show that seriously reflected upon, they have a tendency to fracture the received account of the world. Dreams and mirror-images are obvious examples. Once such phenomena have stimulated the mind to reflexion they may be returned to the world, as, say, the Freudian theory does with dreams or the theory of optics with mirror-images. But enough traces of puzzlement remain for the handling of talk about dreams and mirror-images to resemble a little the handling of edged tools. *Alice in Wonderland* is in the mode of a dream, and *Through the Looking-Glass* is just what it says it is. Both dreams and looking-glasses may give us a bit of a fright and may thus serve as images and symbols of climactic occasions for the soul.

The mirror-image and the dream may come together in the autobiographical mode. 'If I looked into a mirror, and did not see my face, I should have the sort of feeling which actually comes upon me, when I look into this living busy world, and see no reflexion of its Creator.' Thus Newman in the *Apologia*, as he looks out upon the world of men. To look into a mirror and find it blank seems an experience that belongs to nightmare, and we may also remember that uncanny creatures are not reflected in glass or water. There are other passages concerned with mirror-images in Newman. In the *Apologia* he tells us that in the Long Vacation of 1839 he saw modern Christendom reflected in the glass of 'the middle of the fifth century'. 'I saw my face in that mirror, and I was a monophysite.' Here, to the strangeness and the terror is added guilt; for the stranger-heretic that looks back at him from the mirror is himself, but not himself as he has hitherto supposed himself to be.

We may suppose that belief in the thesis of man's epistemological solitude produces a sense of extreme anxiety of the kind depicted by Hume and evinced by Newman. We live in an uncertainly illuminated darkness and suffer from melancholy and delirium; such feelings are not tolerable for long and we therefore look for a deliverance. This is provided: by God in Descartes, by Nature in Hume. But since there is something dodgy about the way in which we are delivered, a retreat into the isolated self is always possible. After all, it is a part of the argument that we have *been there*, and where we have once been we may be again. Again, by taste or temperament we may actually take pleasure in the thought of our epistemological solitude; it may seem a trifle distinguished, may intensify the drama of existence and offer to free us from the claims of the social world and the thought of the perils of the natural. It is a cave within which to hide.

Thoughts of our epistemological solitude seem to leave us, then, with a kind of picture that disposes us to have certain affective states. Does the picture depend upon the arguments in such a way that we have to say, once the arguments are gone, that the picture is dissolved? Perhaps we are left with verbal sequences that can be misread as describing a possible picture, but are like 'round square' when seen for what they are; and 'round square' is not a possible picture. ('At the round earth's imagin'd corners, blow/ Your trumpets, Angells . . .', depends for its force on our recognizing the impossibility of here combining 'round' and 'square'.)

I take the extreme case that on one reading is offered by the passage by Proust. We may be inclined to suppose that what is said is what in another sense of the expression can't be said. This is close to

> He thought he saw a Rattlesnake
> That questioned him in Greek:
> He looked again, and found it was
> The Middle of Next Week.
> (Lewis Carroll, *Sylvie and Bruno*, ch. vi)

That a rattlesnake should turn out to be on closer inspection the middle of next week relies for its effect upon, so to speak, a switch of categories, whereas the rattlesnake's speaking Greek is merely wild, like the head of the horse Falada speaking from its place above the town gate. What is distinctive about the work of Carroll is that he goes in for magical processes, such as the talking of serpents, but then undermines the ethos of the fairy tale by the switch of categories, that is, to use Elizabeth Sewell's way of putting it, we go from Magic to Nonsense.[2]

Now, one peculiarity of the Proust example is that it is self-referring. When the narrator refers to himself as thinking himself to be 'une église, un quatuor, la rivalité de François Ier et de Charles-Quint', we are inclined to suppose that all the identifications are nonsense and do not seek the

---

[2] Cf. Elizabeth Sewell, *The Field of Nonsense*, London, 1952, *passim*.

analogue of magical transformation. But we cannot settle this matter just by inspecting the text. Whereas the intention in Lewis Carroll is to amuse, to entertain, to exercise the mind's muscles, even to instruct (that there may be self-revelation is outside the intentions of which Carroll is fully conscious), the intention in Proust is to tell us in quite a serious way how it was with the narrator. And what reasons could we have for distrusting him, or for supposing that what he intends is mere abracadabra? In dreams and in waking reverie we ceaselessly merge with and separate from the contents of our musings. Here is a learned child who is released in his thinking from deliberation and purpose. Any difficulty we may have in accepting what he tells us will come from our first assigning the passage to the autobiographical mode and then on *a priori* grounds asserting the impossibility of what is related. If other signals are given, we don't commonly have the same difficulty. If poetry is signalled, we accept

I find I incorporate gneiss, coal, long-threaded moss, fruits, grains, esculent roots,
And am stucco'd with quadrupeds and birds all over...
   (Walt Whitman, 'Song of Myself', *Leaves of Grass*, New York, 1912, p. 54)

We still have difficulty over the narrator's telling us that 'j'étais moi-même ce dont parlait l'ouvrage', for the 'j'étais moi-même' is so emphatic; it isn't as though the narrator were to say in a joking way 'My dear, it was the fall of the Roman Empire', or of his signature on a document 'That was when I crossed my Rubicon.' Here the metaphorical uses are condensed simile and a combination of linguistic skill, and general information enables us to catch on to what is said without difficulty. In such cases there is, as it were, a hidden system of mediation, or an acquired skill, which enables us to range over the field of discourse and bring together (as writers or speakers) what is disparate or grasp such conjunctions (as reader or hearer). There is resistance on occasion, for it is a part of the pleasure and excitement generated by such tropes, where they are not made familiar by repetition, that there is the analogue of coyness and surrender in the transaction. This is not the case with Nonsense, where the pleasure seems a different one; for in our recognizing a particular conjunction as Nonsense we set aside the possibility of making an identification that goes beyond the merely grammatical. But when it makes no sense to say that A is x or that N ϕs, to *say* it is still something, and such a saying has in it a power, in a certain context, to produce a felt disorder of the imagination, even an intense feeling of anxiety. (This is one of the notes of modernity in poetry – see Eliot and Wallace Stevens, for example – where the device of Nonsense is used in just such a way.) Hence Tolstoy is provoked, by the purely nonsensical figure of an existing relation to objects that do not exist, in to a state of derangement.

Proust's utterances, though, are not comparable to such figures as 'it was the fall of the Roman Empire'; but it would be odd to take them as nonsensical, for they do not seem designed to provoke anxiety or amusement in the reader; the intention is to tell us how it was with the narrator over a given period. I think we have to notice that he is telling us how it was with him when he was half-asleep, when the rules of an alert consciousness no longer bind. It is as though there lies behind us in our waking life a hidden condition, one that can show itself in moments of reverie or breakdown or going to sleep or waking up. Nonsense, which involves our recognizing that certain collocations have no sense, does not appear for the one giving the account, for there are no rules to be flouted. All the same, as readers, *we* are subject to the rules. This means, first, that we note that what is said is about a state of half-conscious reverie, and secondly, that what is said is about a state in which the customary rules do not bind. But what as statement, given a standard context, remains puzzling, may betray what isn't stated, that is, may function as symptom and symbol. Here we are given, as though they were opening themes in a complex piece of music, the themes of religion, music, the French past, themes that will throughout the rest of the novel both disorder and harmonize the life of one who is here remembering the time when, sent to bed early, he dozed over his books.

(Proust was himself fully aware of the problems raised by this identification of the narrator with 'une église' etc. He elaborates (passage quoted p. 159 above):

Cette croyance survivait pendant quelques secondes à mon reveil; elle ne choquait pas ma raison, mais pesait comme des écailles sur mes yeux et les empêchait de se rendre compte que le bougeoir n'était plus allumé. Puis elle commencait à me devenir inintelligible, comme après la métempsycose les pensées d'une existence antérieure; le sujet du livre se détachait de moi, j'étais libre de m'y appliquer ou non ...)

I have argued that the thesis of epistemological solitude engenders and is accompanied by certain schematic pictures of the self; and that the question to be answered is how far the picture is sustainable apart from the philosophical arguments that purport to establish the thesis; and there is also the slightly different question: is the picture constituted by the arguments in such a way that the supposed picture fails *as a picture* once the arguments are gone?

At the beginning of the second part of the *Discours* Descartes places before us a picture with a definite structure ('comme en un tableau') and uses the picture to state a norm for inquiry and to insinuate a preference for one structure rather than another. He contrasts two cities: one has grown bit by bit over a long period of time, with twisted streets and many different styles of architecture, products of the minds of a multitude of authors, having no unity of style and plan; the other is the work of a single mind, which traces out a perspicuous city with compass and ruler, a city one in plan and style. The unplanned city is an image of what in philosophy we have received from tradition since Plato, with all its irregularities, patchings, discordances of style, dark corners, all that irritates and frustrates one for whom mathematics is the model for all scientific accounts of man and the world. It is of course immensely interesting that it is also a part of the autobiographical account that Descartes, like the rest of us, has to *live* in the unplanned city of tradition. This is reflected in the resolutions as to morality and practice which he adopts at the start of the enterprise of methodical doubt. If, following Wittgenstein, we use the city of tradition as an image of those interconnected forms of life that show themselves, and hide themselves, in the natural languages, then the image of another city would count as the vision of the perfect language in which we can utter what is free of contradiction, obscurity, and ambiguity.

There is a curious passage in the *Philosophical Investigations* (I.18, p. 8ᵉ) in which Wittgenstein uses, though for quite different purposes, the image of the ancient city of language, 'a maze of little streets and squares, of old and new houses, and of houses with additions from various periods', and speaks of 'the symbolism of chemistry and the notation of the infinitesimal calculus' as 'suburbs of our language'. The implication of this way of using the images is that we should add to what we already have, even though the new suburbs may seem more perspicuous than the complicated centre, whereas Descartes suggests we should either desert the old city or raze it to the ground.

Such pictures as these haunt us. It is as though they are not just illustrations, teaching devices, standing in an isometric relation to an argument that can be stated, in principle at least, independently. They are rather constitutive of the argument, not merely heuristic devices. We may even move from the thought of the city to the thought of rising above it and seeing it as a face looking up at us; and this would be an image of the attempt to go beyond the limits of language and the world.

We have noted that Descartes himself chooses to live, at least provisionally, in the ancient city of tradition, or language. His resolution is expressed in four maxims that have the effect of lulling us into a state of complacency (this is perhaps especially the effect of the third), so that we may be exposed to the full effect of the invitation to take our dreams seriously and to cling to the *Cogito* as our only support. Then, of course, everything is given back to us: the world, our bodies and our senses, dreams that are no more than dreams. At times we may suspect that the four maxims are a way of saying that methodical doubt is only a game, the perspicuous city a phantasm of the drawing-board. It is as though Descartes reassures us that after all we don't have to move out of the ancient city. We can live in it, perhaps with a few streets widened and straightened, the cathedral liturgy more handsomely and intelligibly performed, the clerks in the old palace doing their tax accounts on a more rational method, and the public lighting improved.

In finding the traditional city perplexing, we are not wrong. Perhaps we should never have seen the many-layered city of language for what it was without our feeling the pressure of arguments that once seemed compelling, even if now, towards the end of the twentieth century, we are inclined to find them sophistical. It wouldn't be too much to say that Wittgenstein, after the *Tractatus*, is *obsessed* with the arguments of the Cartesians and empiricists and that for him they have a maieutic function.

The dialectic of within and without can take many forms. One man's inwardness is not that of another. But in some form the within/without relation, and in the background or the foreground the pathos of epistemological solitude, show themselves implicitly or explicitly in all those modes of autobiography with a strong autopsychographical component. It seemed for a time that the deep doubts inspired by the Cartesian critique were compatible with – perhaps even strengthened – the intellectual certainties, the sense of decorum in the arts and polite society, the ground rules of the republic of letters. Even then, there is Pascal, a troublesome witness to a tradition that goes back to Augustine (as of course does Descartes through his connexion with the Oratory and with his literary dependence upon the text of Augustine for the *Cogito*), and Pascal returns with force in the nineteenth century, with romanticism and the great outburst of autopsychography, the shift, we might say, from *l'esprit de géometrie* to *l'esprit de finesse*.[3]

The to and fro movement between what is within and what is without, with all its confusions, is perhaps not so much a consequence of philosophically induced anxieties as of the character – the necessary character – of the natural languages. Our language about what is within is for the most part drawn from expressions that have their primary use in application to the life of the body and to public transactions. We *call back* the image of an absent face, we *draw out* consequences and *press home* the conclusions of arguments; to be in ignorance is to be in *darkness* and to come to know is to be brought into the *light*, affections are *warm* and hatred is *burning* or *cold*; and the family of expressions used in our talk about mental images are applicable because we are already acquainted with shadows,

---

[3] On the possible relations between the work of Pascal and Newman see my 'Pascal and Newman', *University of Leeds Review*, Vol. 12, No. 2, October 1969.

drawings, and reflexions in water and looking-glasses. My reference is to what we *say* about mental images, not to such images themselves: these have, since Galton's *Inquiries into Human Faculty and its Development* (1883), been known to be radically different as between different subjects: not everyone, for example, is a 'visualizer'. At the same time, it seems necessary that phenomenological accounts of perceivings of bodies should have a priority over systematic (geometrical, mechanical, physico-chemical...) accounts of bodies and processes. It is only as and how we pick out kinds of things in the world that we have the power to construct systematic accounts of bodies and processes. Of course, *picking out* is not something we do without our having first been drilled and then taught in the use of language.

To attempt autobiography in the sense which has interested me is to be committed to reflexion on philosophical perplexities that have haunted us throughout our lives or at particular times. This is notoriously the case with Augustine, who raises questions about time, memory, personal identity, and how we come to understand language. It is a matter of common observation that young children do raise such questions, though for the most part they lose the taste for them with adolescence, or, if they cherish them, they are more likely to put them into poetry than into philosophy. If they come in later life to give them a philosophical form, it will probably be because they have encountered things in the philosophers that seem to render their perplexities in a plausible way. And I believe it is, commonly, what they get from the philosophers that makes their perplexities a burden. This is above all to be seen in the paradoxes of scepticism that persuade us to think the thesis of epistemological solitude, paradoxes that draw their energy from the thesis once it has been stated.

What remains when the argument is gone, whether reduced to emptiness by analysis or banished in some other way, is a set of pictures. Those pictures we have looked at may at least in part be such that without the arguments we should not have organized them in just that way. For example, the inner world of Locke's epistemology is coloured, resonant, fragrant, so that our isolation from the physical world that explains the inner world is absolute, for the doctrine that ideas of primary and secondary qualities are representations cannot be stated without a paralogism. It has been argued, most forcefully by Dr Luce,[4] that Berkeley's picture of the world and the self overcomes this defect, even that the picture is what we should have had if our epistemological innocence had never been violated by philosophy. This has never seemed to me plausible. What is now inward and hidden is the Will, human and Divine; to think that phenomenal sequences are causally linked is to project in to

[4] A. A. Luce, *Berkeley's Immaterialism*, London, 1975.

the world what belongs to our inwardness. But once the pictures are constructed and given, once they have entered into tradition, they survive as sketches of possibility when the arguments have, quite properly, been discarded. Some verbal formulations of the pictures may be abandoned for purely formal reasons, that is, they do not really compose a picture, as with 'round square'; but not many. Once a picture has, as it were, been constructed and launched, it may float on the sea of discourse indefinitely, as a source of perplexity or clarification. It becomes active in the history of culture and flourishes in those literary forms which most press us to self-scrutiny and to a disinterested curiosity about the world.

The essence of a discarded philosophical theory may remain with us as a picture. This is what stays with us when we have lived through the arguments in imagination, and this is why it seems proper to tell the story of one's philosophical development *comme en un tableau*. If the picture still has a brightness, a vibrancy, that seems surprising after we have (say) finished reading Austin's *Sense and Sensibilia*, then it may mean that we ought to look once again at the argument with which the picture has historically been connected, though in some cases we may suspect this isn't worth the trouble. Another way of looking again at the picture, once we have decided it is worth re-examining, is to try to remember how it was with us when, in childhood or in youth, we were first seized with a sense of the overwhelming strangeness of our life in the world, when we might hope to catch unawares *le néant*, or when we might have conceived that our sensible life was a deception wrought by the angels, or when we were unable to distinguish ourselves from the content of our musings.

INDEX

DATE LOANED

JAN. 25. 1992			
SEP. 02. 1992			
GAYLORD 3563			PRINTED IN U.S.A.